Images of AMERICA in Revolutionary FRANCE

This volume is part of a series of publications resulting from the Bicentennial celebration of Georgetown University (1789-1989). The Seminar on which it draws was sponsored and supported by Georgetown University's Bicentennial Office.

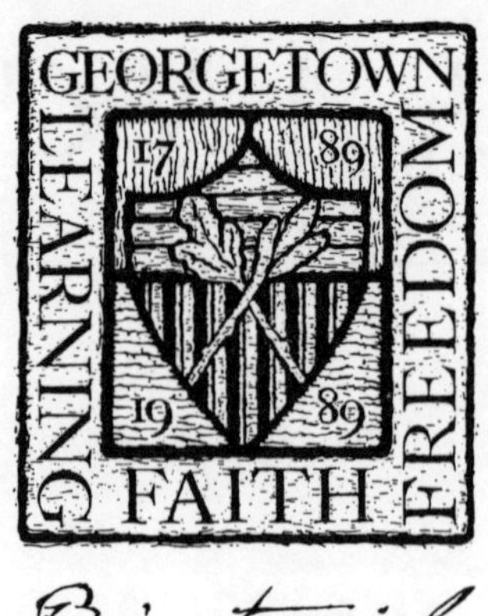

Images of AMERICA in Revolutionary FRANCE

Michèle R. Morris, Editor

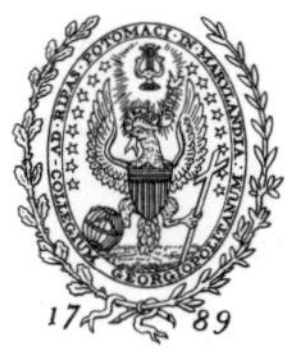

GEORGETOWN UNIVERSITY PRESS
Washington, D.C.

Printed in the United States of America

Library of Congress Cataloging-in-Publication Data

Images of America in revolutionary France / Michele R. Morris, Editor.
p. cm.
Based on papers presented at a conference held at Georgetown University, Apr. 30-May 2, 1989.
Text in English and French.
Includes bibliographical references.
ISBN 0-87840-497-X
1. United States--Foreign public opinion, French--History--18th century--Congresses. 2. French--United States--History--18th century--Congresses. 3. Public opinion--France--History--18th century--Congresses. I. Morris, Michele R.
E183.8.F8I55 1990
944.04--dc20 90-3689
CIP

Contents

Preface

Knowing and understanding the image or images others hold of us is an important component of self-knowledge. Such respected American historians as Henry Steele Commager and Oscar Handlin, to name only two, recognized this dimension long ago in their studies of America.[1] This orientation is still favored by many scholars. Indeed, a recent history of the U.S. is entitled *Images of American Society* and a number of other works appear under similar titles.[2] Other studies have looked at America's image from a French perspective: most readers will be familiar with the pioneering works of Gilbert Chinard, Bernard Fay, Gilbert Fess, and Durand Echeverria whose *Mirage in the West* (1957) remains a classic.[3] More recently, Echeverria updated his conclusions in a thoughtful essay,[4] in which he suggested that scholarly investigation of intercultural images would be more productive if it centered on psychological, social and cultural motives.

---

1. Henry Steel Commager, *America in Perspective: The United States through Foreign Eyes* (New York: Random House, 1947); Oscar Handlin, *This Was America. True Accounts of People and Places, Manners and Customs, as Recorded by European Travelers to the Western Shore in the Eighteenth, Nineteenth, and Twentieth Centuries* (Cambridge: Harvard Univ. Press, 1949).

2. George D. Lillibridge, *Images of American Society: A History of the United States* (Boston: Houghton Mifflin, 1976). Recent studies or anthologies of foreign travelers' notes include: Marc Pachter and Frances Wrin, eds., *Abroad in America: Visitors to the New Nation, 1776-1911* (Washington: National Portrait Gallery, Smithsonian Institution, 1976); Robert Downs, *Images of America, Travelers from Abroad in the New World* (Urbana and Chicago: Univ. of Illinois Press, 1987); Robert Blow, ed., *Abroad in America, Literary Discoverers of the New World from the Past 500 Years* (Oxford: Lennard, 1987).

3. Gilbert Chinard, *L'Amérique et le rêve exotique dans la littérature au XVIIe et XVIIIe siècles* (Paris: Droz, 1913); Bernard Fay, *L'Esprit révolutionnaire en France et aux Etats-Unis à la fin du XVIIIe siècle* (Paris: Champion, 1924); Gilbert M. Fess, *The American Revolution in Creative French Literature (1775-1937)* (Columbia: Univ. of Missouri Press, 1941); Durand Echeverria, *Mirage in the West: a History of the French Image of American Society to 1815* (Princeton: Princeton University Press, 1957).

4. Durand Echeverria, "The French Image of American Society to 1815: Some Tentative Revisions," in Paul J. Korshin, ed., *The American Revolution and Eighteenth-Century Culture* (New York: AMS Press, 1976), 241-65.

The 1976 American bicentennial celebrations stimulated much further research in this area: a colloquium on the American influence in France in the late eighteenth century was held at La Fayette's ancestral home. The Bicentennial issue of *The French Review* focused on "Historical and Literary Relations between France and the United States" and that of *Annales de Bretagne* (1977) was devoted to the French vision of the American War of Independence. In an important article, François Furet, following in Echeverria's footsteps, reexamined the impact of the American experience on French culture, arguing that the American dream went from revolutionary messianism to social science observation before dying in literature.[5] Finally, the immensely diverse papers presented at the various International Congresses on the Enlightenment have at times addressed a number of issues related to our topic, notably during the fourth congress (Yale, 1975) and the sixth (Brussels, 1983): Roger Mercier's 1975 topic, "Image de l'autre et image de soi-même dans le discours ethnologique du XVIIIe siècle" (*SVEC* 154) was further investigated during an entire session on "The European and the discovery of the other" at Brussels.

Aware of the benefits of such an intercultural dimension, curriculum planners have introduced courses reflecting this wider perspective: thus, eight years ago, Georgetown University inaugurated a series of courses under the general heading of "Images of America," in which students are led to reflect upon the images of their own society as projected in other cultures, thereby enriching their own understanding of both the native and the "other" societies.

Not surprisingly then, when Georgetown University started planning its own bicentennial activities, several French and History professors, thinking that the coincidence of our 200th anniversary with that of the French Revolution should not go unnoticed, chose this intercultural perspective to convene a scholarly conference linking the Georgetown Bicentenial themes of "learning, faith and freedom" with the French Revolution. While the 200th anniversary of the latter prompted intense scholarly activity, much of it focused on developments in France and on the impact of the 1789 Revolution on the rest of the world. Therefore our planning committee decided to call for papers updating existing scholarship on "Images of America in France at the Time of the Revolution" around these three themes. The ongoing work conducted by individuals or scholars affiliated with the Ecole des Hautes Etudes en Sciences Sociales, the Institut d'Histoire de la Révolution Française, the Centre de Recherches Révolutionnaires et Romantiques, the Groupe de Recherches sur la Littérature des Voyages, as well as by numerous American *dix-huitièmistes*,

5. François Furet, "De l'homme sauvage à l'homme historique: l'expérience américaine dans la culture française," *Annales: Economies, Sociétés, Civilisations* (juillet-août 1978): 729-39.

historians and social scientists, is proof of the relevance and vitality of this topic.

The Georgetown Bicentennial Conference of April 30-May 2, 1989 capitalized on these efforts and was resolutely interdisciplinary as well as intercultural. Our conference provided a forum for meetings between North American and European scholars. A number of these have long been prominent and made many significant contributions to their respective fields, while others, talented younger scholars, are now gaining national and international recognition. The sessions witnessed lively exchanges of views between speakers, commentators and the audience.

Each session was ably moderated by history, language and literature scholars from a wide range of institutions, and others served as commentators: Alan Karras, Susan Mahoney, Madeleine Simons (all of Georgetown University), Madeleine Therrien (University of Maryland), Robert Ginsberg (Pennsylvania State University), John Brown and the Rev. Joseph Moody (Catholic University Emeriti), Dena Goodman (Center for Literary and Cultural Studies, Harvard University), James Friguglietti (Eastern Montana College), and Cecil P. Courtney (Cambridge University, England). They have all earned our gratitude for their expert and spirited participation.

The conference could not have been been so successful without the unfailing and tireless support of many members of the Georgetown community. Special thanks are due to the Bicentennial Director, Rev. Charles S. Currie, S.J. and to Dr. Kathleen Lesko: their enthusiastic encouragement, skill and persistence guided and sustained us throughout. Dr. James Alatis, Dean of the School of Languages and Linguistics, and his entire staff were helpful in numerous ways, and their long experience in hosting scholarly conferences was invaluable. The conference co-director, Dr. Sandra Horvath-Peterson, of the History Department, shared our work from the start, helping with research, scholarly and public contacts, hospitality arrangements, and the myriad other details involved. She contributed much of her precious time, while planning the subsequent, much larger meeting hosted by Georgetown University, the International Congress on the History of the French Revolution. Also deserving of our deep gratitude are members of the administrative staff in the French Department, Pamela Kaleugher, and Maureen Gavel, assisted by Christel Bernoud and Jacqueline Coates. The meetings ran smoothly, thanks primarily to Jacquelyn Tanner, director of Language Learning and Technology, who provided expert technical support and assistance. To all those mentioned and the many others who generously contributed their time and effort, my heartfelt thanks.

Finally, the publication of this volume was made possible in part by the generosity of the Bicentennial committee. The Georgetown University Press, its director, Rev. John Breslin, S.J., its editors, Deborah Peterson and Eleanor Waters, and Chris Quigley, who prepared the graphics, were always ready to offer their valuable advice and assistance. Special thanks are due to Madeleine Therrien, who carefully appraised most of the manuscripts as advisory reader. The typescript was prepared by Pamela Kaleugher, whose skill and patience are exemplary. I am profoundly grateful to them all.

The present volume offers the revised version of the papers delivered during the conference. Space limitations do not allow us to print the comments and discussions which followed the formal addresses. However, we are fortunate in being able to include some of the illustrations which accompanied Prof. Roman's paper, "Journal de voyage de Louis-Philippe en Amérique: impressions de jeunesse" and Dr. Fritz Daguillard's slide presentation and commentary, "La Révolution de Saint-Domingue et l'évolution de l'image du Noir." Dr. Daguillard, a Washington physician, had kindly consented to share his impressive collection of prints and graphics, "The Black Presence in the French Revolution." We express our deep gratitude to them both for their gracious cooperation.

The essays are organized around the themes which dominated our conference, though they do not follow exactly the order in which they were given then. By way of introduction to French images of America, the reader will learn of the early French connection of Georgetown in Fr. James Hennesey's study of John Carroll and other American and French clergy at the time of the university's founding. The image of Revolutionary France as held by Georgetown's founder was not an exemplary one, due to profound disagreement on certain issues, especially the free exercise of religion and political stability. These very issues are among those considered in the mirror images of America in France that the following papers examine.

The plural form, "images," should be emphasized: instead of one set view of America, we find a multiplicity of representations. Many different images emerge, colored, of course, by the identity, personality, experience and motivations of those who conceived and projected them. Some images are gained from direct contact, such as those of missionaries and soldiers; others are derived from second-hand knowledge, such as oral accounts, press reports, books, plays, and even songs.

The theme of learning about America runs through most of this volume: learning about the peoples of the new American republic, about political and commercial ideas and practices, about the land as it was seen by various travelers. Early French visitors to America were not tourists, but missionaries, soldiers, or people associated with military expeditions, traders. Their accounts, those of Charlevoix, La Hontan, Chastellux, Michaux have been rather widely read, translated, and studied. Others, less well-known, come to light here. First we look at the images drawn by an early traveler and missionary, Lafitau, the father of modern ethnology, whose work on the "American Savages" was to prove so influential during the revolutionary period. Madeleine Simons writes of the Jesuit missionary and of his vision and understanding of American Indians, pointing to a "Saussurean" interest in the Iroquois language. Her striking interpretation provides an entirely new and original approach. A very different traveler was the young Duc d'Orléans, who journeyed with his brothers through part of the new United States. Aurelia Roman illustrated her presentation with slides showing some of the young duc de Montpensier's artistic talent. In her paper, she focuses particularly on the views of the future King Louis-Philippe on Blacks and Indians, especially on the condition of the Indian woman. Later in the book, another image of Indians appears in François Moureau's examination of Billardon de Sauvigny's play, *Hirza ou les Illinois*.

Touching on the theme of freedom and human rights, the French vision of Blacks and slavery during the revolutionary period comes up in several papers: Aurelia Roman underscores the Duc d'Orléans' dismay at the sight of slaves; F. Moureau comments on Billardon's *Les Nègres*; J.-J. Fiechter and L. Trenard respectively discuss French officers' and philosophers' apathy or reaction to this human rights issue. Michèle Duchet was to speak on the Enlightenment philosophers' position on slavery. Though her absence was regretted, her work was often mentioned during the conference and two excellent papers addressed the issue. First, Régis Antoine analyzes the views of various travelers and thinkers on the conduct of the Blacks, using the term to mean both the behavior of the slaves and the leadership of their masters. The views and positions on slavery of the French colonists, administrators and traders were strongly shaped by their own desire for financial success. France was, after all, a powerful colonial nation, with many profitable investments in Louisiana and the West Indies. Commercial and personal interests were not always compatible with the enlightened approach advocated by such *philosophes* as Brissot (founder of *La Société des Amis des Noirs*), Condorcet, or Diderot. Next, Jean Ehrard focuses on the latter writer and thoughtfully examines the apparent contradictions and changes in Diderot's position on the question of slavery, as it evolved throughout the various editions of l'*Encyclopédie* and in other pieces. Ehrard interprets Diderot's contemptuous silence as strong condemnation of a practice he found abhorrent, but also as a sign of optimism, since a free people cannot continue to deny freedom to another. The Abbé Raynal, the author of the influential *Histoire des Deux-Indes*, is unavoidably linked to Diderot, and subsequent papers by Daniel Price and Claude Fohlen also explore Raynal's position on this issue.

Echeverria emphasized the importance of understanding the motivations of those who proposed images of America. In addition to those of Antoine and Ehrard, the following two essays illustrate this orientation. Jean-Jacques Fiechter's paper on the officers in Rochambeau's army, and the first part of Louis Trenard's study shed light on the motivations and impressions of European soldiers who participated in the campaigns of the American

Revolutionary War and they both deflate traditional interpretations of heroic behavior. Though some of the European officers' accounts of the American campaign have been studied and are relatively well known,[6] others remain unexplored. Jean-Jacques Fiechter used many unpublished manuscripts, diaries and reports of a number of young officers in the Rochambeau expeditionary forces. The reality of everyday campaign life helped dispel any myths these young officers might have held. Louis Trenard also analyzes the images formed and projected by the many Lyonnais who had direct or indirect contact with America: politicians, journalists, Freemasons, philosophes and members of various academies. In the decades preceding the French Revolution, the impact of the American Revolution on France was enhanced by the expansion of the press and the proliferation of clubs and lodges (such as the masonic lodge of the "Nine Sisters" to which Franklin belonged). The academies that flourished before and after 1789 provided another forum for discussion. The Marseilles Academy proposed a debate on the effect of trade, and in Lyon the Abbé Raynal essentially asked "Was America a Mistake?"[7] On balance, in the Lyon Academy, America was viewed as a model or as a laboratory where social programs could be tested. Until the early 1790s, America remained a model for Roland, Brissot and their group. For the oppressed, such as the imprisoned Manon Roland, the America dream became that of a refuge.

Raynal, though frequently mentioned in our conference, has been rather neglected in recent scholarship. Therefore we devoted a whole session to him. He is the focus of the next two papers. Daniel Price, placing Raynal in the entire European Enlightenment context of trade and ideology, writes on the concept of trade as developed in the various editions of his then widely read *Histoire des Deux-Indes*. He carefully presents Raynal's position as evolving, since in the third edition he viewed trade negatively, as it brings corruption, decline and finally destruction. In this respect, Price differs from Roger Mercier, who made a more optimistic assessment in 1978.[8] Claude Fohlen then concentrates on Thomas Paine's reaction to the errors he found in the Abbé's interpretations in the 1781 edition of *L'Histoire*. Raynal saw religion in the service of freedom in the American Revolution, and Paine vehemently disagreed. A lively debate is thus brought to light and Raynal's position is

---

6. For example, Howard C. Rice, Jr. and Anne S.K. Brown, translators and editors, *The American Campaigns of Rochambeau's Army, 1780, 1781, 1782, 1783*, 2 vols. (Princeton & Providence: Princeton Univ. Press & Brown Univ. Press, 1972). See also *infra*, 78, note 49.

7. See Henry Steele Commager and Elmo Giordanetti, *Was America a Mistake? An Eighteenth-Century Controversy* (Columbia: Univ. of South Carolina Press, 1967). The book examines the answers to Raynal's question on the discovery of America by Buffon, de Pauw, Perrety, Roubaud, Chastellux, Condorcet and Mandrillon.

8. See Roger Mercier, "L'Amérique et les Américains dans l'"Histoire des deux Indes' de l'abbé Raynal," *Revue française d'Histoire d'Outre Mer* 65 (1978), 240: 309-24.

reevaluated: Fohlen gives more weight to the philosophical contributions of Crèvecoeur and Paine than to those of Raynal.

In addition to clubs, lodges and academies, the press was instrumental in disseminating first and second-hand information on the newly independent colonies. The influential periodical, the *Journal encyclopédique*, is a prominent example which gave the public at large as well as legislators much material for debate. Jacques Wagner, who has already studied America in the *JE* from 1757 to 1778 elsewhere, now surveys the years 1773-1793, and highlights the contrasting views of the moderate journalists and of the enthusiastically pro-American, Brissot. Joan Lenardon probes the numerous references in the *Journal* to the American War of Independence, its protagonists and interpreters, and examines the *JE* writers' understanding of causality for the war; Raynal, Paine and Adams, among others, were frequent contributors.

The second part of her paper addresses the question of faith and religious freedom, which often came up in the *Journal*'s pages. She finds the *JE*'s position closer to such moderates as John Andrews and the Abbé de Mably than to the more revolutionary Tom Paine, who was adamantly opposed to the institutionalized union of church and state. Next, Jacques Grès-Gayer analyzes the uncompromising position of the French Gallicans on the question of separation of church and state, and their lack of understanding and sympathy for the democratization of the American Catholic clergy.

If indeed, as Echeverria believes, the American model was used by the French either to promote reform through comparison with the new republic, or to promote self-esteem by rejecting that model as inappropriate, some of our essays easily fall in each of the two categories. On the side of reform, we find Ehrard's discussion of Diderot's views on slavery, Fohlen's examination of the controversy between Raynal and Paine. The contrary views, those which argue that the American model does not fit the European circumstances, are represented in the two essays on the *Journal encyclopédique*, in Grès-Gayer's paper on religious liberties and in Edna Lemay's essay on French deputies.

Debates in the French Assembly often centered, of course, on political institutions and liberties. In her paper on Démeunier, an admirer and disciple of Lafitau, Edna Lemay, a specialist on the Constituent Assembly, examines how the French deputies and the public viewed the American War and early democratic experience, and how these views shaped their rhetoric, their ideas, and their legislative endeavors.

Finally, to give fuller meaning to the word "images," we turn to cultural representations, which reach into a more indirect or symbolic level. François Moureau, whose research has often focused on the stage, returns to a dramatic author whom Gilbert Chinard had already studied, Billardon de Sauvigny. While Chinard had examined the play, *Washington*, Moureau analyzes Billardon's other American plays, presenting images of the Illini, of Blacks, and of French soldiers in Rochambeau's and La Fayette's armies.

Interestingly, he underlines the political use of Billardon's plays for military and patriotic propaganda. Béatrice Didier, who recently published several works on music and festive celebrations during the French Revolution, writes on the intricate relationship between words and music and on the American themes, such as the cult of Franklin and La Fayette, in songs and hymns of that period. The American image in this area is definitely mythical.

The papers presented here fit tightly together, though they show widely diverse points of view on ideas, customs, structures, and representations of the young American republic. Far from being only a "distant mirror," they vividly show how the new American society was perceived in France during a time of considerable upheaval, as a societal and political exemplar, as an unreachable or unsuitable model, as an experiment, as a dream or a refuge, and how France indeed perceived itself in turn. Their reading will sustain the findings of Echeverria, Furet, Godechot and others, that is, evolution from pre-revolutionary pro-Americanism to a less enthusiastic admiration in the 1790s, yet these essays help flesh out a more nuanced and detailed picture. They provide additional pieces to the complex puzzle that is still being assembled.

Michèle R. Morris
Department of French

Neither the Bourbons nor the Revolution: Georgetown's Jesuit Founders

James Hennesey, S.J.

France was a country not unknown to the band of Catholic priests who founded the academy at Georgetown on the Potomac. Without exception, they began their education in that kingdom. The founder, John Carroll, was a schoolboy at the English Jesuit college at St. Omer in French Flanders–St. Omers, the English called it–from 1748 to 1753, when Louis XV was king, and he was then a Jesuit novice and scholastic at nearby Watten until 1757. Georgetown's first Jesuit president, the Lancashireman Robert Molyneux, followed Carroll to Watten in 1757, and so had a nearer experience of the expulsion of the Jesuits, including the English exiles, from France in the course of the years 1762-1766. Robert Plunkett, the first president, had been a secular seminarian at Douai in France–Dowey the English pronounced it–who became a Jesuit in 1769 and left the order on August 21, 1773, six days after its total suppression had been promulgated in Rome, but before the promulgation in the Low Countries. He completed his studies at Douai and was ordained priest there. Others among the Maryland ex-Jesuits had similar backgrounds.[1]

It is not surprising that the earliest references found to France have to do with the expulsion of the Jesuits. It was a major event in the life of the English Jesuit province. After 169 years at St. Omers, their one and only college had been transferred to Bruges in the Austrian Netherlands, while the novitiate settled at Ghent in 1766. But there is surprisingly little rancor in references to

1. James Hennesey, S.J., "Several Youth Sent from Here: Native-Born Priests and Religious of English America, 1634-1776," in Nelson H. Minnich *et al.*, eds. *Studies in Catholic History in Honor of John Tracy Ellis* (Wilmington: Michael Glazier, 1985), 1-26; Philip S. Hurley, S.J., "Father Robert Molyneux, 1738-1808," *Woodstock Letters*, 67 (1938), 271-92; P.R. Harris, ed., *Douai College Documents, 1639-1794* (London: Catholic Record Society, 1972); Geoffrey Holt, S.J., *St. Omers and Bruges Colleges, 1593-1773: A Biographical Dictionary* (London: Catholic Record Society, 1979), 210.

the French Bourbons. In a 1764 letter to his brother Daniel, addressed from the principality of Liège, John Carroll noted the death of Louis XV's mistress, the Marquise de Pompadour, and reported that the French Jesuits hoped for a turn in their fortunes "since the great ladie's death." They counted on the intercession of the queen, Marie Lesczynska, her children, the bishops, the "prime nobility," and "every order of magistrates in the different cities and towns where the Jesuits were heretofore established."[2] They hoped in vain, as it turned out. But the American priests maintained a consistent position. They criticized the "irresolute behavior" and the "lack of vigor" of French ministers and the "family compact" of the three united courts, France, Spain and Naples, but the royal family itself escaped censure.[3] Extolling the virtues of the queen's father, Stanislaus of Poland and Lorraine at a later date, Carroll once more fastened on the memory of la Pompadour, noting the disgrace of her protégé, the Duc de Choiseul, and the reform of the *parlements* that accompanied it.[4]

For Joseph II, the Holy Roman Emperor, there was no such sympathy. Carroll wrote scornfully of "the character of justice and impartial administration" which that monarch "so much affects," and wondered if his pretensions were only a cloak for "rivetting still faster and faster on his subjects the chains of despotism." The totalitarian prince was in his estimate a "despotical tyrant."[5] Years later, he had not changed his mind. Emperor Joseph's character was "opprobrious and paltry, in the extreme."[6] He was convinced that it was "so new a thing for crowned heads to be just, or rather for them who govern under them," and in 1782 was boasting to his English correspondent, the dedicated monarchist, Charles Plowden, "You see, I have contracted the language of a Republican."[7] That did not prevent him from expressing sympathy for Louis XVI, "the virtuous and beneficent," whose "deplorable fate should draw tears of blood from every American heart."[8] After the death of the Emperor Leopold in 1792, he scarcely concealed his hope that "the feelings of his son [Emperor Francis] may be quicker for the insults imposed on the blood of Austria, thro' the ill treatment of his aunt, the Q[ueen] of France."[9]

---

2. Thomas O'Brien Hanley, S.J., ed., *The John Carroll Papers*, 3 vols. (Notre Dame: The University of Notre Dame Press, 1976), 1: 4. Henceforth, *JCP*.

3. *JCP* 1: 6.

4. *JCP* 1: 13.

5. *JCP* 1: 78, 1: 65.

6. *JCP* 1: 434.

7. *JCP* 1: 65.

8. *JCP* 2: 304.

9. *JCP* 2: 52.

The American Revolution had completed the metamorphosis of John Carroll from Anglo-American to plain American gentleman. Long before France's Revolution, he saw that in the Old World:

> ...the spirit of irreligion...and...of innovation is still prevailing. The reigning principle among the people is a spirit of independence not only of unlawful (which is commendable) but of all authority; and amongst rulers in Europe, it is a spirit of concentrating all jurisdiction within themselves, that they may be uncontrollable in the exercise of every act of despotism.[10]

Carroll was not insensitive to the advantages of life in France. He wrote to Benjamin Franklin at Versailles: "You are undoubtedly happy in the Society of many agreeable persons and in the enjoyments furnished by a fine civilized country," but he urged the statesman to come home to "this Western world," where there was "a new order of things," where flourished "a new combination of ideas and pursuits," where "indeed it will be truly *the new world*."[11]

Carroll wrestled with the idea of revolution. When he was asked to accompany Congress's commissioners to Canada in the spring of 1776, he was reluctant. One reason was his clerical status, the occasion for the invitation. John Adams thought he was just the man to offset the prohibitions against aiding the Americans levelled by Bishop Briand of Quebec. Carroll mused:

> I have observed that when the ministers of Religion leave the duties of their profession to take a busy part in political matters, they generally fall into contempt; and sometimes even bring discredit to the cause, in whose service they are engaged.

A second reason was even more compelling. He did not think that the Canadians had grievances sufficient to justify rebellion, or, if they did, they had not used first the route of petitions and remonstrances, necessary "before it can be lawful to have recourse to arms and change of government."[12] When in 1790, patriots in Brabant and Flanders scored momentary success in their revolt against the Austrians, he was happy, but without explaining the justification.[13] He applauded Edmund Burke's *Reflections on the French Revolution*, noting the "keenness of his censure and the brilliancy of his wit," and was particularly glad to see him take on Rev. Richard Price who had, at a London meeting-house, praised the conduct of "the savage wretches, who committed the murders, and insulted their Sovereigns at Versailles." Burke's

---

10. *JCP* 1: 64.
11. *JCP* 1: 51.
12. *JCP* 1: 46.
13. *JCP* 1: 433-34.

was "a severe, tho' just Philippic." He had, however, some reservations about Burke's arguments as they applied to the American revolutionary experience. Burke seemed to suggest that almost any indignity must be suffered before attempting a change. Nor was Carroll prepared to admit that the system of parliamentary representation prevailing in the British system was fair.[14]

He returned to the topic on reception of the news of a commemoration of the anniversary of the storming of the Bastille. It was a mistake, Carroll thought, "to celebrate with so much parade the memory of a revolution which is connected with principles destructive of the government and constitution of England." The next step would be "to follow the example, without discriminating, what was praiseworthy, from that, which was subversive of all order, and licentiously wicked."[15] Finally, turning to a matter on which he regularly disagreed with his British friend, he defended Irish rebellion against England:

> It is not right, perhaps, as you observe for the present generation to use violent means to redress, because the past generation was most inhumanly treated: but surely it is lawful for 3,000,000 of people, on whom that treatment is still continued, to use a very firm and even, if necessary, an intimidating tone, to work out their recovery of the common rights of citizenship.

But no analogy was to be made with the "French Democrates":

> No one would have blamed these had they confined themselves to the necessary means of delivering themselves from real despotism: but they proceeded farther and overturned their government, founded on the general agreement of the nation, and on the respective rights of the different orders of the community.

This was not the case in Ireland. The "great body of the nation" had never agreed to live under the present laws. Irish people were "disfranchised and degraded by a most insufferable tyranny." The continuation of that system of oppression authorized "the most decisive measure of redress."[16] He obviously did not feel that France was a parallel case.

Carroll was not in sympathy with the Revolution in France. But he was not quite so violently opposed to it as was another American Jesuit, one who after independence had remained in England, Nicholas Sewall. He advocated a propaganda campaign against "the writings of T. Paine and such fellows," and

---

14. *JCP* 1: 500-01.
15. *JCP* 1: 523.
16. *JCP* 2: 40-41.

the employment of "proper people in every part of the Kingdom" to win over the populace. "Better is a half million spent in this sort of secret service, than two million in force of arms and loss of blood." But if necessary, "Another great, and the only sure means to prevent insurrection in England, will be to crush the Republic in France, which must be effected by a grand coalition of all the European powers."[17] Closer to home, the 86-year old patriarch of the Maryland clergy, Thomas Digges, was of a similar, if less sanguinary, mind. The émigré Duc de la Rochefoucauld paid him a visit the Wednesday in Passion Week, 1797. The old man was a gracious host, the dinner "very sparing, quite Catholic and consequently not very restorative," and the conversation equally unappetizing. Digges informed Louis XVI's general that France was peopled with atheists and villains, the Revolution was punishment for its sins, and the true cause of its calamity was not the writings of Voltaire and Rousseau, but the destruction of the Jesuits.[18]

Liking for France, which, except in the recriminations of old Father Digges, had survived the expulsion of the Jesuits, increased during the American Revolution. While Carroll had to warn his friend Plowden not to believe everything he read of French influence in the British press,[19] warm friendships grew up, especially in Philadelphia, where Father Robert Molyneux, the English-speaking pastor (there was also a German-speaking pastor), served as English tutor to Anne-César de la Luzerne, the French diplomatic agent, so that he was "often among the brilliant company at his hotel," and able to test "his natural talents for elegant life and manners."[20] In return the French diplomat facilitated correspondence between the American priests and Rome. A final bond Carroll referred to in a 1781 letter to the Governor of Maryland, Thomas Simm Lee, when he wrote: "Three of my mother's grandsons are with the Marquis [de La Fayette]." They were his sister's sons, serving in the Virginia campaign.[21]

Sadness and criticism over events in France soon became prominent in John Carroll's letters. In March 1788, he wrote his friend Plowden that construction of the academy would begin that summer "on one of the most

---

17. *Archives of the British Jesuit Province*, London. Letters: Frs. Stone, Sewall, Connell. Nicholas Sewall to Joseph Dunn, Preston, November 11, 1790. Nicholas Sewall, S.J. (1745-1834), later Provincial of England, was one of two wealthy American Jesuit brothers. He was a regular correspondent with, and kindred spirit of, his brother, Charles, S.J., a director of Georgetown College. In a letter to Nicholas on November 21, 1803, Charles referred to Napoleon as "the Corsican despot," and reported the presence in Baltimore of his brother Jerome, "a little, insignificant, dissipated youth of about 19 years of age" (*Archives of the British Jesuit Province*, London: Maryland. Charles to Nicholas Sewall, St. Thomas Manor, November 21, 1803).

18. François Alexandre Frédéric, Duc de la Rochefoucauld-Liancourt, *Travels in North America*, 2: 306-08, in *American Catholic Historical Researches* 8 (1891): 72-74.

19. *JCP* 1: 197.

20. Hurley, 277-79; *JCP* 1: 56.

21. *JCP* 1: 59.

lovely situations that imagination can frame," but of France he had only to regret "her present state of humiliation," and "the despicable figure" the country made since the death in the previous year of "that great and good man, the comte de Vergennes."[22] More was to come, all of it negative.

Writing to Plowden on October 23, 1789, he wondered how religion would fare in the midst of the "convulsions in France," and he feared that his worst apprehensions were being realized. This led to a diatribe on the state of French religiosity:

> I have long thought that almost every man in that kingdom above the rank of mediocrity, and many even of these, are lost to every feeling of Religion. We have many of them in this town, Traders and others. It is the case generally throughout the United States. They are every where a scandal to Religion, with very few exceptions; not only that, but they disseminate, as much as they can, all the principles of irreligion, of contempt for the church, and disregard for the duties, which both command.

Not only that, but the continental French had been a bad example to the "numerous body of Acadians, of French Neutrals, and their descendants, who being expelled by the English from Nova Scotia in the war of 1755, settled and increased here" [in Baltimore].

But religious prospects were not all bad. The academy was coming along well, and Carroll hoped for a start-up in the following summer. He predicted the school would be "our main sheet anchor for Religion."[23]

Carroll's promotion to the episcopacy and his trip to England for episcopal ordination prompted further reflections. Making his apologies to the papal nuncio in France, Archbishop Antonio Dugnani, for not having asked him to do the honors, he explained that "before my departure from America, the troubles of France were described to us as so frightful that I believed your Excellency would no longer be there."[24] It was at this time that Carroll contracted with the Sulpicians to come to the United States, and he several times regretted that he owed "so great a blessing" to the "lamentable catastrophe in France." He was fearful that the news get out that "the Gentlemen of St. Sulpice intend so many things for Religion," lest "they may be bereft of the means by the gripping hand of irreligious despotism."[25]

22. *JCP* 1: 275, 273.
23. *JCP* 1: 390.
24. *JCP* 1: 455. Carroll sent similar "regrets" to bishops in Ireland and Quebec. He had never previously mentioned France.
25. *JCP* 1: 466.

In September 1971, Carroll reported on several clerical recruits who had arrived in America fleeing the "devastation of religion in [their] own Country." Several of these he attached to the Baltimore cathedral, where they "attract a great concourse of all denominations by the great decency and exactness, with which they perform all parts of divine service." Still others were settled in Virginia (where John Dubois, future bishop of New York, led a colony) and in the Ohio valley. Bishop Carroll was optimistic about the future of St. Mary's Seminary, an all-French venture, and he reported that, finally, "our George-town academy will be opened next month."[26]

Alarm led to discouragement. In February 1791, he wrote that he had just read Burke's "pamphlet," and that he admired it very much. His conclusions were gloomy: "France is gone. I see it, and I wish it may not be, irrecoverably: for Religion, I mean."[27]

News of the Civil Constitution of the Clergy adopted on July 12, 1790 by the Constituent Assembly and given the royal approval on July 22, did nothing to alleviate John Carroll's anxieties. The vast majority of the French bishops had signified their dissent from the Constitution, and Pius VI condemned it in the brief, *Quod Aliquantum* (March 10, 1791). Had the Constitution done no more "than to assert to a generous people a free government and political happiness," Carroll wrote, it would have his approval, but he agreed that there were clauses in it that altered "the principles of our faith, and violated those rights of spiritual jurisdiction which being derived from God and not from men, are not within the competency of any authority merely human."[28] Years later (in 1809), in the course of correspondence with ex-Constitutional Bishop Henri Grégoire (whom he was careful to address as "Monseigneur"), he explained that the church would be "best preserved in its unity, and integrity, by the intimate union and correspondence between its visible head, and the bishops and pastors diffused over the Christian world."[29]

By March 1792, Carroll was anticipating that the "Princes and emigrants" would have considerable support within France, and reported that the émigrés in Baltimore were "full of impatience and expectation."[30] By June, as the French monarchy was crumbling and the country was moving to the *levée en masse*, he was puzzling what consequences the death of Leopold II and the assassination of Gustavus III of Sweden would have on the resolution of the foreign princes, and he was apprehensive, thinking "that foreign princes will have to be cautious of sending their troops among the French, where their

26. *JCP* 1: 516.
27. *JCP* 1: 492.
28. *JCP* 1: 546.
29. *JCP* 3: 105.
30. *JCP* 2: 22.

habits and even principles of discipline may be corrupted by the cry of liberty."[31]

February 1793 saw him worried at the fate of Liège, where Prince-Bishop Charles van Velbruck had welcomed the ex-Jesuits who reformed there the school formerly at Bruges and before that at St. Omer.[32] "I can hardly suppose," he wrote, "that they, who are animated with diabolical fury against Religion and its ministers, will give a day's respite to an establishment formed by Ex-jesuits and governed by the maxims and in the principles of the abolished Society." But he was upbeat in his estimate of the French émigré clergy. He spoke of their "admirable conduct" and "the influence of religious motives on such Catholics as make their Religion the rule of their conduct," singing the praises of "a Clergy so numerous and having so many ties of blood and interest in France," who now wandered the face of the earth and were so wonderful a spectacle that it was something unheard of in human annals.[33]

Still and all, as he wrote Archbishop John Troy, O.P., of Dublin in July 1794, there was a great threat of "*ecclesiastical*, no less than civil democracy" in the United States. "We are threatened with the dissemination of French political errors; our alliance with them, and the habits of intimacy formed during the [Revolutionary] war between many Americans and some French officers, who have since taken a leading part in their revolution, are active means of spreading the infatuation. It requires all the firmness and integrity of our great President Washington and the persons acting under him," he concluded, "to withstand the torrent." He found in the country much less "effervescence" about France, however, than there had been just a few months earlier. He blamed the earlier enthusiasm on a combination of efforts by French agents and the "lawless depredations on our shipping" perpetrated by Britain.[34] He elaborated on the first of these themes in a second letter to Troy, sent only a week later:

> ...the decency of religious service has been interrupted and disturbed here by the profaneness of numerous French democrats, who, from the West Indies, have inundated our country, and Baltimore in particular. Nor is this the only mischief they have attempted. By indefatigable industry they have succeeded in instituting, within the bosom of our towns, democratical societies, pregnant with all the materials of anarchy and violent hostility against Britain, though evidently adverse to the interests of America.

---

31. *JCP* 2: 52-53.

32. Hubert Chadwick, S.J., *From St. Omers to Stonyhurst: A History of Two Centuries* (London: Burns and Oates, 1962), 362-63.

33. *JCP* 2: 83.

34. *JCP* 2: 120-22.

To counter "the machinations of these societies," Carroll counted on "the firmness, the undaunted courage, the personal influence, and consummate prudence of that wonderful man, our President, Washington." He hoped that Britain would adopt a rational course, "respecting the rights of commerce of neutral nations," and so "strengthen our arms against the violence of the abettors of French politics."[35]

As the years wore on, and revolutionary France began to look more permanent, Carroll's fears increased. In April 1795, he worried that accessions to French strength in new territories, the ships and seamen of Holland, and "the plunder, she has collected by confiscations and the guillotine," might enable France to overcome England, whose royal navy seemed to him to be suffering "great mismanagement."[36] A year later, "the rapid advances of the French in Italy and Germany" astonished him. He thought that fear of the spread of revolutionary principles enfeebled opposition to them:

> Those princes, whose will alone was law heretofore, are afraid of using any authority to prepare against, or defend themselves in times of invasion; they dare not call their subjects into arms, for fear, that the contagion of licentiousness should spread amongst them. Magistrates are deterred from punishing offenders, and officers of maintaining subordination, lest a revolution should happen and they become the victims of their zeal.

"Nothing," he predicted, "will stop the progress of the French, except they should push forward and make attempts against the Russians in Poland."

All this, he mourned, had not taught the émigrés a lesson. Their tragedy

> would not be so painful a consideration could we but behold, that the victims of revolutionary rage kissed the rod of God's vengeance and profited by his rigorous justice over them. Instead of this, I find the Emigrants, with which this, as well as other countries abound, uncorrected by the severe afflictions, under which they are exercised, as much, as they were seduced to forget God in their former prosperity. Religious principles appear to have never had the least hold of their hearts; and this I attribute to the miserable, and libertine education which succeeded the very virtuous one which their Fathers received in the schools of the Society.

He recommended to his correspondent the farewell address of President Washington; he had "far other principles of the necessity of Religion than the superficial French Theorists on government."[37]

---

35. *JCP* 2: 123-24.
36. *JCP* 2: 138.
37. *JCP* 2: 188.

"The College of George-Town" at the same time was hurting for a "supply of capable and virtuous masters," and it had besides lost its president, Robert Molyneux, S.J., who had found the job "too bustling and requiring too much energy for his good-natured and somewhat torpid disposition." But the Sulpician William Du Bourg, "a French Clergyman of abilities and most pleasing character," would replace him.[38]

By 1798, Carroll was feeling more confident about his school. The property had been made over to the Corporation of Roman Catholic Clergymen, founded in 1793, and he looked to the College at Georgetown to provide successors in that corporation, educated in "the same sound principles" as the present members. He was less sanguine about the European situation:

> But that which principally concerns us are the oppressions of Religion. France, Flanders, half Germany, and alas! *Italia la bella*... It is impossible for a contemplative mind, like yours, not to foresee the effects, even after peace, of the present gigantic power of France; and that nothing will be able to withstand their increased strength of territory, population, revenue, and her influential principles. In a word, I see nothing but the hand of God to avert the evils with which the revolution is pregnant.[39]

The situation was better as the year ended. News had come of "Nelson's unexampled victory" in the Battle of the Nile. France, "in spite of all her plunder, gives evident symptoms of a great diminution of power and energy," and even the populace of other countries, so long stunned with the empty noise of liberty and equality, now know the full value of those expressions in the mouth of modern Frenchmen." Carroll had also been reading the Hon. Robert Clifford's translation of *Memoirs Illustrating the History of Jacobinism* by the former French Jesuit Augustin Barruel. The bishop found in this classic formulation of the conspiratorial theory of the French Revolution "a system of impiety which I did not think it was in the heart of man to conceive," but he also thought that "there is too much repetition and verbosity in his reflections." The work, he felt, might have been much shorter.[40]

If the European situation had improved, affairs at Georgetown were in turmoil as 1798 drew to a close. President Du Bourg had come to a parting of the ways with the five Jesuit-connected Directors of the College. It may be that his willingness to spend money was a problem, and there was talk of a Sulpician plot to oust from the college the ex-Jesuits, "who had been at great

---

38. *JCP* 2: 189.

39. *JCP* 2: 233-34.

40. *JCP* 2: 250. Augustin Barruel's work was published in 1798 and in English translation that same year. See Michel Riquet, S.J, "Un Jésuite franc-maçon, historien du Jacobinisme, le p. Augustin Barruel, 1741-1820," *Archivum Historicum Societatis Iesu* 43 (1974): 157-65.

expense in building it," but Bishop Carroll thought that "national attachments, that bane of all communities" was "the original cause of the mischief." The Directors "had too strong prejudices against everything which was derived, in any shape, from France." In fact, in those years of the Adams presidency, anti-French feeling ran very strong in the country. The Alien and Sedition Acts had been passed the previous summer, and the nation was ready to go to war with France.[41] So Georgetown lost a good president and fell into the hands of the brothers Neale, virtuous men, but rigid and severe and totally lacking in either the literary qualities or the affability needed in a college president.[42]

With the Du Bourg resignation, a phase in Georgetown's early "French connection" ended. There was more to come, in the Napoleonic era, with John Carroll alternating between soliciting donations from Bonaparte for the Baltimore cathedral building fund and condemning him for imprisoning two successive popes.[43] Emigrés came and went, some chancing a return to their native France. The early Directors of the College were hardly men with a broad view. Carroll characterized them harshly: "...some, whose violence will listen to no lessons of moderation, and others whose knowledge and observations are too confining to comprehend that anything useful can be learned, beyond what they know..."[44] Their views of international affairs were correspondingly narrow. John Carroll himself remained always a republican. He could understand and support revolution, as, for example, in the United States, in Brabant, perhaps in Ireland. But he did not understand the French Revolution. He opposed it mainly because of the persecution of religion. That was "wild democracy" beyond his approving.[45]

---

41. Annabelle M. Melville, *Louis William Du Bourg*, 2 vols. (Chicago: Loyola University Press, 1986), 1: 68-75; Christopher J. Kauffman, *Tradition and Transformation in Catholic Culture; The Priests of Saint Sulpice in the United States from 1791 to the Present* (New York: Macmillan, 1988), 46-47; *JCP* 2: 248.

42. *JCP* 2: 383; 3: 53.

43. *JCP* 2: 423; 332.

44. *JCP* 2: 318.

45. *JCP* 2: 189.

Joseph-François Lafitau, linguiste présaussurien

Madeleine A. Simons

Redécouvert après une éclipse de deux siècles, le jésuite J.F. Lafitau (1681-1746) est salué aujourd'hui comme le fondateur de l'ethnologie comparée et un pionnier dans l'anthropologie sociale. Son livre, *Moeurs des sauvages américains comparées aux moeurs des premiers temps (1724)*,[1] aujourd'hui disponible en livre de poche,[2] a fait l'objet d'une remarquable édition critique en anglais.[3] Au demeurant, un esprit audacieux qui ose affirmer à l'encontre des "vérités établies" de l'époque des Lumières que les anciens Grecs et les anciens Hébreux étaient des sauvages tout comme les Iroquois. On a tout dit sur l'originalité de la méthode comparative qui, sans être absolument neuve, est appliquée par Lafitau avec une rigueur qu'on n'hésite pas à qualifier aujourd'hui de scientifique. Par contre, on a considéré d'intérêt nul ses remarques sur la langue, objet du dernier chapitre de l'essai, chapitre que Fenton et Moore ont jugé décevant.

Sans doute, on ne peut que déplorer avec eux que le Père Lafitau n'ait pas poursuivi l'oeuvre de ses prédécesseurs missionnaires, Chaumonot pour la grammaire huronne, et Bruyas pour celle des Mohawks, en composant une grammaire iroquoise. Les circonstances ayant fait obstacle à son retour auprès des Iroquois de Sault-Saint-Louis, il a néanmoins songé à écrire un tel ouvrage puisque seuls des vocabulaires rudimentaires avec des mots estropiés avaient été publiés jusqu'alors. Il y a renoncé sachant que le public ne s'intéresse pas à ces langues: un ouvrage sérieux et détaillé serait considéré comme fort ennuyeux, et un abrégé serait trop imparfait. Il nous reste heureusement le

---

1. Joseph-François Lafitau, *Moeurs des sauvages amériquains comparées aux moeurs des premiers temps*, 2 vols. (Paris: Saugrain, 1724). Toutes les citations sont tirées de cette édition (*MSA*). J'ai modernisé l'orthographe.

2. *Moeurs des sauvages américains* (Paris: Maspero, 1983). Introduction, choix de textes et notes par Edna Hindie Lemay.

3. Joseph-François Lafitau, *Customs of the American Indians Compared with the Customs of Primitive Times*, ed. and transl. by William N. Fenton and Elizabeth L. Moore, 2 vols. (Toronto: The Champlain Society, 1974).

chapitre IX, le dernier de l'essai, intitulé *Langue* qui n'est qu'une ébauche sans doute, mais révèle des vues exceptionnelles pour l'époque et un point de vue déjà présaussurien. Parce que les principes généraux qui y sont énoncés nous semblent aujourd'hui évidents, il est difficile d'imaginer une époque où ils n'avaient pas été exprimés, où le lexique de la linguistique générale n'existait pas encore.[4] Si le style de Lafitau nous semble pesant et gauche quand il décrit des phénomènes de langue, c'est que le glossaire approprié lui manquait totalement.

Apprentissage sur le terrain

En 1711, le P. Lafitau, ses études terminées–rhétorique,philosophie, théologie–fait voile vers la Nouvelle France. Il restera 5 ans à Sault-Saint-Louis (1712-1717) près de Montréal, comme missionnaire chez les Iroquois. Il. se met immédiatement à l'étude de leur langue. Toutes les remarques concernant l'apprentissage de cette langue nous sont précieuses car on ne connaît guère de documents de cette époque concernant l'acquisition d'une langue améridienne par un Européen, sur le terrain. Lafitau considère que les moeurs, les usages, les coutumes d'un peuple ne s'apprennent que "par une connaissance parfaite des langues étrangères, une grande habitude de commercer [avoir des échanges sociaux] avec les naturels du pays, et une grande attention à réfléchir sur ces mêmes usages."[5] Il est donc loin de sous-estimer la difficulté de l'entreprise.

Eh quoi, sont-ce là ces vues originales que vous nous annonciez? Oui, précisément. Appliquer des critères d'excellence à des langues considérées comme rudimentaires, et par surcroît, philosopher à leur sujet aurait de quoi surprendre les grammairiens de l'*Encyclopédie*. Qu'il suffise de rappeler que le mathématicien La Condamine, considéré à Paris comme une autorité sur les sauvages parce qu'il avait publié un livre sur l'Amazonie, n'avait que de vagues notions de leurs langues et ne les avait observés que de très loin. Voltaire, on s'y attendait, de son fauteuil de Ferney, ridiculise l'ouvrage du jésuite, dans son *Essai sur les moeurs*. Vous chercherez en vain le nom de Lafitau dans l'*Encyclopédie*. Mais Rousseau et son bon sauvage? Il ne mentionne pas Lafitau, mais cite, comme tout le monde, La Condamine.[6]

Avant de présenter les vues théoriques sur la langue de notre missionnaire et de les mettre côte à côte avec leur expression moderne dans le *Cours de*

---

4. La liste des mots-clés de la linguistique moderne qui apparurent pour la première fois dans le *Cours* est impressionnante. Voir Ferdinand de Saussure, *Cours de linguistique générale* (Paris: Payot, 1975), Introduction, iv.

5. Joseph-François Lafitau, *Histoire des découvertes et conquêtes des Portugais dans le Nouveau Monde* (Paris, 1733), xiv.

6. Charles-M. de La Condamine, *Voyage sur l'Amazone* (Paris: Maspero, 1981).

linguistique générale, il importe donc de rappeler ici l'expérience vécue sur le terrain d'un homme de trente ans pour qui les langues faisaient problème, si l'on en croit Fenton. Il est vrai qu'il ne savait très bien que le latin et l'espagnol; le grec, passablement; l'hébreu, à peine.

Les difficultés d'acquisition des langues amérindiennes. Refus du jargon.

Il s'agit donc d'apprendre une langue qui ne ressemble à aucune des langues qui "passent pour savantes"–l'expression est de Lafitau lui-même. Elle aurait enchanté Saussure. Elle nous renseigne déjà, sur son refus de valoriser certaines langues en leur assignant un génie particulier. L'iroquois ne ressemble, en outre, à aucune des langues vivantes connues, exception faite de celle des Esquimaux et des Basques.

Cependant, pour la plupart des Français de la Nouvelle France, la communication avec les Indiens ne fait pas problème:

> Ils s'expriment par gestes, et par l'usage de certains mots corrompus qui n'existent ni dans l'une ni dans l'autre langue, mais qui par l'usage restent consacrés à certaines significations, qui servent à les faire parvenir au but qu'ils se proposent. Le dictionnaire de ce jargon est fort court. Il y entre des mots empruntés aux langues de toutes les nations avec qui les Français ont commercé. Dans ce curieux idiome, on prend un temps pour un autre, le pluriel pour le singulier, la troisième personne pour la première.[7]

Qu'importe, on finit toujours par se comprendre. Le Français croit alors parler la langue du sauvage et le sauvage la langue du Français. C'est cet idiolecte que les sauvages de Sault-Saint-Louis lui parlent tout d'abord. Il n'y entend rien et leur demande de parler leur langue naturelle, puis s'astreint à l'apprendre. Il n'a malheureusement pas de pédagogie-miracle à proposer: du temps, de l'application, de la réflexion, et la grâce divine...

Lafitau est conscient de l'extrême complexité de ces langues–chaque nation en possède trois: l'une propre au style du Conseil si relevée, si obscure, qu'ils n'entendent souvent pas ce qu'ils disent; la seconde, particulière aux hommes; la troisième, particulière aux femmes. (476) Il ne saurait souscrire à l'opinion acceptée dans les cercles philosophiques que des peuples grossiers n'ont que des langues grossières. L'*Encyclopédie* ne fait pas mention des Iroquois, mais, à l'article *Huron*, on peut lire:

---

7. Lafitau, *MSA*, 475. Il est difficile de ne pas songer ici à certain personnage du *Nom de la Rose*.

> La langue de ces sauvages est gutturale et très pauvre parce qu'ils n'ont connaissance que d'un très petit nombre de choses. Comme chaque nation du Canada, ainsi chaque tribu et chaque bourgade de Hurons porte le nom d'un animal, apparemment parce que tous ces barbares sont persuadés que les hommes viennent des animaux.

L'auteur de l'article a probablement eu en main ces petits lexiques de poche à l'usage des marchands d'eau-de-vie et autres, auxquels Lafitau fait référence. Il mesure le degré de civilisation au nombre de substantifs et le huron n'en possède point.[8]

Premières constatations

a. Les langues amérIdiennes ont une économie (*nomos*, règle), c'est-à-dire qu'elles sont soumises à des règles de fonctionnement très différentes de celles auxquelles il est accoutumé.

b. Les catégories descriptives d'Aristote, ce qu'il appelle les parties d'oraison (noms, verbes, adverbes...) ne s'appliquent pas à ces langues. L'erreur de la plupart des missionnaires est de vouloir appliquer à ces langues les mêmes catégories qu'aux langues qu'ils connaissent, au lieu de les étudier dans leur spécificité: "Les deux langues, huronne et iroquoise n'ont que le verbe qui domine dans toute la langue. Point de nom substantif et adjectif, point de déclinaisons de cas, d'articles..." Etonnement des missionnaires qui cherchent tout d'abord des noms, parce que pour eux, la langue est, par essence nomenclature,[9] avec correspondance parfaite entre les mots et les choses, les "substances". Cette conception est fondée sur un postulat philosophique hérité des Grecs: les idées préexistent aux mots.

c. Enfin, ces langues n'ont pas d'écriture. Point de livres pour les apprendre. Il faut donc se constituer, soi-même, une méthode, préparer une grammaire. Comme on aimerait avoir les carnets du Père Lafitau, là où il notait ses observations journalières sur la langue iroquoise. Il les a certainement utilisés pour la préparation de son livre. Ils devaient être alors au collège Louis-le-Grand avec les notes pour ses autres ouvrages. Ont-ils complètement disparu? Ont-ils été détruits en 1761 quand les Jésuites ont été chassés de France? Transportés à Rome? Les recherches à la bibliothèque vaticane n'ont jusqu'ici rien apporté. On ne peut que conjecturer sur le système de notation qu'il utilisait. Il semble qu'il rendait les sons de la langue huronne avec des sons français approximatifs. Avait-il des signes particuliers pour les différentes consonnes, à la manière du président de Brosses dans

---

8. Selon Denys d'Halicarnasse, grammairien grec, le nom indique l'essence (*ousia*), le verbe, l'accident. Cf. Gérard Genette, *Mimologiques* (Paris: Seuil, 1976), 185, n.3.

9. Cf. Saussure, 97.

son *Traité de la formation mécanique*? Un esprit aussi méthodique avait sûrement un système pour la transcription des phonèmes iroquois.

Un précurseur

De ses observations sur la langue des Iroquois, il tire quelques grands principes de linguistique générale qui seront isolés ci-dessous et mis en parallèle avec leur expression saussurienne, mais dans un ordre différent de celui du *Cours*.

Au chapitre II du *Cours* est énoncée la matière de la linguistique:

> La matière de la linguistique est constituée d'abord par toutes les manifestations du langage humain, qu'il s'agisse des peuples sauvages ou des nations civilisées, des époques archaïques, classiques ou de décadence, en tenant compte, dans chaque période, non seulement du langage correct et du 'beau langage', mais de toutes les formes d'expression. (20)

Comme on l'a souligné plus haut, Lafitau refuse toute classification hiérarchique des langues et rejette l'approche européocentrique.

1. Le comportement linguistique est largement inconscient. Loin d'être simples et grossières, les langues des peuples sauvages révèlent des complexités dont ils ne sont pas eux-mêmes conscients, et auraient été bien incapables d'inventer:

> Il règne dans celle même des peuples les plus grossiers, un ordre et une économie qu'ils n'ont jamais été en état d'introduire d'eux-mêmes par art et par principes, et qu'ils ont encore aujourd'hui, sans être en état de les bien comprendre; de manière qu'ils paraissent tout surpris lorsque les missionnaires qui les ont pénétrées par un long usage, par une étude constante, et encore plus par le secours d'en haut, leur font remarquer dans leur langue propre cette *connexion méthodique* qu'ils n'avaient jamais aperçue.[10]

Saussure: "la réflexion n'intervient pas dans la pratique d'un idiome; que les sujets sont, dans une large mesure, inconscients des lois de la langue; et s'ils ne s'en rendent pas compte, comment pourraient-ils les modifier?" (106)

2. Cette *connexion méthodique* indique que la langue est systémique. Saussure: "Une langue constitue un système... Ce système est un mécanisme complexe; l'on ne peut le saisir que par la réflexion; ceux-là mêmes qui en font un usage journalier l'ignorent profondément." (107)

---

10. Lafitau, *MSA*, 459. Je souligne.

3. Aux observations sur les structures, Lafitau joint des observations sur ce que nous appelons aujourd'hui les différences phonémiques. Les Iroquois travestissent notre langue parce qu'ils ne peuvent pas en reproduire les sons avec exactitude. Exemple: *Lucifer* est prononcé *Roufikouer*; *Ponce Pilate*, *Konskouirat*. Mais, de même qu'ils travestissent notre langue, nous travestissons la leur. Lafitau soupçonne qu'il y a de la méthode dans ce travesti. Il se rend compte que la substitution d'un phonème pour un autre est systématique, elle aussi. Il s'agit d'une permutation. Ils n'ont pas de labiales dit-il, et leur substituent des sons qui leur paraissent semblables. Qu'on essaie d'imaginer ces Indiens qui ont une grande facilité à parler la bouche ouverte et (*sic*) en tenant le calumet entre les dents... Lafitau exagère peut-être à moins qu'il n'ait écrit par erreur *et* au lieu de *ou*. On imagine assez mal le calumet dans une bouche ouverte. Conscient de ces différences, il suggère une phonologie comparative, mais n'insiste pas sur la nécessité de reproduire exactement les sons et ne suggère pas d'écriture phonologique.

Saussure ne la jugeait pas nécessaire: "En dehors de la science, l'exactitude phonologique n'est pas très désirable." (57) En effet, le sens est produit par un jeu d'oppositions des expressions acoustiques. Cette découverte d'un système différentiel producteur de sens, notre missionnaire ne la soupçonnait pas, au surplus ne pouvait pas la penser.

Il ne dissimule pas que les efforts linguistiques des missionnaires sont parfois la cause d'un fol amusement chez les Indiens. Mais son apprentissage ardu lui permet de comprendre, non seulement la méconnaissance des Européens à l'égard des Indiens, mais celle des historiens de l'antiquité à l'égard de ceux qu'ils nomment les barbares. Les Grecs et les Romains les ont décrits à distance, sans les bien connaître, et, surtout, sans connaître leur langue. Le barbare est celui qui ne parle pas le grec et ne produit que des sons inintelligibles *bar...bar...* Lafitau se méfie donc de ces témoignages incontestés pendant des siècles. Or,

> ils sont si peu fidèles dans le récit qu'ils nous ont fait des moeurs et des coutumes des barbares qu'ils *voyaient de trop loin* pour les bien connaître, auront plus facilement estropié les mots de leurs langues que les figures de leurs personnes dont il nous ont souvent fait des grotesques et des monstres par leur trop grande crédulité."[11]

Pour Lafitau, l'ère du soupçon a déjà commencé. La leçon, ici, est claire, si la syntaxe nous semble un peu confuse. S'il est plus facile de caricaturer une langue que l'on ne comprend pas qu'une personne qu'on peut examiner *de visu*, on sait ce qu'il faut penser des témoignages antiques sur les barbares

---

11. Lafitau, *MSA*, 465. Je souligne.

dont les langues étaient si méprisées. L'ignorance des langues amérindiennes ne peut manquer de causer de semblables méconnaissances. La méthode comparative débouche ici sur l'évaluation critique des sources.

4. Le premier grand principe saussurien, l'arbitraire du signe[12] linguistique, est exprimé par Lafitau d'une manière presque moderne:

> Le langage[13] en un sens, est une chose purement *arbitraire*, et les termes dont il est composé, n'étant que des *signes institués* pour représenter les choses auxquelles ils ont été attachés ne signifient rien par eux-mêmes, c'est-à-dire qu'ils sont indifférents, par eux-mêmes, à signifier une chose ou bien une autre, de la même manière que les caractères et les figures, qui sont les images et les signes des termes, n'ont de force et de valeur, qu'autant qu'on est convenu qu'ils auraient une telle signification. De cette sorte les langues peuvent être multipliées, autant qu'il y a de nations, et elles pourraient être si absolument différentes les unes des autres, qu'il n'y aurait pas une expression, un seul mot de l'une dans l'autre, avec la même signification, sans un pur effet de hasard ou de la communication de ces nations qui auraient adopté quelques mots par le commerce qu'elles auraient eu ensemble.[14]

Saussure: "La langue...n'est limitée en rien dans le choix de ses moyens, car on ne voit pas ce qui empêcherait d'associer une idée quelconque avec une suite quelconque de sons." Ce caractère sépare la langue de toutes les autres institutions et explique sa mutabilité:

> située à la fois dans la masse sociale et dans le temps, personne ne peut rien y changer, et, d'autre part, l'arbitraire de ses signes entraîne théoriquement la liberté d'établir n'importe quel rapport entre la matière phonique et les idées. Il en résulte que ces deux éléments unis dans les signes gardent chacun leur vie propre dans une proportion inconnue ailleurs, et que la langue s'altère ou plutôt évolue, sous l'influence de tous les agents qui peuvent atteindre soit les sons soit le sens. (110)

Dans sa réflexion sur les langues, Lafitau ne néglige pas non plus leur dimension historique et évolutive, objet de la cinquième partie du *Cours*. Il remarque que toutes les langues évoluent, mais il remarque aussi que certaines disparaissent, remplacées par celles des conquérants alors que d'autres au contraire survivent. Ainsi aucune des colonies grecques d'Afrique

---

12. On dit aujourd'hui l'immotivation.

13. Il ignore naturellement la distinction entre langage, aptitude naturelle à tous les hommes, et langue, produit social de la faculté du langage. Cf. Saussure, 24-25.

14. Lafitau, *MSA*, 488. Je souligne.

ou de la grande Asie n'ont conservé la langue grecque. (465) Saussure notera qu'en Afrique, la langue punique et la numidique ont survécu autour de Carthage. (267)

Réfléchissant au sort des langues des colonisés, Lafitau signale le danger d'extinction de la langue huronne, du moins sa réduction massive. Ce n'est pas le cri d'alarme de *Tristes Tropiques*, mais une constatation sévère de génocide. Le Père de Brébeuf comptait environ 30 000 âmes de vrais Hurons. Qu'en reste-t-il aujourd'hui? Quant aux Algonquins, il ne reste d'eux que les Iroquois, "les eaux-de-vie les ayant presque complètement détruits." (477)

5. Potentiel de créativité des langues. Les grammairiens et théoriciens des langues au XVIIIe siècle ne se soucient pas d'inclure dans leurs travaux les langues des sauvages. Ils sont bien trop occupés à débattre les mérites respectifs de la syntaxe française et de la syntaxe latine. Fi donc des langues des sauvages![15] Diderot, dans la *Lettre sur les sourds et muets* exprime un gallocentrisme hérité du siècle précédent: "Notre langue est de toutes les langues la plus châtiée, la plus exacte, la plus estimable, celle en un mot qui a retenu le moins de ces négligences que j'appellerais volontiers des reflets de la balbutie des premiers âges."[16] Un siècle plus tard, Renan, pourtant professeur d'hébreu, n'hésite pas à parler de la supériorité des races et des langues indo-européennes récemment étudiées par Bopp et Schlegel avec la méthode comparative.

Lafitau ose intégrer les langues barbares dans la grande famille des langues humaines et sur un pied d'égalité. Son apprentissage sur le terrain lui révèle une totale réciprocité. La langue iroquoise, avec une économie très différente de la française, n'en a pas moins ses beautés et un potentiel illimité de créativité: "Les langues huronne et iroquoise qui n'ont proprement que des verbes, n'en sont pas pour cela moins riches. Il se trouve dans ces verbes un artifice admirable qui supplée à tout le reste, et c'est cet artifice qui fait toute l'économie de ces langues, lesquelles ont leurs beautés comme les nôtres..." (488)

L'époque colonisatrice ne pouvait accueillir de telles remarques. Au XIXe siècle, ce n'est plus la pauvreté des idées que l'on reproche aux langues des Indiens, mais l'horrifiante luxuriance de leurs vocables, hérissés de consonnes comme de flèches au curare: "Les idiomes des hurons, des botocudos et des chesapeaks sont des forêts de consonnes à travers lesquelles, à demi englоutis dans la vase des idées mal rendues, se traînent des mots immenses et hideux,

---

15. Lire à ce sujet, le chapitre "Blanc bonnet *versus* bonnet blanc" dans l'admirable essai de Genette: "Voyage en Cratylie", *Mimologiques*, 183-226.

16. Cité par Genette, 203.

comme rampaient les monstres antédiluviens sous les inextricables végétations du monde primitif."[17]

Esprit scientifique, le P. Lafitau exige l'observation directe et l'étude approfondie des langues indigènes. Il rejette les mythes ethno-centriques et racistes qui prévalaient à son époque et qui triompheront au siècle suivant. Chrétien, il ne peut admettre, comme le fait son illustre compatriote La Condamine,[18] l'existence d'une sous-humanité à placer au niveau des bêtes.

L'Ecole de Langues et Linguistique de Georgetown se devait, à l'occasion du bicentenaire de l'université, de rendre hommage à ce grand jésuite.

---

17. Victor Hugo, justement surnommé "le cyclope français", dans *Le Rhin*, lettre XX, cité par Genette, 399.

18. La Condamine, 62.

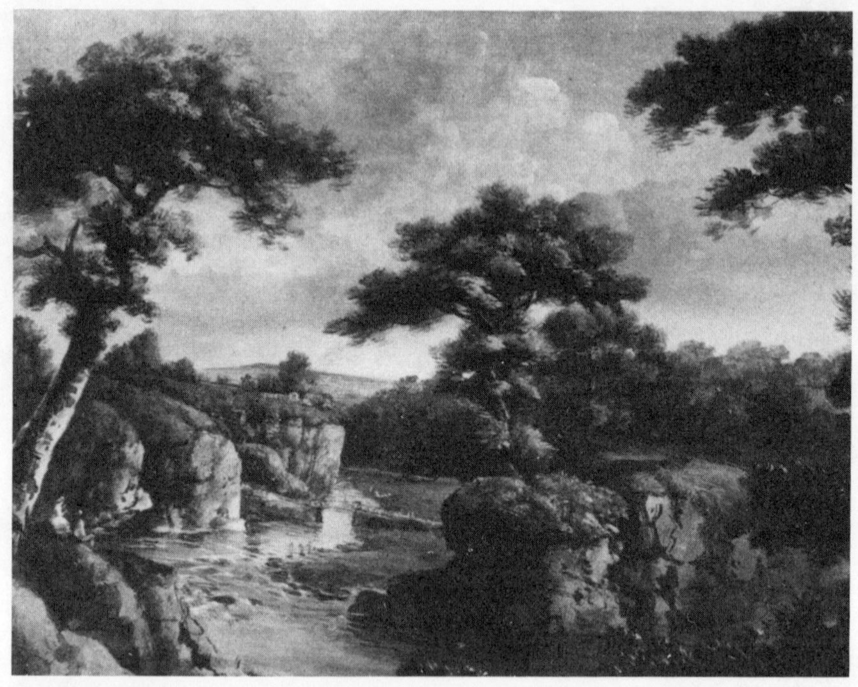

Les petites chutes du Potomac, visitées par les princes le 4 avril 1797 (coll. du Comte de Paris). Cliché Flammarion.

Mondes nouveaux, vices anciens: Journal de voyage de Louis-Philippe en Amérique, impressions de jeunesse

Aurelia Roman[1]

Huit ans après la Révolution française, en 1797, par un timide début de printemps, un groupe pittoresque parcourt à cheval les terres récemment défrichées, ou encore sauvages, de la Virginie, de la Caroline du Nord, du Kentucky et du Tennessee. Ils sont quatre: le duc d'Orléans,[2] futur roi des Français (1830-1848) qui n'a alors que 23 ans, ses deux jeunes frères, le duc de Montpensier, 21 ans, et le comte de Beaujolais, 17 ans, récemment libérés de leurs humides cachots de Marseille, et leur fidèle valet, Beaudoin.

Réfugiés outre Atlantique après l'exécution de leur père, cousin du roi, les trois frères décident d'entreprendre de hardis voyages d'exploration. Aidés financièrement en grande partie par des prêts accordés par Gouverneur Morris, ambassadeur des Etats-Unis en France, et guidés par un itinéraire dressé par l'ancien président George Washington lui-même, les jeunes princes allient la curiosité au courage pour découvrir à leur tour les terres frontières du nouveau monde. Fatigués, parfois "mouillés jusqu'aux os, dévorés par toutes sortes d'insectes,"[3] souvent affamés et dormant là où ils le peuvent,

---

1. A mes amis français du Var et des Etats-Unis.

2. Louis-Philippe (1773-1850), roi des Français entre deux révolutions, appartenait à la branche d'Orléans et descendait directement de Louis XIII. Duc de Valois à sa naissance, il devint duc de Chartres en 1787. Après l'exécution de son père, Philippe-*Egalité* en 1793, il prend le titre de duc d'Orléans et c'est sous ce nom qu'il est connu lors de son voyage en Amérique, ou plutôt comme "Mister Orleans." A l'issue de plusieurs aventures en Suisse et en Laponie, il dut s'embarquer pour l'Amérique le 24 septembre 1796. Le Directoire consentit à mettre en liberté ses deux jeunes frères pour qu'ils le rejoignent à Philadelphie au début de l'année suivante. Ils furent parmi les premiers Français à rendre visite aux Indiens. En 1798 ils furent accueillis avec enthousiasme à la Havane, Cuba, mais de nouveau poursuivis, ils quittèrent Cuba l'année suivante pour aller s'établir en Angleterre. Le futur Louis-Philippe ne regagna la France qu'en 1814. Voir Marguerite Castillon du Perron, *Louis-Philippe et la Révolution Française* (Paris: Perrin, 1963).

3. Nous citons ici le duc de Montpensier qui, à la demande de sa mère, la duchesse d'Orléans, rédigea quelques pages sur la partie finale de leur voyage en Amérique du Nord. Voir

chez un cultivateur, dans une pauvre auberge ou à la belle étoile, ils n'oublient pas de prendre des notes dans leurs carnets de voyage.

Le jeune Louis-Philippe et ses deux frères entreprirent ainsi trois grands voyages,[4] du Canada jusqu'à la Nouvelle Orléans et plus tard jusqu'à Cuba. De leurs impressions écrites il ne nous reste plus qu'un seul journal[5] formé de deux cahiers, les notes de Louis-Philippe couvrant la période du 2 mars au 21 mai 1797, date à laquelle il tombe malade et renonce à écrire. Ce journal, qui comprend 203 pages, fait partie des archives de la Maison d'Orléans, récemment ouvertes au public.

Esprit intelligent et habile observateur, instruit et formé par une des femmes les plus douées de son temps, la Comtesse de Genlis, le jeune Louis-Philippe réussit à laisser dans ses notes une grande richesse de détails concrets et d'observations personnelles sur le paysage et les hommes. Il y mêle descriptions physiques et dialogues pleins d'humour, impressions vigoureuses et réflexions perspicaces, captivant l'intérêt à chaque page.

L'importance et la fascination de ces mémoires de voyage sont encore rehaussées par la présence de reproductions des dessins et peintures du frère de l'auteur, Antoine-Philippe, duc de Montpensier. Ancien élève du peintre David, Montpensier révéla son talent dès son plus jeune âge. Inspiré par le paysage américain, il remplit fébrilement plusieurs cahiers d'esquisses au cours du voyage. Ces précieux croquis, "vrai reportage en images", ont disparu aujourd'hui. Il en est de même pour la plupart des gouaches et peintures à l'huile qui en dérivèrent, oeuvres exécutées par Montpensier lui-même, ou par d'autres peintres engagés par Louis-Philippe pour son grandiose projet d'épopée illustrée, mais presque toutes détruites par la révolution de 1848. Il en reste quelques-unes encore à la New York Historical Society, notamment la plus belle, la vue des Chutes du Niagara, que les princes visitèrent le 21 juin 1797. D'autres oeuvres se trouvent dans la collection privée du Comte de Paris ou aux Archives Nationales de France. Si la postérité a gardé justement certaines de ces impressions mémorables, c'est parce qu'à son retour en

---

Louis-Philippe, *Journal de mon voyage d'Amérique* (Paris: Flammarion, 1976), 145-48.

4. Le Musée de l'Histoire de France établit la carte exacte de ces voyages pour l'exposition "Louis-Philippe" (Archives Nationales, 1974-1975). Cette carte est reproduite dans le *Journal*, mentionné ci-dessus, à la fin de l'excellente présentation du volume faite par Suzanne d'Huart, conservatrice des Archives de la Maison de France et Jean-Pierre Babelon, conservateur du Musée de l'Histoire de France.

5. Le journal de Louis-Philippe fut publié pour la première fois en 1976 (note 2). Il fut traduit en anglais et parut dans une élégante édition illustrée des planches en couleurs sous le titre *Diary of my Travels in America*, translated from French by Stephen Becker, Preface by Henry Steele Commager (New York: Delacorte Press, 1977).

Angleterre, en 1800, Montpensier eut l'occasion de s'initier au nouveau procédé de la lithographie.[6]

Nous insisterons sur un dernier point flatteur pour nous, en cette année du bicentenaire de l'Université Georgetown, la découverte dans le journal de Louis-Philippe d'une remarque sur notre école, le premier collège catholique de la jeune république américaine. En effet, le 4 avril 1797, le lendemain de son arrivée dans la région de Washington, Louis-Philippe note dans son *Journal* que la future capitale tracée par un compatriote, Pierre l'Enfant, se trouve en rivalité avec Georgetown: "Georgetown est une jolie ville bâtie en amphithéâtre, sur la rive gauche du Potowmack... Il y a au-dessus de Georgetown un collège de Catholiques qui est établi dans un bâtiment assez considérable pour ce pays-ci." (50) C'est, croyons-nous, la première fois qu'un futur chef d'état européen prend connaissance de notre université, l'inscrit dans ses souvenirs de voyage et note l'ampleur du bâtiment à l'échelle non seulement de la capitale, mais du pays. C'est donc une vision prophétique, pour cet établissement qui garde effectivement une place "considérable" dans "ce pays" depuis deux siècles.

Conditions de voyage; les Noirs

Voilà donc nos héros prêts à affronter "the wilderness", comme dit l'auteur, qui emploie souvent des phrases en anglais. Le soir, à la lumière d'une lampe ou d'une bougie, Louis-Philippe se contraint à noter les événements de la journée: pluie ou beau temps, chemin parcouru, région traversée, végétation et cultures. Il remarque les rivières grossies par les pluies et les forêts épaisses, l'aspect pauvre et sévère des maisons des premiers *settlers* (colons), les repas modestes et souvent peu appétissants de lard frit et de maïs. Il s'étonne avec une certaine ironie de dévorer avec appétit des "morceaux de boeuf séché dont un chien voudrait à peine" et se félicite de se délecter de gibier frais chez certains officiers ou fermiers pour lesquels il avait des lettres de recommandation. Doué d'une mémoire remarquable et d'un incontestable talent de conteur, il reconstruit en saynètes animées nombre de discussions. Parfois les compagnons de voyage rencontrés se lancent dans des critiques amères contre le gouvernement fédéral qui les "accable de taxes pour payer un tas de gens inutiles et conduit indignement leurs intérêts politiques." (134)

Mais ce qui nous intéresse surtout sont les quelques réflexions de Louis-Philippe témoignant déjà d'un changement sensible d'orientation. Lui qui dans sa première jeunesse avait été séduit par les Jacobins, lui dont le père,

---

6. Selon Jean-Pierre Babelon, ce fut Montpensier, à Londres, qui parmi les premiers artistes, sinon le premier, utilisa ce procédé pour la diffusion de ses dessins, signés APDO: Antoine-Philippe d'Orléans et datés de 1804, l'An un de la lithographie.

Philippe-*Egalité*, avait voté pour la mort de son cousin, le roi Louis XVI, s'oriente de plus en plus vers le conservatisme. C'est ainsi qu'il note au cours de son passage dans le Kentucky, le soir du 17 mai:

> Nous ne fîmes que 22 milles dans la journée: une forte pluie nous ayant surpris dans une baraque abominable même dans ce pays-ci, nous nous y arrêtâmes. L'hôte était un Allemand pennsylvanien et sa femme une bavarde insupportable... Une conversation sur les infortunes des gens de l'ouest s'établit alors parmi la société et chacun déraisonna à son aise. Ils se trouvent grevés d'impôts quoiqu'il n'y ait pas de peuple civilisé qui en paie aussi peu à beaucoup près. Ils trouvent même inutile de payer pour le soutien du gouvernement particulier du Kentucky. Ils parlent partout avec la même aigreur du gouvernement des riches négociants de l'est et répètent ces misérables lieux communs jacobins, que les pauvres travaillent et que les riches profitent. (140)

Ce changement d'orientation ne signifie nullement que Louis-Philippe trouvât naturelles, par exemple, l'exploitation des Noirs ou les ruses des Blancs pour enlever leurs terres aux Indiens. En effet, ses réflexions concernant les Noirs et les Indiens dénotent un intérêt prépondérant pour les problèmes sociaux ainsi qu'un esprit sensible à l'injustice sociale.

C'est ainsi que lors de son agréable visite chez l'ancien président Washington, entre les 5 et 9 avril, Louis-Philippe remarque les nombreux Noirs qui y travaillent:

> Le général possède dix mille acres de terre autour de Mount Vernon... Il y a environ 400 nègres... Ces malheureux peuplent beaucoup et leur nombre augmente... Le dernier recensement de la Virginie a donné pour résultat 770 000 habitants. On compte qu'il y en a presque les trois quarts qui sont noirs. (53-54)

Et le jeune homme de 23 ans ajoute avec une vision digne de Tocqueville:

> Cette proportion est effrayante et sera tôt ou tard fatale aux états du Sud. Les idées de liberté sont déjà répandues parmi eux et il paraît que les Quakers [et d'autres] sont les propagateurs de cette doctrine... Le cuisinier du général s'est échappé étant à Philadelphie et a laissé à Mount Vernon une petite fille de six ans. Cette petite fille répondit à Beaudoin qui lui disait qu'elle devait être bien fâchée de ne plus voir son père: "Oh, sir, I am very glad, because he is free now". Le général Washington a interdit l'usage du fouet envers ses nègres, mais malheureusement cet exemple a été peu suivi. On ne regarde pas ici un nègre comme un autre homme. Quand ils rencontrent un blanc, ils le saluent de loin et fort bas

> et paraissent souvent étonnés que nous leur rendions le salut, car ici personne ne le fait. Toute la culture de la Virginie se fait par des nègres que l'on loge...dans de mauvaises cabanes de bois qu'on appelle ici *quarters*. Ces cabanes fourmillent...de petits négrillons couverts de haillons que nos mendiants ne porteraient pas. Comment s'étonner ensuite que les nègres soient paresseux puisque leur travail ne leur profite jamais et qu'au contraire c'est l'avantage de ceux qu'en général ils doivent haïr. (54-55)[7]

Si Louis-Philippe n'approuve pas le mécontement des Américains critiquant le système des impôts, le réalisme de sa description des Noirs et sa révolte contre leur inhumaine condition rappellent bien les célèbres pages de La Bruyère sur les paysans français du temps de Louis XIV.

Les Indiens

Enfin, le 30 avril les trois frères, l'imagination sans doute remplie des récits extraordinaires sur "les sauvages de l'Amérique", arrivent sur les bords du Tennessee, près de Maryville, à Tellico Block House, autrement dit Fort Wilkinson, dans le pays des Indiens Cherokees.

Cette partie du *Journal* se présente comme la plus importante du texte, tant par le nombre de pages que par la richesse de ses renseignements. Louis-Philippe, ancien professeur de collège en Suisse, fait pratiquement un cours sur trois tribus indiennes, les Cherokees, les Chickasaws et les Choctaws.

Après avoir brièvement dépeint la réception chez le commandant américain de la garnison où ils mangent pour la première fois du dindon sauvage, il raconte la longue conversation sur les coutumes des Cherokees. Il écoute et prend des notes avec attention mais se propose de vérifier ces informations et de ne rapporter dans ses mémoires que ce qu'il aura vu de ses yeux.

Dès l'abord, il précise: "Je préfère le mot de 'nation' indienne à celui de 'sauvages', épithète que ces peuples ne méritent en aucune manière."

Linguiste amateur et ethnologue scrupuleux, il se fait répéter plusieurs fois par les Indiens le nom correct de leur tribu ainsi que ceux des autres tribus connues dans le pays:

> J'ai fait prononcer devant moi les noms des deux nations du nord par des Indiens et ils ont dit avec leur accent cahoté Tchero-Khi, Tchikeso. Je ne compte ces quatre nations que pour trois peuples, parce que les Tchoctaws et les Tchikesaws qui habitent la partie voisine du Mississippi, ont

7. Dans le *Maryland Journal* de l'époque, M. C. du Perron relève dans les petites annonces commerciales: "A côté d'une réclame de pommes de terre, d'un cru particulièrement bon, sont proposés en un seul lot quatorze nègres, des huitres et du charbon"! (148)

> absolument la même langue à quelques mots près, très peu importants... Cette conformité de langues s'étend aussi aux usages et elle a établi entre les deux nations une alliance étroite et une grande amitié qu'ils ne se rappellent pas d'avoir rompue. (86)

Et voilà le futur roi des Français qui s'asseoit avec les Indiens du village de Tokono pour fumer la pipe et pour s'amuser à apprendre comment nommer l'herbe qu'ils fument. Il donne non moins de six variantes dans six langues:

> Nous fumâmes ce que les Tcherokees appellent *Taluma*, les Tchikanos *Mosutchek*, les Indiens du Nord *Kalikinek*, les Américains *Little Shoemake*, les Français d'Amérique *Appapona* et, enfin, nous autres Français, nous l'appelons *le Sumac*! (108)

En fumant tranquillement avec les Indiens, une sorte de camaraderie s'établit et les voyageurs s'entendent rebaptiser par leurs nouveaux amis. Louis-Philippe, protecteur de ses deux jeunes frères est nommé le Père, *Atôta*. On le prend également pour un Espagnol, un *Squouannah*, mais il leur explique qu'il est Français, c'est-à-dire un *Krenché*. C'est ainsi que pour la première fois dans un journal qui n'est point intime, nous avons un portrait indirect de l'auteur:

> Apparement que mon teint noir, ma barbe un peu longue et mes cheveux sans poudre me donnaient l'air espagnol; mais ce qui m'étonna beaucoup fut la promptitude avec laquelle ils découvrirent que nous n'étions pas Américains. (101)

Lorsque Louis-Philippe regarde à son tour les Indiens il les trouve d'un aspect physique très agréable "lestes" et "agiles", car, remarque-t-il, ils se nourrissent beaucoup mieux que les Blancs: "leur nourriture est même meilleure que la nôtre." (88) D'ailleurs, ils "apportent continuellement au magasin de la garnison du gibier frais, des oeufs, des légumes et des fruits dans la saison." (101) L'hospitalité spontanée et sincère des Indiens le touche, car dans toutes les petites maisons où entrent les voyageurs on leur offre immédiatement "des fraises délicieuses et en abondance en ce début de mai" et du pain de maïs, très bon et dans lequel il y avait des fèves. A la surprise des visiteurs français, les Indiens appelaient ce pain *Gatô*. "Dans quelque temps, note l'auteur, ils auront des melons d'eau d'un parfum exquis." (109-10) Autour de leurs maisons ils cultivent du maïs, des pommes de terre et du tabac. Leur charmant village de Tokono inspire une belle toile à Montpensier, aujourd'hui perdue.

Laissons de côté les longues et minutieuses descriptions des maisons indiennes. Il est plus important de souligner son enthousiasme pour les paysages des terres indiennes du Tennessee "richement couvertes d'un grand tapis vert terminé par des collines brisées et à l'horizon des montagnes que l'éloignement fait paraître bleues." Une rivière tranquille traverse cette riche terre, rivière "bordée d'acacias de diverses espèces, de marronniers, de vignes sauvages et d'arbres étrangers qui donnent à ce joli paysage l'apparence d'un beau jardin anglais." (103-04)

Cette description édénique des terres indiennes rapprocherait notre auteur de bien d'autres voyageurs qui idéalisèrent la terre du nouveau monde, mais elle s'arrête brusquement car ce réaliste sait poser les questions essentielles et regarder au-delà des apparences. Il constate ainsi deux réalités choquantes: la convoitise des Blancs et la condition de la femme indienne.

En discutant avec l'interprète indien, Louis-Philippe apprend ainsi que les Indiens vivent dans la frayeur que la puissance des Blancs ne finisse par écraser leur peuple.[8] Quand il demande si les Indiens ont des lois, on lui répond: "qu'il n'en faut que pour les méchants et il n'y a que des méchants comme les Blancs qui en ont."(117) Et s'il souligne la richesse des terres indiennes c'est pour nous faire mieux comprendre pourquoi les Blancs leur cherchent continuellement querelle, car ils veulent s'en emparer, n'hésitant pour cela à faire la guerre.

Le sujet de la guerre est d'ailleurs longuement discuté et le jeune Louis-Philippe frissonne à la pensée des massacres commis des deux côtés. Quant aux Indiens:

> Leur manière de faire la guerre est féroce, ils ne font que rarement des prisonniers. Dans la dernière guerre ils en ont fait quelques-uns qui furent pour la plupart conduits à Detroit...et vendus à des marchands canadiens qui les revendirent ensuite aux Américains... Quelque affreux et révoltant que soit ce système, on conçoit ce qui a poussé les Indiens à des cruautés; car les massacres font parmi eux un tort irréparable... Ils disent même qu'ils ne savent plus comment s'y prendre avec les Blancs,...car les pertes des Blancs sont réparées sur le champ et rien n'arrête l'augmentation de ce peuple dans leur voisinage... Tous les voisins ambitionnent les terres qu'ils occupent dans le Tennessee. (92-93)

---

8. Le temps nous a malheureusement permis de vérifier que ces craintes étaient fondées. Au cours de l'hiver de 1838-1839 les survivants de cette tribu ont été expulsés de leurs terres et chassés jusqu'en Oklahoma. Des milliers sont morts en chemin. Ce calvaire demeure connu dans l'histoire sous le nom de "the trail of tears" (le chemin des larmes). Voir James Paul Allen & Eugene James Turner, *We the People: an Atlas of America's Ethnic Diversity* (New York: MacMIllan, 1988), 29.

Les promesses faites par les traités ne sont pas respectées par les Blancs qui cherchent toujours à provoquer les Indiens par des assassinats et à déclencher ainsi une nouvelle guerre pour accaparer d'autres terrains. Dans leurs efforts extraordinaires pour survivre, les Indiens acceptent même que les Blancs s'établissent parmi eux et leur offrent leurs femmes:

> Il y a beaucoup de Blancs qui vivent parmi les Indiens. Il faut seulement qu'ils prennent une femme indienne (ou plusieurs si cela leur convient) et en cas de guerre qu'ils aillent à l'armée.[9] Chez les Tcherokees et, je pense, chez tous les Indiens, les familles se comptent par les femmes au lieu de se compter par les hommes comme parmi nous. Ils prétendent qu'il n'y a que cela de sûr. La conséquence en est que les enfants des Blancs et des Indiennes sont Indiens comme les autres. Ils ont une couleur moins foncée que les autres. Les Américains les appellent *half breeds*. (95)

La femme indienne

Ne nous trompons pas sur la situation de la femme chez les Indiens. Si les familles peuvent se compter par les femmes, pour des raisons évidemment pratiques, celles-ci ne jouissent, selon Louis-Philippe, d'aucun respect dans la société des Cherokees. Objet de plaisir et bête de somme, la femme est traitée avec mépris par l'homme:

> Un Indien peut avoir autant de femmes qu'il peut en nourrir; il les prend et les chasse comme des servantes et les quitte de même quand cela convient... Si la femme d'un Tcherokee couche avec un autre homme, il se contente de la chasser sans rien dire à l'homme, trouvant au-dessous de sa dignité de se quereller pour une femme. (90)

La condition de la femme indienne chez les Cherokees se rapproche de celle des Noirs. Les femmes font toutes les tâches ménagères, ainsi que tous les travaux exigés par la culture de la terre, pendant que les hommes, allongés ou assis, fument et causent tranquillement ou s'amusent à des jeux sportifs. Louis-Philippe emploie exactement la même phrase pour les Noirs que pour les femmes indiennes, lorsqu'il écrit que "tout travail est fait par eux!" Ajoutons encore que selon les informations de l'auteur, les Indiens possédaient également quelques esclaves noirs. La consommation du whisky ne serait donc pas la seule influence pernicieuse de la société "civilisée" des

9. Il s'agit, bien sûr, des groupes de combat indiens. John Watts, chef de guerre des Cherokees, redouté des Blancs, était lui même, le fils d'un Blanc.

Blancs sur les "sauvages", ils auraient également succombé aux avantages de l'esclavage...

Le voyageur français consacre des notes contradictoires et souvent amusantes à la femme indienne: elle est tout d'abord belle et coquette, et selon lui, même une Française n'aurait rien à lui apprendre. Elle sert à table et essaie de séduire l'officier américain, mais disparaît une fois qu'elle a déposé tous les plats, elle peut avoir l'oreille légèrement coupée par un mari jaloux, mais elle est libre de le quitter et de vendre ses services à un autre homme. Elle peut même devenir l'épouse d'un Blanc qui choisit de s'intégrer à la vie du village indien. Quoi qu'elle fasse cependant, la liberté toute relative des moeurs qui lui est accordée ne lui vaut que le mépris:

> Il est extraordinaire que cette liberté de concubinage et cette polygamie aient toujours pour conséquence de faire tomber les femmes dans le mépris des hommes et de leur ôter toute espèce d'influence. Ceci est un pronostic fâcheux pour les femmes françaises pour qui les nouvelles lois sur le divorce ont fait du mariage le concubinage indien. (91)

Y a-t-il alors de l'espoir pour les femmes? Le jeune prince, éduqué d'après les principes rousseauistes, conseille aux femmes de s'élever au-dessus de leur condition de dépendance en inspirant aux hommes "des sentiments" d'amour et non en se les attachant "par les plaisirs qu'elles leur donnent". C'est donc par "la magie de l'amour" et non par la jouissance ou par son travail que la femme peut se faire respecter. (91)

Il est très intéressant de rapprocher ces observations sur la condition misérable de la femme indienne faites par le jeune Louis-Philippe et un texte Diderot, *Sur les Femmes* (1772).[10] A un quart de siècle de distance ces écrits réalistes offrent un contraste frappant avec l'image par trop répandue d'une Indienne romantique à la manière d'Atala. L'Indienne de Diderot se défend pathétiquement devant un missionnaire jésuite:

> Représente-toi bien, père, les peines qui sont réservées à une Indienne parmi ces Indiens. Ils nous accompagnent dans les champs avec leur arc et leurs flèches. Nous y allons, nous, chargées d'un enfant qui pend à nos mamelles, et d'un autre que nous portons dans une corbeille. Ils vont tuer un oiseau ou prendre un poisson. Nous bêchons la terre, nous; et après avoir supporté toute la fatigue de la culture, nous supportons toute celle de la moisson. Ils reviennement le soir sans aucun fardeau; nous, nous leur apportons des racines pour leur nourriture et du maïs... De retour...ils

---

10. Essai de Diderot, suscité par celui d'Antoine Thomas, et publié dans *La Correspondance littéraire* de Grimm. Voir Diderot, *Romans et Contes*, 3 vols. (Paris: Dubuisson, 1963) vol. 3.

vont s'entretenir avec leurs amis; nous, nous allons chercher du bois et de l'eau pour préparer leur souper. Ont-ils mangé, ils s'endorment; nous, nous passons presque toute la nuit à moudre le maïs et à leur faire la chica; et quelle est la récompense de nos veilles? Ils boivent leur chica, ils s'enivrent, et quand ils sont ivres, ils nous traînent par les cheveux et nous foulent aux pieds. Ah! père, plût à Dieu que ma mère m'eût étouffée en naissant! (159-160)

Les ressemblances entre le texte de Louis-Philippe et celui de Diderot sont étonnantes et paraissent donc correspondre à la vie réelle de la femme indienne. Et si les Indiens ont beaucoup souffert à cause des Blancs, les femmes indiennes, enfermées dans une situation sans issue, ont eu un sort incomparablement plus tragique.

Après la visite de deux jours chez les Indiens, le 1er et le 2 mai, Louis-Philippe et ses compagnons continuèrent leur voyage jusqu'à Nashville. De là ils remontèrent vers le nord, faisant halte aux chutes du Niagara–qu'ils virent en juillet–pour revenir à Philadelphie, leur point de départ.

Si le journal est inachevé, s'arrêtant net le 21 mai à Bardstown, dans le Kentucky, il demeure cependant dans son ensemble un témoignage des plus précieux.

En dernière analyse la valeur de ce document de voyage réside dans la singulière perspicacité de son auteur. A peine vingt ans après la naissance de la république américaine, il a su saisir de façon précise les puissances contraires en lutte et prophétiser les axes de tension qui résulteraient de leur choc: aspiration à la liberté et à la démocratie d'une part, exploitation inhumaine des esclaves de l'autre, tension qui conduira trois générations plus tard à la guerre de sécession; désir profond de paix et idéalisme humanitaire d'un côté, pillage et anéantissement de la nation indienne de l'autre.

Intelligence aiguë des événements, intuition inquiète du caractère des hommes du nouveau monde, perplexité devant la violence raciste dont il fut témoin, voilà ce qui amena Louis-Philippe à conclure à l'ingouvernabilité de la jeune nation américaine, telle qu'elle lui apparut, tiraillée entre la créativité généreuse et les puissances de mort.

Reste à découvrir dans une recherche future, l'exacte mesure de l'évolution entre les prises de positions politiques et philosophiques si ardemment défendues par le jeune voyageur dans son journal, et celles qu'adoptera le "roi-citoyen" quelque trente ans plus tard.

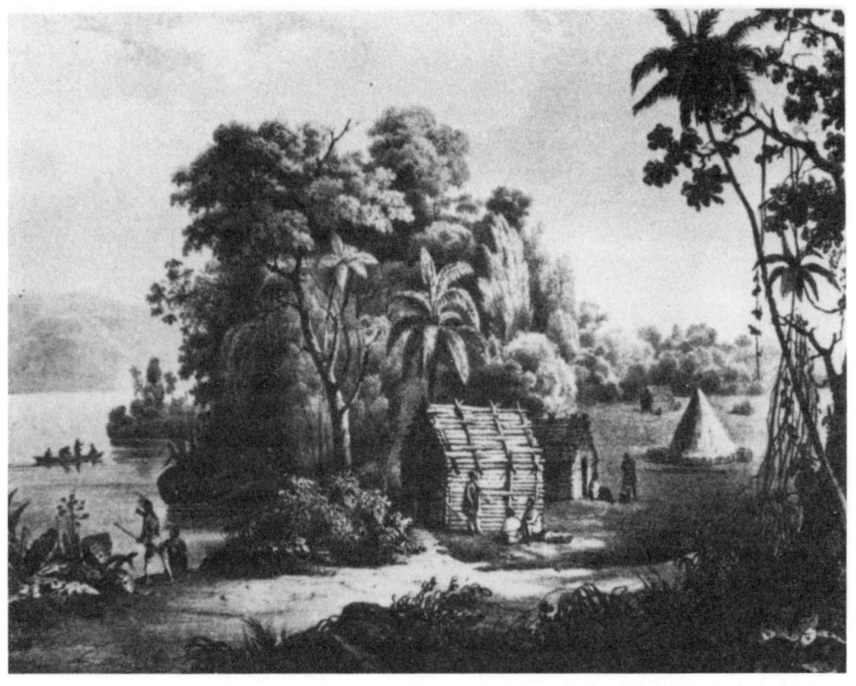

Vue du village des Indiens Cherokee à Tokono, sur les bords du Tennessee, que les princes visitèrent le 1 et le 2 mai 1797. Cliché Service Photographique des Archives Nationales.

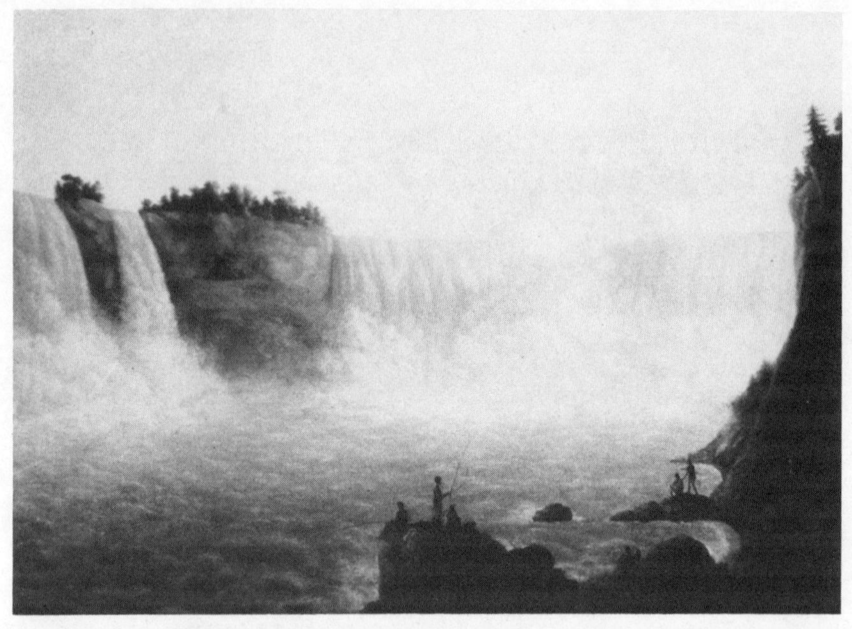

Vue des Chutes du Niagara, que les princes visitèrent le 21 juin 1797 (Musée de la New York Historical Society). Cliché du musée.

La conduite du Noir américain selon les voyageurs français du XVIIIe siècle

Régis Antoine

Commentons deux mots de ce titre: d'abord le terme "américain" qui au XVIIIe siècle signifie plus souvent habitant des Antilles qu'habitant de la Terre-Ferme, et ce sera un des buts du présent exposé que de confronter ce qui se disait sur le Noir des îles à sucre et ce qui se disait sur celui des colonies en voie de regroupement après l'indépendance sous le nom d'Etats-Unis. Autre précision: la "conduite du Noir" veut dire aussi bien la manière dont il se conduit que celle dont on le "conduit travailler", pour reprendre une expression en usage dans les contrats des commandeurs. Mais dans la réalité comme dans les textes auxquels nous avons à faire, l'une ne va pas sans retentir sur l'autre, comme on le verra successivement pour ce qui concerne la condition des esclaves, le comportement à tenir à leur égard en cas de révolte, et enfin le problème de leur affranchissement.

Je ne reprendrai pas l'analyse de textes directement politiques comme ceux de commissaires envoyés à Saint-Domingue pendant la Révolution française ou, en sens inverse, ceux des délégués américains aux assemblées parisiennes, ou ceux des pamphlétaires coloniaux rapatriés en métropole. Pour autant, la douzaine de voyageurs ici retenus ne doivent pas être considérés comme des touristes dilettantes, car l'exotisme américain dont Gilbert Chinard a parlé dans ses ouvrages[1] n'est généralement pas leur fait. Ce sont des hommes en situation, soit impliqués à un titre ou à un autre dans l'économie de plantation, soit délégués pour réaliser une enquête, soit témoins plus ou moins profondément impressionnés par leurs lectures et par les scènes auxquelles ils assistent.

---

1. Gilbert Chinard, *L'Amérique et le rêve exotique dans la littérature française au XVIIe et au XVIIIe siècle* (1913; Paris: Droz, 1934). Pour la même raison, John R. Carpenter, l'*Histoire de la Littérature française sur la Louisiane de 1673 à 1766* (Paris: Nizet, 1966), ne recoupe pas notre propos.

Il s'agit aussi, à une exception près, de textes qui se situent entre la publication de l'*Esprit des Lois*, en 1748, et les années 1802-1807, si riches en événements pour le sujet qui nous occupe. Dans ce laps d'un demi-siècle, les auteurs sont confrontés avec d'une part, des situations stables ou stabilisées, qui tendraient à montrer que vaille que vaille, l'histoire se serait arrêtée dans certains territoires situés entre le Massachusetts et les Guyanes. Précisons: en Louisiane ce sont toujours les mêmes colons qui pratiquent la même agriculture esclavagiste, que le statut soit français jusqu'en 1762, espagnol de 1762 à 1800, français de nouveau, puis américain après 1803. Et le Code Noir y survit jusqu'au moment, en 1806, où Charles Robin met la dernière main à ses *Voyages à l'intérieur de la Louisiane*.[2] A la Martinique, on ne note aucune solution de continuité dans le processus servile, que l'île soit anglaise ou française. Et d'autres types de situation perdurent, comme ces accords, tacites ou explicites que les autorités coloniales ont passés çà et là avec des collectivités libres d'esclaves marrons: en Guyane avec les Bonis, à Saint-Domingue entre ceux des "grands bois" et Monsieur de Bellecombe et, vraisemblablement, à la périphérie de la Nouvelle-Orléans.

Mais les voyageurs ou résidents temporaires étaient aussi témoins de modifications radicales dans la condition des Noirs: affranchissement octroyé par les Quakers en Pennsylvanie, abolition arrachée sur place à Saint-Domingue, abolition entérinée à Paris après quatre années d'atermoiements au sein des assemblées révolutionnaires. Et du fait de la guerre, l'exil aux Etats-Unis et en Louisiane d'un bon nombre d'anciens colons dominguiens leur fait découvrir les situations diversifiées du Massachusetts, de Virginie, et de la colonie espagnole.

Pour ajouter à cette disparate, rappelons le cas de la Guadeloupe, qui connaît la liberté générale pendant huit années, avant la décision restauratrice de Bonaparte en 1802, et la tragédie qui s'ensuit.

Quelle stimulation pour l'esprit que ces contradictions formidables de situations sur le continent comme dans les îles: là des hommes demeurés à l'écart de la citoyenneté, qu'ils aient été libérés ou laissés dans l'état de servitude; ailleurs la résolution dramatique, en des sens opposés, des épopées noires, selon qu'il s'agissait de la Guadeloupe écrasée par la répression, ou d'Haïti où, comme devait l'écrire Aimé Césaire, "la négritude se mit debout pour la première fois".[3]

Dans la plupart des cas de figure, les perspectives réformistes, leurs ajustements mesquins ou leurs maquettes prestigieuses (les *Réflexions sur*

---

2. Charles-César Robin, *Voyages dans l'intérieur de la Louisiane, de la Floride occidentale et dans les îles de la Martinique et de Saint-Domingue*, 13 vols. (Paris: F. Buisson, 1807).

3. Aimé Césaire, *Cahier d'un retour au pays natal* (*Volontés*, 1939; Paris: *Présence africaine*, 1971), 67.

l'esclavage des Nègres, que Condorcet fit paraître en 1781), le réformisme donc ne pesa pas lourd face à la violence historique.

Si l'on ajoute à cette pesée d'ensemble la charge biographique de la plupart de nos écrivains-voyageurs, on comprendra que le lyrisme, la prise de hauteur philosophique aient tenu peu de place dans les relations, face à l'esprit positif, qui se nourrit d'un concret regardé à travers le prisme des intérêts personnels.

Les manuels de planteurs

Il en va ainsi, et en premier lieu, pour ce qui concerne la description des conditions de vie des Noirs cultivateurs, aux Antilles comme en Amérique septentrionale.

Parlons d'abord des manuels de planteurs, littérature pratique diffusée dans le monde colonial francophone, voire plus largement quand l'ouvrage est traduit, et dont la circulation est amplifiée à la fin du siècle par la dispersion des colons de la grande île. Car, il convient de le rappeler, le futur Haïti constituait alors la colonie majeure et centrale, la première aussi dans la hiérarchie des productions culturelles aussi bien qu'économiques, en regard de quoi les aléas et l'immensité de la Louisiane ne constituaient qu'une zone seconde. Donc les manuels de planteurs dominguiens devenus voyageurs malgré eux, ouvrages issus d'une expérience reconnue dans l'ordre de l'agriculture esclavagiste, vont faire autorité en différents territoires quelle qu'ait été leur tendance: esprit de violence ou esprit de douceur.

C'est à cette deuxième catégorie qu'appartient *Le Planteur de café de Saint-Domingue*, de P.J. Laborie.[4] L'auteur s'est réfugié à la Jamaïque, et a rédigé son ouvrage en français, avant qu'il ne soit traduit en anglais et publié à Londres, puis traduit en espagnol à Cuba. Laborie, imprégné d'humanisme chrétien, veut limiter à trois coups de fouet la capacité de punir que détiennent les commandeurs; il étend jusqu'à trois années le temps d'acclimatation et d'apprentissage des esclaves nouvellement arrivés d'Afrique, et prévoit de faire construire pour eux des cases "à demi-africaines". A l'inverse, *Le Parfait Indigotier*, de l'impitoyable Elie Monnereau,[5] sera repris terme à terme, quarante ans plus tard, par un ancien gérant d'habitation, Ducoeurjoly. Celui-ci, avec son *Manuel des Habitants de Saint-Domingue*, paru en 1802, répond aux espoirs que suscite parmi les planteurs le rétablissement de l'esclavage et l'envoi d'un corps expéditionnaire dans la colonie. Ducoeurjoly passe vite sur sa remarque: "il faut être humain envers son semblable. Le nègre est un homme comme nous."[6] Il faudrait, ajoute-t-il, ne

4. J.P. Laborie, *The Coffee Planter of Saint-Domingue* (London: Cadel, 1798).
5. Elie Monnereau, *Le Parfait Indigotier* (Marseille: J. Mossy, 1765).
6. Ducoeurjoly, *Manuel des Habitants de Saint-Domingue* (Paris, 1802), 1: 53.

le châtier qu'en connaissance de cause, mais: "on a plus souvent fait d'excellents sujets par la crainte que par une douceur toujours mal placée." (1, 41)

C'est également une visée pragmatique qui commande de "traiter avec modération les nouveaux débarqués". Aussi, "l'antidote" indispensable à cet impératif catégorique, se faire craindre, est-il: "égayer les nègres", qui devient ainsi la seconde obligation des conducteurs d'esclaves. La raison en est expliquée au principe, l'origine africaine: "Il faut les égayer afin qu'ils fassent moins attention au joug qu'ils vont porter, et qu'on doit leur faire envisager comme préférable à l'état de liberté, ordinairement malheureux, d'où ils sortent." (1, 38)

Du même esprit de précaution et d'économie de la force de travail procède la recommandation: "donner à chacun la femme qu'il aime". Par elle, Ducoeurjoly permet de mieux lire, c'est-à-dire d'écarter toute préoccupation sensible, la remarque de Raynal: "mettre les plaisirs de l'amour à la portée de tous les noirs"[7] qui s'ajoute à un conseil plus général: Pour rendre l'esclavage utile, il faut du moins le rendre doux. (216)

Le même souci de l'intérêt bien compris conduit un autre ancien habitant de Saint-Domingue, le citoyen Avalle, à utiliser avec plus ou moins de pertinence en 1799 deux concepts qui avaient été chers à Saint-Just, et à les étendre aux colonies américaines: "Le propriétaire leur doit en échange le *bonheur*; son intérêt même le porte à suivre les lois de l'*égalité*."[8]

Le clergé missionnaire

Au-delà de ceux que l'on pourrait appeler les "voyageurs de commerce" coloniaux, il est un secteur de pensée qui appelle examen: le clergé missionnaire, le clergé envoyé au Nouveau-Monde "sur l'ordre du Roi", selon la formule consacrée. Son appréciation de la condition des Noirs esclaves sera ici questionnée dans la confrontation qui a surgi entre deux représentants du même ordre ecclésiastique, les jésuites. L'un, le père Le Pers, est obscur résident à Saint-Domingue; l'autre est le célèbre Xavier de Charlevoix, qui a voyagé sur le continent et dans les îles.

De 1720 à 1723, Charlevoix a envoyé des lettres à la duchesse de Lesdiguières, qui seront réunies et publiées en 1744 dans son *Journal historique d'un Voyage dans l'Amérique septentrionale*. Etant données les dates de rédaction, on comprend qu'aucune mention ne soit faite des Noirs cultivateurs. Quant à son *Histoire de la Nouvelle-France*, à laquelle le *Journal*

---

7. Guillaume-Thomas Raynal, *Histoire philosophique et politique des établissements et du commerce des Européens dans les deux Indes* (ed. 1783), Livre 11, ch. 30, 222.

8. Avalle, *Ouvrage du citoyen Avalle, sur l'importance des colonies française aux Antilles* (Paris, an VII). C'est nous qui soulignons *bonheur* et *égalité*.

est joint, elle ne parle des Noirs d'origine africaine qu'en tant que recrues militaires dans les guerres menées contre les Indiens sauvages. L'ouvrage de Charlevoix qui nous retiendra donc est l'*Histoire de l'Ile espagnole de Saint-Domingue* parue en 1730, pour le traitement que l'auteur y fait subir à des manuscrits que lui avait fournis le Père Le Pers, et qu'il modifie considérablement dans un sens de cruauté accrue, et de strict ajustement à l'esprit esclavagiste.

On est à proprement parler stupéfait de passer des remarques évangéliques, demeurées inédites: "la douceur a grâce partout, partout elle est nécessaire",[9] aux obsessions anti-philanthropiques du Père Charlevoix: les Noirs, "rebut de la nature", sont des "machines dont il faut remonter les ressorts... Quelque peu qu'ils mangent et qu'ils dorment, ils sont également forts et durs au travail".[10] Bien sûr le fouet est indispensable à l'esclave: "Il faut lui faire sentir à coups de fouet qu'il a des maîtres." (1, 287) "...Mais il faut recommencer souvent." (2, 500)

Là où Le Pers apparaissait comme un anti-esclavagiste: "Rien n'abrutit plus que l'esclavage. C'est au contraire plus ou moins de liberté, soutenue de plus ou moins de culture et d'éducation qui donne plus ou moins d'esprit. C'est ce que nous remarquons aux Iles parmi les nègres libres,"[11] le Père Charlevoix ne manque pas de dresser une barrière de haine entre les races, notamment lorsqu'il évoque une révolte: "Canailles, vils esclaves dont tout le sang ne vengerait pas assez la mort d'un seul Français." (2, 123)

Si on se reporte au contraire à ce que le même Charlevoix dira des Indiens dans son *Histoire de la Nouvelle-France* (1744), on remarque que les termes du discours sont bouleversés, puisqu'il voit leurs sociétés plus douces et plus égalitaires que celle de ses compatriotes.

Ce n'est pas seulement l'objet ethnographique qui a changé, l'Américain au lieu de l'Africain, c'est aussi une critique par ricochet de la société blanche, c'est enfin tout le système de valeurs de l'écrivain, dès lors qu'il ne parle plus de la propriété intangible du Blanc. Racisme, esclavagisme, tel est malheureusement le message que l'*Histoire de l'Ile Espagnole* aura transmis à Buffon, à Voltaire, qui citent volontiers le jésuite parmi leurs références.

Trouvera-t-on en regard de ces textes imbus d'esprit colon des relations de voyage idéologiquement plus libres? Prenons le cas le plus favorable, celui d'un officier d'origine comtoise, Girod-Chantrans, qui selon l'historien Gabriel Debien s'est travesti en Suisse, probablement pour se situer le plus

---

9. Le Pers, *Mémoires pour l'Histoire de Saint-Domingue*, ms (Paris: Bibliothèque Nationale, Paris, n.a.f.) 8990 fo 67; ms *Histoire de l'Isle de Saint-Domingue*, n.a.f. 8991.

10. Pierre-François Xavier de Charlevoix, *Histoire de l'Isle espagnole de Saint-Domingue*, 2 vols. (Paris: Guérin, 1730-1731), 2: 501.

11. Fo 71. Pour une étude d'ensemble, cf. Régis Antoine, *Les Ecrivains français et les Antilles* (Paris: Maisonneuve et Larose, 1979).

extérieurement possible par rapport à l'appartenance française, et donc à l'esprit "national" que Le Pers critiquait chez Charlevoix. Dans son *Voyage d'un Suisse dans différentes colonies d'Amérique*, publié en 1785,[12] Girod-Chantrans écrit en effet avec quelque humour: "le peuple français est le seul navigateur qui accumule ainsi les hommes en mer". Ce qu'il appelle selon l'expression communément usitée "le gouvernement des nègres" lui apparaît comme une "machine curieuse toujours montée...rarement le trouve-t-on exempt de cruautés." Et cherchant des limites objectives aux abus des maîtres, il déclare lucidement: "l'habitant sera despote autant qu'il est possible." (134) Singulièrement il juge les esclaves plus libres dans leurs amours que ne le sont les planteurs, mais ce libertinage même est source d'épuisement et de mélancolie pour des individus d'une complexion "moins forte que lascive". Seules échappent à la malédiction attachée à l'amour dans les colonies, les liaisons que les maîtres entretiennent dans le monde des gens de couleur, au sein duquel, ajoute notre voyageur, il conviendrait de déclarer libres tous ceux qui sont de peau moins foncée que les mulâtres. Et pour se faire une idée réaliste de la condition des esclaves, il faudrait s'en tenir au seul jugement qui soit fiable, celui des nouveaux débarqués. Comme on s'en doute, il s'agit d'un voeu tout à fait gratuit, les Africains déportés, grands voyageurs s'il en fût au XVIIIe siècle, et témoins capitaux, n'ayant disposé ni de la parole ni a fortiori de la capacité d'écrire, autrement que par le truchement tout à fait artificiel de la prosopopée, dans quelques textes humanitaires.

Les autres textes de voyageurs ou de résidents temporaires qui traitent de la condition des Noirs sont eux aussi marqués d'écarts subjectivistes par rapport à ce que les travaux des historiens américains nous apprennent aujourd'hui.[13] Ainsi Jean-Bernard Bossu, qui a voyagé à l'île de la Grenade, à Saint-Domingue et surtout en Louisiane, est connu pour les épisodes pittoresques qu'il a insérés dans les 500 pages de ses *Nouveaux Voyages aux Indes occidentales* et les 400 pages de ses *Nouveaux Voyages dans l'Amérique septentrionale*.[14] D'un côté il prétend avoir connu à Saint-Domingue le colon Chaperon "qui fit entrer un de ses nègres dans un four chaud", et il ne manque pas de relater la vente dans cette colonie d'esclaves nus, méticuleusement visités avant l'étampage. Cependant il a pu remarquer une cruauté des maîtres dans l'immense territoire qui venait d'être acquis par

---

12. Justin Girod-Chantrans, *Voyage d'un Suisse dans différentes colonies d'Amérique pendant la dernière guerre* (Neufchâtel: Imprimerie de la Société Typographique, 1785).

13. Notamment à notre connaissance de John Spenser Basset, *The Southern Plantation Overseer as revealed in his letters* (Northampton: Smith College, 1925; New York: Negro Universities Press, 1968); Charles S. Sydnor, *Slavery in Mississippi* (New York: D. Appleton-Century, 1933); Rosser H. Taylor, *Slaveholding in North Carolina: An Economic View* (Chapel Hill: University of North Carolina Press, 1926); et *Louisiana Historical Quarterly*.

14. Jean-Bernard Bossu, *Nouveaux Voyages aux Indes occidentales* (Paris: Le Jay, 1768); *Nouveaux Voyages dans l'Amérique septentrionale* (Amsterdam: Changuion, 1777).

l'Espagne: "J'ai vu à la Louisiane des habitants jouer leurs esclaves au brelan. Il y en eut un, à ce que l'on m'a raconté, qui troqua un Nègre contre un chien de chasse dont il avait envie. Le Nègre, indigné de ce parallèle, se pendit dans les bois." (372)

Mais ce sont des démêlés avec la hiérarchie militaire, et non pas une dénonciation de l'esclavage dans le Nouveau-Monde, qui vaudront à l'auteur des *Nouveaux Voyages* d'être embastillé à son retour en France. Car, et je joue sur les titres de précédents ouvrages relatifs à la Louisiane, Bossu découvrant après Hennepin[15] "un très grand pays", est comme Charlevoix moins attiré par le tableau de la servitude noire en Nouvelle-France que par ce que Lafitau appelait les "Moeurs des Sauvages Amériquains".[16]

Crèvecoeur, Chastellux et Brissot

Vingt ans plus tard, à la veille de la Révolution française, les choses ont changé. L'insurrection à Saint-Domingue n'a pas encore commencé, mais les textes des Français voyageurs ou résidents peuvent être plus directement utilisés par la propagande négrophile à titre de documentation topique. C'est ainsi que Brissot de Warville, animateur de la "Société des Amis des Noirs" et futur leader girondin, nourrira sa réflexion de deux jugements croisés sur l'agriculture esclavagiste en Virginie.

Le premier émane des *Lettres d'un Cultivateur américain*,[17] de Michel-Guillaume Jean de Crèvecoeur, publiées en français en 1784, auxquelles Brissot se réfèrera dans son ouvrage publié sept ans plus tard: *Nouveaux Voyage dans les Etats-Unis*. Crèvecoeur a résidé onze ans (de 1769 à 1780) dans la colonie de New York, loin donc des champs d'indigo et de riz qu'il mentionne pour situer ses préoccupations humanitaires. Ce n'est pas une excuse à ses yeux pour demeurer indifférent au sort des Noirs: "De cette riante capitale, écrit-il, on n'entend pas le bruit des fouets dont on presse ces malheureuses victimes à un travail excessif. La race favorisée de la nature boit, mange et vit heureuse, pendant que l'autre remue la terre..." (2, 373)

Manquant peut-être d'éléments concrets pour sa dénonciation, lui qui en tant que fermier n'utilisait pas le travail servile, Crèvecoeur se contente d'élever une protestation pathétique: "Quel spectacle affreux la misère n'offre-t-elle pas dans les campagnes!" (2, 365)

---

15. P. Louis Hennepin, *Nouvelle découverte d'un très grand pays situé dans l'Amérique entre le Nouveau Mexique et la mer glaciale* (Utrecht: G. Brodelet, 1697).

16. Joseph-François Lafitau, *Moeurs des Sauvages Amériquains comparées aux moeurs des premiers temps*, 2 vols. (Paris: Saugrain, 1724).

17. Michel-Guillaume Jean, dit Saint-John de Crèvecoeur, *Letters from an American Farmer*, (London: T. Davies, 1782); édition française (Paris: Cuchet, 1784).

Il a vu, ou a entendu parler des esclaves: "exposés comme les chevaux à la foire, vendus et marqués d'un fer rouge. On les conduit ensuite sur les plantations, où ils sont condamnés à mourir de faim, à languir pendant plusieurs années." (2, 374)

Au corpus bien connu des arguments des négrophiles, Crèvecoeur présente l'intérêt d'ajouter l'opposition, terme à terme, de la condition des exploiteurs et de celle des exploités; les premiers "ne voient, ne sentent, n'entendent rien des maux et des gémissements de ces pauvres esclaves, qui par leurs pénibles travaux font naître toutes leurs richesses. Ici, les fatigues perpétuelles et les horreurs de l'esclavage ne sont jamais appréciées." (2, 373)

Pour insuffisante et répétitive qu'elle puisse paraître à l'historien des idées, la rhétorique de Crèvecoeur, reprise par d'autres bouches et d'autres plumes, acquiert une force nouvelle et ne manque pas de faire avancer l'histoire, plus rapidement en cette fin de siècle que ce que l'on pourrait déduire, pour les décennies précédentes, de la place occupée par les récits de voyage dans les bibliothèques privées.[18]

Deuxième regard: celui de François de Chastellux, tel que Brissot le découvrait dans le *Voyage de M. le Marquis de Chastellux dans l'Amérique septentrionale* paru à Paris en 1786, auquel l'idéologue négrophile répondait la même année par son *Examen critique des voyages de Chastellux*. Le marquis, officier passionné des idées d'Helvétius, avait pourtant tracé un tableau lénifiant du processus esclavagiste en Virginie:

> On n'entend pas habituellement comme à Saint-Domingue et à la Jamaïque le bruit des fouets et les cris des malheureux dont on déchire le corps par lambeaux. C'est qu'en général le peuple de Virginie est plus doux que celui des îles à sucre, qui est tout composé de gens avides et pressés de faire fortune, pour s'en retourner ensuite en Europe. C'est que le produit de la culture n'étant pas d'une si grande valeur, le travail n'est pas exigé avec tant de sévérité.[19]

Chastellux joint donc un argument économique judicieux au leit-motif du "bruit des fouets", dont la prégnance sur l'opinion publique française éclairée devait, à la fin de l'Ancien Régime, aboutir à modifier la réglementation de la violence privée coloniale: la même année 1786, une ordonnance royale interdisait aux maîtres de mutiler, de tuer, de donner plus de cinquante coups de fouet...

---

18. Cf Daniel Mornet, "Les enseignements des bibliothèques privées (1750-1780)", *RHLF*, 17 (juillet-sept. 1910): 459-96; Michèle Duchet, *Anthropologie et histoire au Siècle des Lumières* (Paris: Maspero, 1971).

19. François-J. de Chastellux, *Voyages de M. le Marquis de Chastellux dans l'Amérique septentrionale dans les années 1780, 1781 et 1782*, 2 vols. (Paris: Prault, 1786), 2, 144.

Chastellux a su aussi répercuter un certain état de la conscience humanitaire au Nouveau-Monde, placée devant le pénible devoir de faire du revenu. Ses planteurs virginiens, en général, "paraissent affligés d'avoir des Nègres, et parlent sans cesse d'abolir l'esclavage, et de chercher un autre moyen de faire valoir leurs terres." (2, 145)

S'emparant de ce texte, Brissot disqualifie le prétendu pouvoir d'une race sur l'autre; et tant pis selon lui si la recherche de l'égalité entre les hommes passe par la violence et par l'initiative armée des esclaves révoltés. Précisons que cinq ans plus tard, lorsque l'insurrection aura réellement pris corps dans la plaine du Cap, Brissot sera infiniment plus gêné, et cessera de la justifier. Mais entre-temps, il était à son tour devenu voyageur: en avril 1788 il avait entrepris une mission d'enquête comme délégué des Amis des Noirs, et c'est devant l'Assemblée de la Société des Amis des Noirs qu'il avait présenté en février 1789 son *Mémoire sur les Noirs de l'Amérique septentrionale* dans lequel il relevait des situations contradictoires. Il avait vu des esclaves doucement traités aux Etats-Unis; il en avait vus qui "passaient le dimanche...entièrement dans l'inaction. L'inaction est leur souverain bonheur, aussi travaillent-ils peu et nonchalamment." (32)

Il avait vu dans le Maryland et en Virginie "des cadavres noirs ambulants". (40) Et dans les états du Sud, des Noirs "dans un état d'abjection et d'abrutissement difficile à peindre. Beaucoup sont nus, mal nourris, logés dans de misérables huttes, couchés sur la paille." (31)

Autre contradiction: Brissot qui ne se voulait "ni enthousiaste ni frondeur" se plaisait, en philosophe, à considérer les cases des Noirs libres "où la tyrannie ne fait point verser de pleurs." (29) Mais l'abolition ne règle pas tout, remarquait-il car le préjugé de couleur limite toujours les possibilités de promotion sociale du Noir.

En définitive le *Mémoire* de Brissot assurait sa cohésion: l'esclavage est un ensemble de situations intolérable, et l'on voit ici combien l'idéologie motrice du voyage a su absorber les contradictions secondaires perçues pendant le séjour. Et le cas Brissot montre comment le "vu" de 1788, tressé avec le "lu", c'est-à-dire le témoignage des autres (Crèvecoeur, Chastellux), permet un certain déploiement du proclamé (*Mémoire*, *Voyage dans les Etats-Unis*), avant que n'apparaissent des butoirs du débat post-insurrectionnel, et donc les limites du négrophilisme girondin. Qu'on ait bien en tête le fait que, jusqu'à la grande épreuve de 1791, la philanthropie s'était surtout nourrie d'énoncés produits en métropole, par des auteurs éloignés des ateliers d'esclaves, écrivant des textes flamboyants de pathétisme facile et de compromissions visionnaires avec des révoltés virtuels, ce qui explique de notoires rétractions, plus tard. Sur place en revanche, et depuis les *Nouveaux Voyages aux Iles de l'Amérique* du Père Labat en 1772, et les *Mémoires historiques sur la Louisiane* de Le Mascrier, en 1753, parmi donc les écrivains résidents avait prévalu l'esprit précautionneux, ou conjuratoire, face au spectre de la contre-violence noire. En 1758 déjà, Le Page du Pratz, qui avait séjourné seize années en tant que régisseur de l'habitation du Roi près de la Nouvelle-Orléans, insistait sur les précautions qu'il avait prises pour éviter la délinquance et la turbulence des esclaves il fit briser leurs pirogues et abolir leurs assemblées. Il les mit également dans un camp entouré de palissades. Or une conjuration se déclare, menée par le premier commandeur, et qui menace de se généraliser: les Nègres voulurent se défaire des Français et s'établir à leur place. D'autres Noirs étaient passés aux Illinois, esquissant peut-être une alliance singulièrement prometteuse; aussi fit-on "souffrir les mèches ardentes" aux conjurés, puis cette roue française qui devait jusqu'en 1789 servir de remède ultime aux troubles coloniaux.[20]

Moreau de Saint-Méry et Berquin-Duvallon

Que fait d'autre Brissot en 1791, qui était pourtant revenu plein d'usage et raison de son voyage? L'initiative historique des Haïtiens, si elle ne glace pas tout à fait sa plume comme elle fait pour tant d'autres, conduit quand même l'Ami des Noirs à approuver l'envoi de troupes de répression. On peut voir là les prémisses de cette permanence structurelle qui a été appelée dans un récent colloque "colonialisme de la gauche conservatrice".[21]

Devant l'événement dominguien, l'attitude de deux représentants du monde colonial, dictée par l'intérêt de classe, a plus de mal à se faire passer pour de la responsabilité politique. L'un est le célèbre Moreau de Saint-Méry, né à la Martinique, passé à Saint-Domingue où il a été juriste officiel des autorités, puis envoyé en députation en France dans les trois premières années de la Révolution, puis émigré aux Etats-Unis. L'autre, Berquin-Duvallon, est un colon de la grande île, qui a dû s'intégrer plus ou moins bien à la "colonie espagnole du Mississippi", dont il publiera une *Vue* en 1803.[22]

La première remarque que nous ferons est que Moreau de Saint-Méry, publiant à Philadelphie en 1797 une imposante *Description de la Partie française de l'Ile de Saint-Domingue*, décide de ne rien changer au manuscrit rédigé avant l'insurrection, ce qui confère au texte publié un étrange parfum "Restauration" avant la lettre: annulées, les six années de révolte généralisée; figés au statu quo ante, les rapports entre races et classes. Et voilà que de 1793 à 1798, Moreau effectue un "Voyage aux Etats-Unis de l'Amérique",

---

20. Le Page du Pratz, *Histoire de la Louisiane* (Paris: de Bure l'aîné, 1758).

21. Colloque *Révolution, esclavage, colonisation, libérations nationales*, AFASPA-Université de Paris VIII, 24-26 février 1989.

22. Berquin-Duvallon, *Vue de la colonie espagnole du Mississippi...en l'année 1802, par un observateur résidant sur les lieux* (Paris: Imprimerie expéditive, 1803).

pour reprendre le titre d'un autre de ses manuscrits.[23] Il se dit d'abord heureux de retrouver à Norfolk, Virginie, une ambiance analogue à celle qu'il avait connue dans les îles. Mais il est également frappé de l'état d'avilissement et de saleté des nègres, qu'il juge châtiés "arbitrairement". Le loup esclavagiste, qui avait fait paraître un recueil de *Loix et Constitutions de Saint-Domingue* jugé par Brissot comme un "monument de barbarie",[24] s'était-il fait berger? Non, puisque c'est au niveau des spéculations consolatriçes qu'il se démarque des méthodistes, qui ont le tort selon lui de ne pas promettre à l'esclave "un autre monde meilleur", et dont la croyance menace cet esclave "de ne lui faire goûter l'égalité avec son maître qu'en enfer". On le voit: pour être passé du Cercle des Philadelphes, au Cap, à la ville de Philadelphie, Moreau de Saint-Méry n'en continue pas moins à se faire une singulière idée de l'amour de ses "frères".

Quant à Berquin-Duvallon, la Louisiane ne l'a pas poétiquement inspiré comme avait fait la colonie dominguienne.[25] Là où un autre exilé, Louis Ducrot, sut fonder en 1794 *Le Moniteur de la Louisiane*, il tient à souligner sa situation d'étranger. Car Berquin est un de ces évacués qui ont amené avec eux des esclaves domestiques, dans un pays où la législation coloniale a interdit l'importation de nouveaux nègres, ce qui détruisait un certain nombre de leurs espérances, comme en témoignent des correspondances privées.[26] Berquin représente ces planteurs que fustigera Charles Robin: "Parmi les fugitifs de Saint-Domingue venus à la Louisiane, il s'en est trouvé que des esclaves avaient suivis par attachement. La récompense de ces trop fidèles serviteurs a été d'être ensuite inhumainement vendus."[27]

Apprenons donc à lire notre ci-devant planteur. D'un territoire à l'autre, il fait glisser des expressions telles que "bon nègre", auxquelles, bien entendu, il continue de donner un sens très précis: "Le bon nègre durant les deux heures de relâche qui lui sont accordées [en Louisiane] ne perd pas son temps. Il va travailler à un coin de terre où il a planté des vivres pour son bénéfice." (265) Et lorsqu'il écrit: "Les noirs de Louisiane sont moins souples, plus âpres et plus décidés que ceux de Saint-Domingue", (262) comprenons que les Noirs des îles ont plus de valeur sur le marché du travail, ce qu'une correspondance d'exilé confirme: "les débris de nos nègres se louent mieux".[28]

---

23. Médéric-Louis-Elie Moreau de Saint-Méry, "Voyage aux Etats-Unis de l'Amérique", ms (New Haven: Yale Historical Publications, 1913).

24. Jacques-Pierre Brissot de Warville, *Note sur l'administration des planteurs*.

25. Berquin-Duvallon, *Recueil de poésies d'un colon de Saint-Domingue* (Paris: Imprimerie expéditive, an XI, 1802).

26. Maurice Begouen Demeaux, *Stanislas Foache, négociant de Saint-Domingue* (Paris: Larose, 1951).

27. Charles Robin, *Voyage dans l'intérieur de la Louisiane...*, 3: 204.

28. Begouen Demeaux, *Stanislas Foache*.

Berquin-Duvallon se donne le luxe de critiquer les colons du continent, "trop parcimonieux", conformément à ce qu'un autre voyageur, Perrin du Lac, esclavagiste lui aussi, signale sur l'avarice des maîtres louisianais.[29] Mais quand il affirme que l'esclavage hic et nunc est "plus dur qu'à Saint-Domingue", s'agit-il chez Berquin d'un plaidoyer pro-domo d'un préjugé national, ou d'une embellie rétrospective et nostalgique, puisqu'on sait par exemple le supplice des quatre piquets, dénoncé pour la Louisiane dans les mêmes années par Charles Robin, n'avait pas laissé d'être communément appliqué dans la grande colonie insulaire? Non, des hommes comme Berquin-Duvallon n'ont pas été ébranlés dans leurs convictions: de ses avatars personnels, qui sont ceux de toute une caste, il tire une conclusion finaude: "il n'y a qu'à remplacer le mot esclavage par le mot servitude". Dix ans de guerre révolutionnaire n'ont pas gommé ses jugements les plus obsolètes concernant les Noirs et leur "irrésistible propension, instinct machinal, qui les dispose et les attache à la servitude." (258)

Plus généralement, n'attendons pas un renouvellement de l'anthropologie chez ces voyageurs vaincus et réduits à l'ombre d'eux-mêmes par la perte de leurs possessions. Un demi-siècle plus tôt, Nicolas Bossu avait recueilli des anecdotes traitant de la dignité nègre, dans les îles comme sur la Terre-Ferme; dans son ouvrage de 1772, *De l'Amérique et des Américains*, le "voyageur-philosophe" Pierre Poivre avait âprement discuté l'idée de la dégénérescence des non-Européens. On note au contraire, chez nos voyageurs qui écrivent parmi les bouleversements de la dernière décennie du siècle, des options anthropologiques figées: Berquin voit les Noirs comme une espèce d'hommes destinés à l'esclavage.

Et Moreau de Saint-Méry se refuse à commenter les remarques d'ordre culturel que dans son livre *Danse*,[30] il a consacrées à la langoureuse "chica", qui lui semble pourtant l'expression de la personnalité nègre commune aux colonies noires du continent et à celles des îles. Et si Perrin du Lac rapporte dans son *Voyage dans les deux Louisianes* des faits qui témoignent de la perversité des maîtres blancs, il faudra lire sans ironie son conseil extra-humanitaire concernant les esclaves: "ayons au moins pour eux les soins que nous avons pour les quadrupèdes dont nous nous servons." (411)

L'abolition de l'esclavage

Le grand problème qui suscite tant de crispations anachroniques est celui de l'abolition de l'esclavage. Répétons-le, la plupart de ceux qui se sont

29. François Marie Perrin du Lac, *Voyage dans les deux Louisianes et chez les nations sauvages du Missouri* (Paris: Capelle et Renand, 1805).

30. Moreau de Saint-Méry, *Danse*, article extrait d'un ouvrage ayant pour titre *Répertoire des nations coloniales* (Philadelphie: l'auteur, 1796).

déplacés en divers territoires à l'économie esclavagiste et qui veulent en cette fin de siècle témoigner par l'écrit ont été personnellement engagés dans le processus colonial ou marchand. Aussi leurs préjugés, leur amertume, leurs espoirs de revanche récupératrice entravent-ils leur indépendance d'esprit, allant jusqu'à stériliser l'expérience née du déplacement.

L'officier Chastellux avait pourtant ouvert la voie en 1786 à des réflexions fécondes sur les rapports, ou plutôt les contradictions entre droit de propriété et liberté individuelle, à partir de ce que lui offrait le spectacle de la Virginie. D'une part, il observait la hiérarchie des races confondue avec celle des classes: "l'affranchissement ne peut faire cesser cette malheureuse distinction; aussi ne voit-on pas que les Nègres soient très empressés d'obtenir leur liberté." (2, 147)

"La véritable force sera toujours du côté de la propriété", remarquait-il, et Chastellux analysait philosophiquement le statut de citoyenneté des nouveaux états, au moment où s'élaborait la Constitution de 1787; le Virginien "est toujours un homme libre qui a part au gouvernement, et qui commande à quelques nègres, de façon qu'il réunit ces deux qualités distinctives de citoyen et de maître." (2, 46)

Seule la conclusion de Chastellux apparaissait comme fantasmatique: effacer la couleur noire par le métissage généralisé et ainsi se débarasser des Nègres pour abolir l'esclavage.

Un an plus tard, cette pseudo-solution par le dépérissement démographique passait sous la plume de l'abbé Genty, dans son livre *L'Influence de la découverte de l'Amérique sur le bonheur du genre humain*: "Hélas, ce n'est que par l'extinction progressive de la race noire qu'on parviendra au terme où le prix de l'esclavage surpassera celui qu'on en peut tirer".[31]

C'était offrir une perspective véritablement sinistre à une catégorie d'hommes qui étaient sur le point de s'affirmer d'une manière particulièrement impétueuse. Car, quelques années plus tard, la guerre de décolonisation, processus de violence noire émancipatrice, se déclenche à Saint-Domingue, et jette le désarroi dans la réflexion politique des personnes déplacées.

Perrin du Lac campe sur ses positions esclavagistes, et se permet même de conseiller les autorités américaines et Louisiane: "Après la cruelle expérience de Saint-Domingue...je suis loin d'engager aucun gouvernement à relâcher les liens de l'esclavage; on doit les laisser subsister dans leur intégrité, ou perdre les colonies." (409)

---

31. Louis Genty, *L'Influence de la découverte de l'Amérique sur le bonheur du genre humain* (Paris: Nyon, 1788), 331.

Quant à Moreau de Saint-Méry, son *Voyage aux Etats-Unis* le montre désemparé, agité d'observations contradictoires. D'une part il note qu'au Massachusetts, "La liberté générale n'a eu aucun effet fâcheux. Les esclaves sont devenus ouvriers...aucun d'eux n'est allé se faire esclave dans les autres états, ni n'a péri de misère." (326)

Mais c'est pour en tirer une conclusion sur la relativité géographique des statuts civils: "Ces états semblent vouloir donner un grand exemple des inconvénients d'accorder la liberté à des esclaves qui sont employés dans la culture, comme dans la partie sud des Etats-Unis." (333)

Enfin, il formule des regrets dont l'inutilité surprend chez cet homme de pensée: "il aurait été plus avantageux pour les peuples qu'on n'ait jamais parlé de liberté." (334)

Malouet, qui avait voyagé et séjourné à Saint-Domingue et en Guyane en qualité d'ordonnateur, et qui était lié au parti colon, s'était rendu célèbre au-delà des milieux administratifs par son *Mémoire sur l'esclavage des nègres*, paru en 1788. Lui aussi notait que: "Les Pennsylvaniens ont affranchi; ils ont fait sans aucun danger, et avec un grand avantage au contraire, un acte conséquent à leurs principes, à leur culture, à leur population; ils ont affranchi leurs nègres, qui ne sont pas dans leur pays un instrument nécessaire de culture". Mais il précisait aussitôt: "Qu'avons-nous de commun aux îles du Vent et sous le Vent avec les Habitants de la Nouvelle-Angleterre?"[32]

Très singulièrement, il s'en remettait à l'initiative étrangère pour instituer un nouveau Code Noir qui serait imposé au reste du monde par les principales puissances coloniales: France, Espagne, Angleterre: "Comme les Anglais nous ont précédés dans tous les calculs de l'économie rurale et politique...ce peuple penseur trouvera le premier les modifications convenables à la servitude nécessaire des Noirs." (150)

L'histoire en a décidé autrement et en 1797, Malouet se retrouve à Londres en situation de double exil. Ses prévisions, ses stratégies administratives ayant été bousculées, sa vision se fait apocalyptique, et par sa brochure intitulée *Quel sera pour les Colons de l'Amérique le résultat de la Révolution française*, il est probablement celui qui envisage avec le plus d'acuité un mouvement pan-nègre aux Amériques:

> Le roman de la liberté se terminera par la permanence d'une armée noire... C'est la perte totale des établissements européens en Amérique qui se présente comme dénouement de ce drame, il n'y a point d'enceinte, point de vaisseaux garde-côtes qui puissent empêcher la communication électrique de l'anarchie organisée (sic) entre les différentes tribus de nègres répandues dans les Antilles... Les Européens doivent se préparer

---

32. Pierre-Victor, baron Malouet, *Mémoire sur l'esclavage des nègres* (Neufchâtel, 1788), 44.

à abandonner le golfe du Mexique ou à s'y tenir constamment en état de guerre.

Soit relative stabilisation dix ans plus tard, soit incapacité de penser la totalité, le naturaliste Charles Robin, auteur des *Voyages dans l'intérieur de la Louisiane...*, songe à des solutions différenciées, selon les territoires.

Pour Saint-Domingue, il avance l'idée d'une partition, plutôt qu'une guerre de reconquête: "Pourquoi ne vous borneriez-vous pas à un état défensif envers les noirs insurgés?" (1, 269)

Pour les petites îles, où il est plus facile de résister à l'insurrection que sur les continents, notamment en Louisiane, il compte sur une imposante force militaire de répression, combinée avec des réformes empiriques, "à moins que de nouveaux principes, de nouvelles moeurs, de nouvelles lois mûrement réfléchies, sagement et circonspectement (sic) exécutées, n'amènent dans les colonies un nouvel ordre de choses." (1, 41)

En définitive, pour l'historien des idées et des sensibilités, pauvre peut sembler le bilan de ces relations de voyage et de séjour parmi les champs de canne, d'indigo ou de tabac. Avant le soulèvement de 1791, toute la conduite à tenir envers les esclaves tient en ces mots: châtier, égayer, ne pas abuser, c'est-à-dire au sens premier ne pas mésuser des noirs bossales[33] ou créoles. Par ailleurs, les situations contrastées dans l'espace comme dans le temps que les voyageurs ont eu l'occasion de vivre, ne se sont pas résolues pour eux en conclusions pratiques ou théoriques: les exemples différenciés de Pennsylvanie et de Virginie, de New York ou Baltimore et du Cap-Français, ne les ont pas conduits à élaborer un système cohérent pour le "gouvernement des noirs". Brissot lui-même, pourtant porteur d'une doctrine, va se faire surprendre par l'événement et en demeurer quelque peu prisonnier.

Les situations personnelles renforcent encore cette espèce de loi qui veut que l'écriture du concret aboutit très souvent à justifier le déjà-là, le voyage, le témoignage constituant paradoxalement un obstacle à la critique fondamentale: dans la quasi-totalité des cas la réflexion in situ piétine ou régresse par rapport aux acquis théoriques de Montesquieu, Diderot et Rousseau.

En dernière analyse, et depuis la crispation des expossédants jusqu'aux protestations plus ou moins indignées contre les abus et même l'existence de l'esclavage, l'idéologie de nos voyageurs ne connaît-elle pas les hésitations et les oppositions homologues de celles qui furent au coeur de deux réalisations de la pensée bourgeoise française de l'époque: l'*Encyclopédie*, la Révolution? La Révolution, y compris cette journée à la fois ambiguë et unanime de

---

33. Nés en Afrique.

pluviôse an II, qui vit à leur tour se mettre debout, pour l'abolition, la gauche montagnarde de l'Assemblée et les représentants des colons présents dans les tribunes.

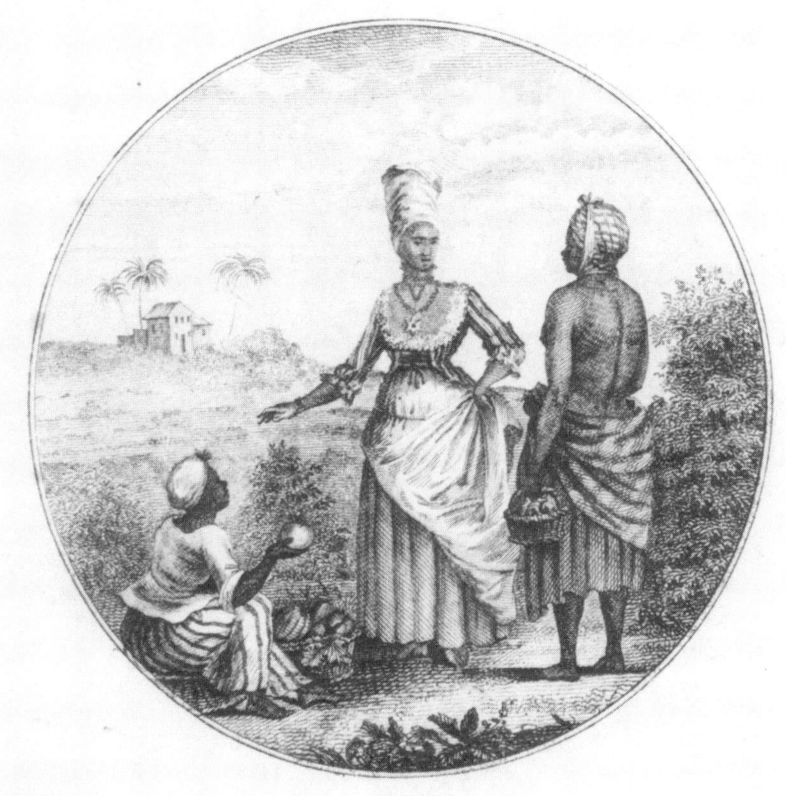

ABOVE AND FOLLOWING PAGE: Nicholas Ponce, *Slave and Free Women of the West Indies,* 1791 (collection of Dr. Fritz Daguillard). These prints are based on original works by Brunias, an Italian-born English artist who visited the West Indies in the late 18th century at the invitation of the Governor of the island of Dominica. Half of the island being French, the costumes shown here most likely reflect the styles worn in the French West Indies at that time. Free women of the island were known for their elaborate and elegant attire.

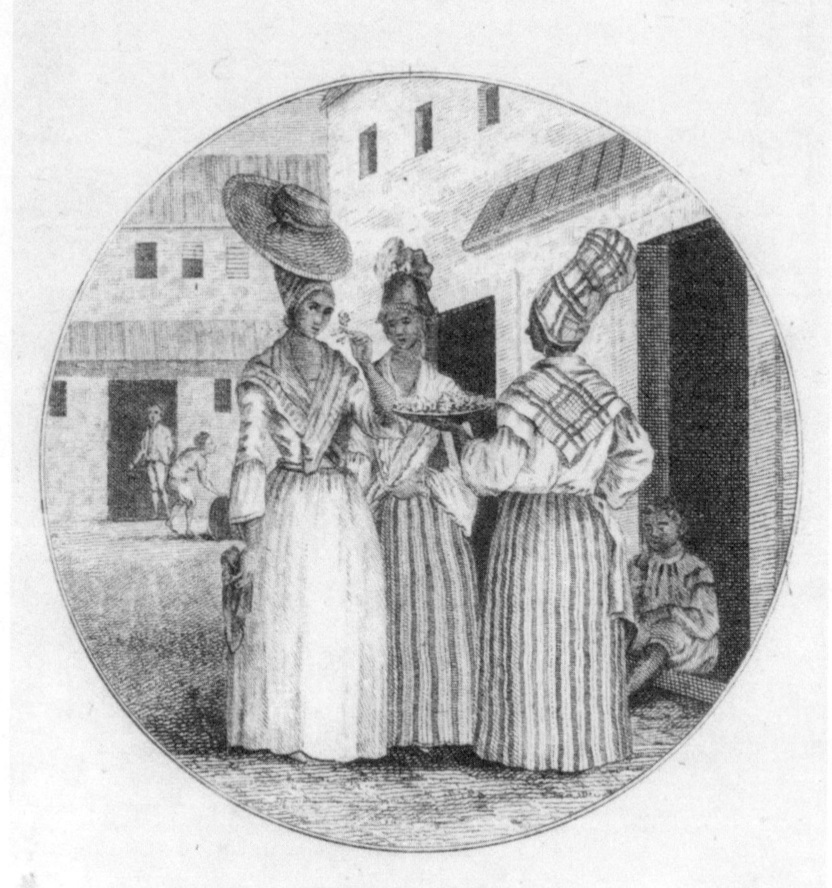

COSTUMES

DES AFFRANCHIES ET DES ESCLAVES

des Colonies.

A propos d'un silence: Diderot, l'indépendance américaine et l'esclavage colonial

Jean Ehrard

Lumières et indépendance américaine. Lumières et esclavage colonial: ces deux directions de recherche sont aujourd'hui bien explorées et balisées. Mais peut-être de façon trop autonome. N'avons-nous pas toujours un peu tendance à oublier que le vent de la liberté qui soufflait d'Amérique dans la décennie précédant la Révolution venait d'un pays esclavagiste? Certes, le paradoxe n'avait pu ne pas heurter alors quelques esprits aussi généreux qu'éclairés: on sait les vaines démarches de La Fayette auprès de Washington, lui-même propriétaire d'esclaves dans son domaine de Mount Vernon.[1] Il y a pourtant encore à chercher, et à dire, sur le point d'articulation, dans la conscience française, de deux convictions également fortes, du moins parmi l'avant-garde des philosophes et de leurs disciples: le soutien fervent à la liberté américaine et une répulsion croissante pour l'esclavage des Noirs. Comment ces deux images de l'Amérique ont-elles pu se combiner, sinon se concilier, comment en tout cas se situaient-elles l'une par rapport à l'autre? Le cas de Diderot me semble susceptible de fournir quelques éléments de réponse: non que je prétende apporter au plan textuel quelque révélation–toutes les pages qui concernent le sujet sont bien connues, mais par le simple rapprochement de textes qui habituellement ne relèvent pas tous du même champ de recherche.

Présent dans de nombreux articles, généralement brefs, de l'*Encyclopédie*, le continent nord-américain inspire aux collaborateurs de Diderot une double série de réflexions, les unes d'ordre anthropologique, les autres d'ordre politique. Les "Américains"–et le mot, alors, désigne exclusivement les indigènes–donnent matière à un portrait composite, sinon contradictoire, de l'homme à l'état sauvage: hospitalier, courageux jusqu'à l'héroïsme, mais

---

1. Voir Albert Krebs, "La Fayette et l'abolition de l'esclavage", *La France et l'esprit de 76*, Actes du colloque de Chavagenac-La-Fayette établis et présentés par Daniel Royot (Faculté des Lettres et Sciences Humaines de Clermont-Ferrand, Clermont-Ferrand, 1977), 95-112.

paresseux, inconstant, cruel et féroce jusqu'à l'anthropophagie. L'appréciation de sa mentalité religieuse est encore plus contrastée: Jaucourt, inspiré par La Hontan, tire vers une sorte de déisme très raisonnable la "philosophie des Canadiens"; d'Holbach ridiculise au contraire la superstition des Algonquins, des Hurons et des Iroquois, à propos desquels Jaucourt le rejoint du reste... Mais ce même auteur insiste surtout sur la "liberté naturelle" que les sauvages ont su conserver aussi bien à l'égard des colons européens que dans leur propre organisation qui ne connaît "ni roi, ni chef".[2] Diderot ne se pose pas ce type de questions dans l'article **Amérique*, d'une remarquable sécheresse; de même ne considère-t-il les sauvages d'Amérique du Nord que du point de vue physique dans le panorama des races que présente l'article **Humaine espèce (Hist. nat.)*. C'est seulement dans l'article *Caraïbes, ou cannibales*, s'il est bien de lui, que sa curiosité, guidée par celle de Montaigne, se porte vers les moeurs d'une peuplade américaine; à cette époque Diderot engrange la documentation, mais le temps de la méditation approfondie qu'il mènera plus tard sur le bonheur comparé du civilisé et du sauvage n'est pas encore venu. Antérieur à l'entreprise encyclopédique, le débat sur la légitimité et l'utilité des colonies se développe en revanche dans le *Dictionnaire raisonné des sciences, des arts et des métiers*. Véron de Forbonnais y justifie, sans états d'âme, le système du Pacte colonial et de l'Exclusif. Sans doute précise-t-il: "Il faut encore que le sort des habitants soit très doux, en compensation de leurs travaux et de leur fidélité." Mais cette exigence concerne les seuls colons, non les "anciens habitants" qu'il a d'abord été nécessaire de chasser (art. *Colonie. Hist. anc. mod. et commer.*). Quelques années plus tard Damilaville dénonce au contraire l'injustice de principe et les effets pernicieux des conquêtes coloniales: affaiblissant le conquérant en divisant sa puissance, elles exterminent ou corrompent les occupants légitimes (art. *Population. Phys. Polit. Morale.*)

Quelques lignes de Damilaville sur les vices exportés outre-mer par les Européens ont déjà un peu des accents du *Supplément au Voyage de Bougainville*. Mais dans les années 1770 l'actualité politique immédiate est beaucoup moins la condition des peuples colonisés que la question des rapports entre colons et métropole. C'est l'époque où les tensions entre l'Angleterre et ses colonies américaines se font de plus en plus vives. L'*Encyclopédie* ne les avait guère prévues. Ainsi dans l'article *Virginie* (*Géog. mod.*) le chevalier de Jaucourt s'abritait derrière l'autorité de David Hume

---

2. Nous ne pouvons, ici, qu'effleurer la question: voir notamment les articles *Sauvages (Hist. mod.)*, non signé, *Sauvages (Géog. mod.)*, *Canadiens (philosophie des)* et *Iroquois*, qui sont du chevalier de Jaucourt, et l'article *Michabou*, du baron d'Holbach. Sur tout cela voir Michèle Duchet, *Anthropologie et histoire au siècle des Lumières* (Paris: Maspero, 1971).

pour nier le risque de sécession.[3] Mais dès 1769 Diderot donnait pour sa part un pronostic inverse: "c'est une grande querelle que celle de l'Angleterre avec ses colonies. Savez-vous mon ami [Grimm], par où nature veut qu'elle finisse? Par une rupture?"[4] Depuis plusieurs années, par l'intermédiaire du baron d'Holbach, Diderot s'était lié avec le "Gracchus" britannique, le radical John Wilkes.[5] Après avoir admiré en lui le défenseur de la liberté anglaise, il en vient tout naturellement, en accord avec l'opinion publique française, à applaudir à ses discours parlementaires en faveur des colons révoltés.[6] Deux ans plus tard il insère dans l'*Essai sur Sénèque* sa célèbre apostrophe aux insurgents d'Amérique, reprise sous une forme un peu différente en 1780, dans la troisième édition de l'*Histoire des deux Indes*: adresse enthousiaste à la jeune nation, conviction que la libre Amérique est désormais à la fois un refuge pour les Européens opprimés et un exemple redoutable pour leurs tyrans, mais aussi mise en garde contre les menaces que ne manqueraient pas de faire peser sur la liberté américaine "l'accroissement énorme et l'inégale distribution de la richesse".[7] Quelle mélancolie pour le Philosophe que de se savoir lui-même trop âgé pour visiter jamais cette "contrée héroïque"![8]

On notera dans ces lignes ardentes une petite mutation sémantique qui n'est pas sans intérêt: les "braves Américains" dont Diderot admire tant le courage civique sont bien entendu les anciens colons anglais, et non plus les peuplades dont ceux-ci avaient usurpé les terres, ces "Américains", au sens traditionnel du nom, sur "le goût antiphysique" desquels il s'interrogeait à la veille de la guerre d'indépendance.[9] Comme au théâtre, dans quelque drame

---

3. Voir aussi, du même auteur, l'article *Pennsylvanie*, tout à la gloire du "second Lycurgue" et, par ricochet, des Anglais. Raynal n'est pas meilleur prophète: en 1770 l'*Histoire des deux Indes* (Livre XVIII) considère la sécession comme improbable et très peu souhaitable.

4. Compte rendu des *Lettres d'un fermier de Pennsylvanie aux habitants de l'Amérique septentrionale*, de Dickinson, trad. de l'anglais: texte destiné à la *Correspondance littéraire*, mais resté inédit jusqu'en 1798. Diderot, *Oeuvres complètes*, éd. R. Lewinter (Paris: Club français du Livre, 1971) 8: 357.

5. Les deux hommes ont dû se rencontrer pour la première fois à Paris, chez le baron au printemps 1763. (Voir Diderot, *Correspondance*, éd. G. Roth, 16 vols. (Paris: Minuit, 1958) 4: 250. Nombreuses allusions à Wilkes et quelques lettres de Diderot à son adresse dans les volumes suivants: le surnom de "Gracchus" apparaît dans une lettre du 19 octobre 1771; (*Correspondance*, 9: 210).

6. *Correspondance*, juin 1776, 14: 198.

7. *Essai sur les règnes de Claude et Néron...*, II, 74 (Diderot, *Oeuvres complètes*, éd. H. Dieckmann, J. Varloot, 27 vols. (Paris: Hermann, 1986) 25: 355-56). Voir aussi 25: 417-18; Raynal, *Histoire philosophique et politique des établissements et du commerce des Européens dans les deux Indes*, Nelle édit. (Genève: Pellet, 1780), t.9, livre XVIII (voir Denis Diderot, *Mélanges et morceaux divers. Contributions à l'Histoire des deux Indes*, edizione a cura di Gianluigi Goggi, (Sienne: 1977), 2: 186-87).

8. Goggi, 180.

9. Texte inséré en 1774 dans l'*Histoire des deux Indes* (Livre VI, ch. 7). Ed. 1780, livre VI, ch. 8. D'abord publié dans la *Correspondance littéraire*, le 15 septembre 1772. Cf Diderot, *O.C.* Lewinter, 10: 66 et 86, *Mélanges* Goggi, 2: 329-30 et 366, et Michèle Duchet, *Diderot et L'Histoire*

philosophique, *exit* l'indigène victime de la colonisation, entre le compagnon de Franklin et de Washington...ou plutôt la second silhouette se superpose à la première, si bien que l'image de l'Amérique en est doublement valorisée: une terre de liberté naturelle devient le lieu privilégié de la liberté politique. Ce téléscopage qui transforme l'histoire en mythe relègue dans ses coulisses non seulement les malheurs de l'Indien colonisé, mais le mal absolu de l'esclavage des Noirs. Sur la scène américaine où se joue un raccourci prometteur de l'aventure humaine les esclaves n'ont pas leur place au dénouement. Et s'ils y sont apparus à l'acte précédent, c'est tout au plus en simples figurants. Au printemps 1776 Diderot s'était fait l'écho, à l'adresse de Wilkes, d'informations inquiétantes sur les mesures extrêmes que le gouvernement britannique aurait envisagées: "Il paraît ici un papier qu'on dit être d'un homme important de votre nation; il paraît par ce papier que le projet secret de la mère patrie est de faire égorger la moitié des colons, et de réduire le reste à la condition des nègres".[10] Passée la menace, les nègres disparaissent. Pas un mot, fût-il de simple pitié, de la part du Philosophe dans l'enthousiasme républicain de 1778 et 1780. Il est toujours hasardeux de commenter un silence. De toute évidence le contraste entre le despotisme européen et français, évocateur pour Diderot des plus sinistres années de l'empire romain, et la jeune liberté américaine éclipse alors à ses yeux une réalité déplaisante. Qu'il puisse l'oublier complètement, même le temps d'une *apostrophe* qui par ailleurs dénonce d'avance les progrès du luxe (la possession de domestiques noirs n'en est-elle pas un?), cela fait néanmoins problème: d'autant que les vifs sentiments anti-esclavagistes qui sont siens dans cette même période ne peuvent être mis en doute. Un détour par les colonies françaises d'Amérique aidera peut-être à éclairer le paradoxe.

La condamnation véhémente de l'esclavage colonial par le Diderot des dernières années est le résultat d'une lente maturation.[11] Dans l'*Encyclopédie*

---

des deux Indes: ou L'écriture fragmentaire (Paris: Nizet, 1978), 35.

10. Voir lettre citée à la note 5 (*Correspondance*, 9: 199).

11. Sur les problèmes des colonies et de l'esclavage colonial, et en particulier la position de Diderot, je ne puis que renvoyer aux travaux de: Yves Benot, *Diderot, de l'athéisme à l'anticolonialisme* (1970; 2e éd. Paris: Maspero, 1981); *La Révolution française et la fin des colonies*, (Paris: Editions La Découverte, 1988). - Carminella Biondi, *Mon frère, tu es mon esclave! Théorie schiaviste e dibatti antropologico—razziali nel Settecento francese* (Pisa: Libreria Golicardica, 1973); *Les esclaves sont des hommes. Lotta abolizionista e litteratura negrofila nella Francia del Settecento* (*ibid.*, 1979). Voir aussi, bien sûr, le livre fondamental de Michèle Duchet, *Anthropologie et Histoire...*, les actes du colloque *La Période Révolutionnaire aux Antilles* (1986), éd. Roger Toumson (Université des Antilles et de la Guyane, 1988), et le résumé de la table ronde organisée par Y. Benot au Septième Congrès International des Lumières (Budapest: 1987), *SVEC* 265 (Oxford: The Voltaire Foundation, 1989), 1751-64.

Riches d'informations et de réflexions utiles, les ouvrages de Pierre Pluchon, *Nègres et juifs au XVIIIe siècle. Le racisme au siècle des Lumières* (Paris: Tallandier, 1984) et de Louis Salasa position personnelle ne se distingue guère de celle qui ressort du *Dictionnaire raisonné* dans son ensemble: un débat au moins entr'ouvert, mais sur fond d'indifférence. Une petite dizaine d'encyclopédistes se partagent la cinquantaine d'articles dont le sujet implique une prise en compte des réalités de l'esclavage. Un tiers de ces articles se bornent à parler des produits des îles, en oubliant de mentionner leur mode de production; deux tiers de ceux qui abordent explicitement le sujet le font sur un ton de totale neutralité; seule une petite minorité d'articles s'interrogent sur la légitimité de l'institution esclavagiste, soit pour la condamner avec vigueur, comme le chevalier de Jaucourt le fait dans l'article *Traite des nègres*, inspiré de l'anglais George Wallace,[12] soit pour la justifier à la manière de Le Romain qui énumère dans l'article *Nègres considérés comme esclaves dans les colonies de l'Amérique* les arguments de la bonne conscience; les Noirs des Antilles y sont moins malheureux qu'en Afrique, ce sont de grands enfants etc... Quant à Diderot, il se borne le plus souvent à des articles purement documentaires. Pas un frémissement de sensibilité pour nous apprendre que la traite est considérable au Paraguay (**Acara ou Acaraï*), que les meilleurs nègres viennent d'Angola (**Angola. géog. mod.*), ni pour nous détailler les étapes de la culture et du travail du cacao (**Cacao ou Cacaoyer. Hist. nat.*). L'article **Coton (Hist. nat. bot.)* réussit même la gageure de consacrer dix-neuf colonnes à la production et au traitement des fibres sans utiliser une seule fois le mot *nègre*, laissant le sujet productif dans un élégant indéfini: "un homme...un autre homme...on..." L'article **Humaine espèce (Hist. nat.)* ne prête pas à l'accusation de racisme, puisqu'il attribue principalement au climat, et en second lieu aux habitudes alimentaires et sociales, les différences de couleur entre les hommes, mais l'auteur semble se pincer le nez lorsqu'il évoque la mauvaise odeur des Angolais–par ailleurs, on l'a vu, si solides à la peine...–et la protestation sincère contre l'esclavage sur laquelle le texte se conclut mêle à la compassion quelque condescendance:

> Quoiqu'en général les Nègres aient peu d'esprit, ils ne manquent pas de sentiment. Ils sont sensibles aux bons et aux mauvais traitements. Nous les avons réduits, je ne dis pas à la condition d'esclaves, mais à celles de bêtes de somme; et nous sommes raisonnables! et nous sommes chrétiens!

Molins, *Le Code noir et le calvaire de Canaan* (Paris: P.U.F., 1987), sont malheureusement gâtés, le second surtout, par un parti pris anti-philosophique qui frise, et parfois dépasse, le contre-sens.

12. George Wallace, *System of the principles of the laws of Scotland* (Edinburgh, 1760). Le passage traduit par Jaucourt figure en appendice dans l'ouvrage du pasteur Antoine Benezet, *Some historical account of Guineau...* (Philadelphie, 1771 et Londres, 1772). (Je remercie Y. Benot de ces renseignements qu'il m'a aimablement communiqués à la suite de la publication de mon article "L'*Encyclopédie* et l'esclavage colonial", *La Période Révolutionnaire...*, 229-39).

Reconnaître aux Noirs du "sentiment", c'est interdire à leur égard toute cruauté; leur concéder de faibles facultés intellectuelles, c'est presque les situer à mi-distance de l'homme et de l'animal: d'autant que Diderot qui croit à la continuité de la nature est loin de faire sienne la théorie cartésienne de l'animal-machine... On mesurera le chemin parcouru en quelques années par sa réflexion anthropologique en rapprochant ces lignes de deux autres passages. En réponse à Helvétius qui accordait le monopole de la vertu héroïque aux "peuples plus ou moins policés" son contradicteur raconte l'histoire d'un nègre de Cayenne qui avait préféré s'abattre le poignet d'un coup de hache plutôt que d'obéir à l'ordre de pendre ses compagnons.[13] Quant au préjugé du "peu d'esprit" des nègres, le livre XI de l'*Histoire des deux Indes* en fait justice dès 1770. L'infirmité intellectuelle des esclaves noirs ne vient pas de la nature, mais de la condition qui leur est imposée: "les nègres sont bornés; parce que l'esclavage brise tous les ressorts de l'âme..."[14]

C'est donc dans la période d'intense méditation philosophique, morale et politique qui suit l'achèvement de l'*Encyclopédie* que Diderot met définitivement au point ses idées sur l'esclavage colonial: sur cette question comme sur beaucoup d'autres les années 1770-1780 sont particulièrement fécondes. On peut certes s'étonner de la discrétion avec laquelle le commerce des îles est évoqué, en 1772, dans *Ceci n'est pas un conte*. Pour satisfaire à la cupidité de sa maîtresse Tanié s'expatrie neuf ou dix ans à Saint-Domingue. S'il s'y distingue "par ses lumières et par son équité", le lecteur un peu informé ne peut conserver de doute sur la nature des "affaires" auxquelles il devra de pouvoir rapporter à la Reymer "le produit de ses ventes et de ses travaux." Tout au plus peut-on supposer qu'il ne s'est pas conduit en maître injuste et cruel. Colon ou négociant? Plus ou moins directement Tanié a, en tout cas, été mêlé à la traite, et il est même devenu un notable de l'île ("il entra au Conseil Souverain du Cap.")[15] Ici, pas le moindre mot de pitié sur ceux auxquels il doit sa fortune; pas le moindre recul critique du narrateur... Il faut cependant tenir compte de la logique de la fiction qui fait de Tanié, du "bon Tanié", lui-même une victime, et se rappeler que *Ceci n'est pas un conte* forme

---

13. *Réfutation de l'ouvrage d'Helvétius intitulé De L'Homme, O.C.* Lewinter, 11: 603. (Voir *De L'Homme*, section V, ch. V, 2e proposition). Notons qu'il y a émulation dans l'héroïsme—le maître a d'abord vainement offert la vie sauve à celui des "sauvages marrons" qui accepterait de pendre ses camarades—et aussi contagion de sensibilité—"Tu n'es plus un esclave; tu es mon ami", déclare le maître au nègre amputé, "en l'embrassant"...Le livre XI de l'*Histoire des deux Indes* raconte un autre geste "sublime", le sacrifice d'un esclave marron qui s'est faussement accusé d'un assassinat pour servir son maître, mais résume en trois lignes le fait divers précédent: "on a vu l'un de ces malheureux se couper le poignet d'un coup de hache, plutôt que de racheter sa liberté par le vil ministère de bourreau". (ch. 28)

14. Cf. *Mélanges* Goggi, 2: 234 et 289. Il s'agit du fragment *Sur l'esclavage des nègres*.

15. Diderot, *Contes et entretiens*, éd. Lucette Pérol (Paris: Garnier-Flammarion, 1977), 126-27.

seulement le premier volet d'une trilogie: on ne saurait en juger indépendamment de l'ensemble, et c'est "à la fin"–comme en avertissait en avril 1773 la *Correspondance littéraire*–donc dans le *Supplément au voyage de Bougainville*, qu'on peut espérer en découvrir "la morale et le but secret".[16] Certes, le thème dominant du *Supplément*, les interdits sexuels, est apparemment très éloigné d'un problème que le premier récit de la trilogie effleure sans le poser, et la servitude que refuse le discours pathétique du vieillard est d'abord celle du pays–"le vol de toute une contrée"–plutôt que l'asservissement individuel de ses habitants. Mais deux ou trois expressions suggèrent que dans l'esprit de l'orateur la servitude civile est ici inséparable de la servitude politique: "Un jour ils reviendront...vous enchaîner... Un jour vous [Otaïtiens] servirez sous eux...celui dont tu veux t'emparer comme de la brute..."[17] Déjà, dans le dialogue qui précède ces *Adieux du vieillard*, en réponse à une question sur les Jésuites du Paraguay, l'interlocuteur l'élevait contre la façon dont "ces cruels spartiates en jaquette noire" en usaient avec leurs esclaves indiens;[18] encore est-il difficile de préciser par ce seul passage si l'esclavage est ici mis en cause dans son principe ou seulement pour son excessive dureté. Mais la condamnation absolue portée par Orou contre les préceptes de la morale sexuelle européenne vaut aussi, par sa formulation très générale, contre l'institution esclavagiste elle-même: préceptes "contraires à la nature, parce qu'ils supposent qu'un être pensant, sentant et libre *peut* être la propriété d'un être semblable à lui".[19] Quelques lignes des *Fragments échappés du portefeuille d'un philosophe*, contemporains du *Supplément*, associent explicitement dans un même refus l'asservissement de la femme et le sort fait à l'esclave: "jamais un homme ne peut être la propriété d'un souverain, un enfant la propriété d'un père, une femme la propriété d'un mari, un domestique la propriété d'un maître, un nègre la propriété d'un

---

16. Sur l'unité et le mouvement de la trilogie, voir Jean Ehrard, "Diderot conteur, ou l'art de déplacer la question", *Colloquio internacional Diderot* (Lisbonne, 28-29 janvier 1985), Actes réunis et présentés par Maria Héléna Carvalho Dos Santos (Lisbonne: Universitaria Editoria, 1987), 161-71.

17. *Supplément au voyage de Bougainville*, éd. Herbert Dieckmann (Genève: Droz et Lille: Giard, 1955), 12-14.

18. *Supplément...*, 8. On est loin de Montesquieu qui, tout en relevant avec malice l'esprit de domination de la Société de Jésus, la félicitait de faire le bonheur des Indiens (*De l'Esprit des Lois*, IV, 6). Loin aussi de la conclusion admirative que Jaucourt avait encore donnée, au t.11 de l'*Encyclopédie*, à une présentation légèrement distante des missions du Paraguay (art. *Paraguay, missions du*) (*Géog./Hist.*). Loin enfin du préjugé favorable accordé aux jésuites par un long chapitre de l'*Histoire des deux Indes* elle-même (Livre VIII, ch. 37 de la seconde édition).

Le *Salon* de 1767 (*O.C.* Lewinter, 7: 122) rapprochait déjà la condition des ilotes lacédémoniens de celle des esclaves des colonies, mais pour la juger encore plus malheureuse: "La tyrannie d'un colon d'Amérique est moins cruelle; la condition des nègres moins triste".

19. *Supplément...*, 26.

colon".[20] C'est bien l'argument anti-esclavagiste de Montesquieu, Rousseau et Jaucourt que le sauvage Orou applique aux relations entre les deux sexes: la liberté naturelle est inaliénable.[21]

L'homme n'est pas une chose. Diderot le répète avec force, par l'intermédiaire de Raynal, dans l'*Histoire des deux Indes* où la question de l'esclavage colonial est abordée de front. Grâce au fonds Vandeul de la Bibliothèque Nationale on sait aujourd'hui avec certitude que tout un chapitre du livre XI–*L'esclavage répugne à l'humanité, à la raison et à la justice* (ch. 24 de l'édition de 1780)–vient de Diderot.[22] A première lecture ce chapitre surprend, tant sa fermeté dans le refus, et surtout certains accents révolutionnaires contrastent avec les conseils pratiques sur le bon usage de la traite ou l'adoucissement souhaitable du sort des esclaves que Raynal prodigue par ailleurs. Il ne faut cependant pas en simplifier la démarche. D'abord parce que ce qui est dit dans ce livre XI contre l'esclavage est impérativement à rapprocher d'autres passages de même origine, et en particulier des propos du livre XIII sur l'administration coloniale. Ensuite parce que des nuances qui ne sont pas sans intérêt apparaissent de la première édition à la seconde, et de celle-ci à la troisième. Enfin, et surtout, parce qu'à ces variantes près la même structure complexe se décèle comme une constante de la contribution globale de Diderot à l'*Histoire* sur les colonies et l'esclavage. Car cette contribution est faite en réalité de trois discours qui s'interpénètrent et dont la compatibilité, du moins pour nous, fait problème: une condamnation absolue de l'esclavage; de prudentes propositions de réformes en faveur des Noirs; des propositions de réformes en faveur des colons. A une institution

---

20. *Mélanges* Goggi, 2: 315 (voir note 9). Enumération presqu'à l'identique dans *Sur l'esclavage des nègres*, 2: 235.

21. *De l'Esprit des Lois*, 15: 2. *Discours sur l'origine et les fondements de l'inégalité parmi les hommes*, 2e partie, éd. J.-L. Lecercle (Paris: Les Classiques du Peuple, 1954), 133-34. *Du Contrat social*, I, 4. *Encyclopédie*, art. *Liberté naturelle (Droit naturel)*: longtemps attribué à Diderot, cet article est plus vraisemblablement du chevalier de Jaucourt, selon John Lough ("The problem of the unsigned articles in the *Encyclopédie*", *SVEC* 32 (1965): 347) qui y discerne l'influence de Burlamaqui: voir aussi l'article *Egalité naturelle (Droit naturel)*, du même Jaucourt, et Jean Ehrard, "L'*Encyclopédie* et l'esclavage: deux lectures de Montesquieu", *Enlightenment Essays in Memory of Robert Shackleton* (Oxford: The Voltaire Foundation, 1988), 121-29.

22. Correspond à une partie des fragments manuscrits des *Mélanges* regroupés par M. de Vandeul sous le titre *Sur l'esclavage des nègres*, éd. Goggi, 218-44. Pour le détail de la correspondance entre cet ensemble et les trois éditions principales de l'*Histoire*, voir Goggi, 287-94 (c'est à cette édition que renvoient les références données ici entre parenthèses après les citations), et Duchet, *Diderot et l'Histoire des deux Indes...*, Deuxième partie. Sur le fond, voir les analyses serrées de ce dernier auteur dans *Anthropologie et histoire...*, 170-77. S'il est exact, comme le dit Naigeon (Duchet, *Anthropologie et histoire...*, 175, note 200), que le texte des deux premières éditions est de Pechméja, Diderot se l'approprie en le transformant pour la troisième.

qui lui fait horreur Diderot a été tenté d'opposer "le mépris du silence". (239) L'*Histoire* développe l'idée avec insistance en début de chapitre:

> Montesquieu n'a pu se résoudre à traiter sérieusement la question de l'esclavage. En effet c'est dégrader la raison que de l'employer, on ne dira pas à défendre, mais à combattre même un abus si contraire à la raison. Quiconque justifie un si odieux système, mérite du philosophe un silence plein de mépris, et du nègre un coup de poignard.[23]

Quand le philosophe s'appelle Denis Diderot il ne lui est pourtant pas facile de se taire, surtout quand l'émotion soutient et anime la conviction intellectuelle. Aussi s'emploie-t-il à argumenter: "Démontrons d'avance qu'il n'est point de raison d'état qui puisse autoriser l'esclavage." (219) Plusieurs pages véhémentes récusent les unes après les autres les justifications traditionnelles données par les esclavagistes: les "extravagances atroces" de l'explication théologique qui fait des Noirs les descendants de Caïn; le droit du plus fort, qui légitimerait plutôt la revanche violente des victimes; l'universalité de la pratique, qui ne pourrait suffire à l'innocenter; la prétendue protection des esclaves contre les abus des colons par les lois européennes: "Dans la vérité, le droit d'esclavage est celui de commettre toutes sortes de crimes" (234); le caractère des Noirs dont les faiblesses ou les vices sont en réalité le produit de leur condition; l'esclavage de naissance, le droit des gouvernements, la vente volontaire, tous arguments qui butent sans réplique sur la nature inaliénable de la liberté; les crimes des Africains vendus aux Européens, alors que le despotisme règne en Afrique et que "dans un état despotique, il n'y a de coupable que le desposte" (236); l'amélioration relative de la condition des Noirs déportés en Amérique, "comble de l'extravagance", (237); l'universalité de la servitude dans le monde, comme si celle des Européens égalait celle des esclaves; enfin les bienfaits du baptême acquis aux esclaves en vue de leur salut: "O débonnaire Jésus, eussiez-vous prévu qu'on ferait servir vos douces maximes à la justification de tant d'horreurs!" (238)

Cette réfutation passionnée apparaît déjà, en substance, dans la première édition de l'*Histoire*. Mais il faut attendre la seconde pour qu'elle débouche sur la conclusion logique qu'appelait sa véhémence. La "nature" ne peut se laisser violer indéfiniment sans réagir. Les esclaves marrons ont déjà prouvé leur capacité d'organisation; des cas individuels de représailles par le poison, ou de suicide, ont montré que l'oppression est devenue insupportable: "il ne manque aux nègres qu'un chef assez courageux, pour les conduire à la

23. Dès 1770 ces lignes s'ajoutent dans l'*Histoire* au texte qui nous a été conservé par le manuscrit des *Mélanges*. On notera que leur auteur—quel qu'il soit—ne se trompe pas, à la différence de certains commentateurs d'aujourd'hui, sur la portée du célèbre chapitre *De l'esclavage des nègres* de *L'Esprit des Lois* (XV, 5).

vengeance et au carnage". Cette idée vient, on le sait, de L.-S. Mercier. Sous le titre de *Singulier monument*, son "rêve" de 1770, *L'An deux mille quatre cent quarante* (ch. 22), décrivait, entre autres figures de marbre d'un monument du nouveau Paris, "plusieurs esclaves mutilés, qui criaient vengeance en regardant le ciel" et "sur un magnifique piédestal un nègre, la tête nue, le bras tendu, l'oeil fixe, l'attitude noble, imposante". Le narrateur précise: "Autour de lui étaient les débris de vingt sceptres. A ses pieds on lisait ces mots: *Au vengeur du nouveau monde!*" Après quoi, le héros se fait expliquer comment l'Amérique a été libérée de ses "tyrans" européens par le soulèvement de leurs victimes, sous la conduite d'un "homme immortel..., ange exterminateur à qui le Dieu de justice avait remis son glaive"...[24] A "cet homme étonnant" l'*Histoire* donne un nom: "Où est-il ce grand homme, que la nature doit peut-être à l'honneur de l'espèce humaine? Où est-il ce nouveau Spartacus, qui ne trouvera point de Crassus?" On ne sera pas surpris qu'ici la "nature" ait remplacé le "Dieu de justice" de Mercier. Il est plus important de noter que pour les deux auteurs l'affranchissement des esclaves passe par une insurrection nationale, si bien que la libération civile des personnes va de pair avec la libération politique de l'Amérique. Mais tandis que Mercier suppose l'extermination des oppresseurs, dans un massacre d'apocalyse, l'*Histoire* s'intéresse au sort, peu enviable des survivants: "Alors disparaîtra le *code noir*; et que le *code blanc* sera terrible, si le vainqueur ne consulte que le droit de représailles!" Le texte de 1780 se termine sur la même menace, mais après avoir suivi de plus près celui de Mercier dans l'évocation du carnage libérateur, jusqu'à en être le démarquage.[25] Différences plus importantes entre les deux éditions: la disparition de la référence romaine–le héros n'a plus de nom–sans doute parce que celle-ci évoquait autant la défaite des esclaves que leur révolte; et surtout le ton plus assuré de la prédiction. Non seulement le "peut-être" de 1774 disparaît également, mais à l'interrogation initiale–"Où est-il?"–répond désormais une affirmation insistante: "Il paraîtra, n'en doutons point, il se montrera, il lèvera l'étendard sacré de la liberté..."

---

24. Louis-Sébastien Mercier, *L'An deux mille quatre cent quarante. Rêve s'il en fut jamais*, éd. Raymond Trousson (Bordeaux: Ducros, 1971), 203-06. Voir le commentaire de Joseph Jurt, "L.-S. Mercier et le problème de l'esclavage et des colonies", dans *La Période Révolutionnaire aux Antilles*....

25. Mercier: "La terre de l'Amérique a lu avec avidité le sang qu'elle attendait depuis longtemps, et les ossements de leurs ancêtres lâchement égorgés ont paru s'élever alors et tressaillir de joie". Diderot: "Les champs américains s'enivreront avec transport d'un sang qu'ils atendaient depuis si longtemps, et les ossements de tant d'infortunés, entassés depuis trois siècles, tressailleront de joie".

Notons par ailleurs, avec Goggi, qu'au lieu de "Vainqueur" le manuscrit des *Mélanges* donne "vengeur".

A première vue ce ton de prophète se concilie pourtant mal avec les suggestions réformistes présentées en 1770, et que Diderot et Raynal se gardent de supprimer des deux éditions suivantes. Elles consistent d'une part en un projet d'affranchissement progressif, d'autre part en un appel aux Rois d'Europe pour qu'ils donnent l'exemple de la renonciation à la traite: "Refusez le sceau de votre autorité au trafic infâme et criminel d'hommes convertis en vils troupeaux, et ce commerce disparaîtra." Pour la cohérence des textes le premier point fait encore plus problème que le second, et surtout dans la troisième édition. Car alors même que celle-ci accentue *in fine* le ton messianique de la précédente, elle transforme une simple suggestion en un véritable programme auquel ne manque même pas ce que nous appellerions des mesures complémentaires d'insertion. Dès 1770 l'*Histoire* affirme que la suppression de l'esclavage ne priverait pas les Européens des produits des îles: "Ces productions peuvent être cultivées par des mains libres, et dès lors consommées sans remords." La rédaction est identique en 1774. En 1780 elle se nuance d'un *peut-être* et le futur est remplacé par un conditionnel.[26] On pourrait y lire l'expression d'un léger doute, symétrique du renforcement simultané de la prédiction finale, et propre par là-même à atténuer l'apparente contradiction, si l'exposé du projet qui vient ensuite ne faisait alterner les conditionnels et les futurs: plus vraisemblablement nous avons là une sorte de précaution oratoire, à l'intention des sceptiques qui ne croient pas à la possibilité de faire travailler aux îles des hommes libres. Car en prenant à son compte un objectif "si généralement regardé comme chimérique", Diderot prend parti, comme l'a établi Michèle Duchet, dans un débat d'actualité ouvert au sein de l'administration coloniale française. "L'homme éclairé" dont il résume le projet n'est pas un philosophe, facilement accusé de verser dans les abstractions et les chimères, mais un homme de terrain dont l'expérience devrait se faire entendre dans les bureaux du Ministère.[27] C'est alors que

26. "Il ne *serait* pas même *peut-être* impossible d'obtenir ces productions de vos colonies, sans les peupler d'esclaves. Ces denrées *pourraient* être cueillies par des mains libres, et dès lors consommées sans remords." (*Mélanges* Goggi, 2: 240)

Le même texte de 1780 suggère ce qui arrivera effectivement au XIXe siècle: tirer les produits exotiques directement d'Afrique: mais dans l'esprit de l'auteur il s'agirait, semble-t-il, de libre commerce, et non d'exploitation coloniale.

27. Le baron de Bessner, qui fut notamment inspecteur général en Guyane en 1764 et gouverneur de la colonie en 1781. Son projet d'affranchissement date de 1774; il est discuté en 1779 au Comité de législation pour les colonies, où Malouet le combat après l'avoir soutenu. Voir Duchet, *Anthropologie et histoire...*, 129-35, 154-58, etc. L'auteur souligne que ce projet prend place dans un ensemble d'autres propositions, dont l'*Histoire des deux Indes* se fait également l'écho (134, note 421).

L'idée que l'esclavage est une erreur économique et la conviction de la meilleure productivité du travail libre étaient répandues parmi les Physiocrates et leurs proches. Voir notamment les articles des *Ephémérides du citoyen* mentionnés par Duchet (*Anthropologie et histoire...*, 163 et *sq.*).

prend un contenu très concret l'idée présente dès 1770, mais alors seulement indiquée, d'un affranchissement étalé dans le temps (Diderot parlait, sans autre précision, d'un indépendance recouvrée "successivement"). Les esclaves actuels, "hommes stupides" parce que vieillis dans la servitude, ne sont malheureusement pas susceptibles de se conduire jamais en hommes libres. La liberté sera donc réservée à leurs enfants, et seulement au-delà de la vingt-cinquième année: travail obligatoire pour rembourser les maîtres de leurs dépenses, gratuitement jusqu'à vingt ans, contre salaire les cinq années supplémentaires. Doté alors aux frais de l'Administration d'une cabane et d'un jardin, le "nouveau citoyen" pourra devenir un producteur indépendant; et s'il reste salarié le surcoût de ce travail libre pour l'économie générale sera compensé par une bien meilleure productivité dont tout le monde profitera: "une plus grande masse de travail donnera une plus grande abondance de productions aux colonies, que leurs richesses mettront en état de demander plus de marchandises à la métropole." (241)

Pragmatisme réformateur ou messianisme révolutionnaire? Les deux attitudes seraient inconciliables s'il était sûr qu'il faille interpréter l'annonce du soulèvement libérateur comme un "appel à la révolte".[28] Cette lecture est assurément possible mais, une annonce n'étant pas forcément un "appel", elle ne s'impose pas avec évidence. Peut-être même n'est-elle pas la plus plausible. Diderot n'a rien d'un homme de sang, et on l'imagine mal souhaitant le massacre des colons...[29] Plus vraisemblablement le texte est une mise en garde qui place l'Administration royale et les colons eux-mêmes devant une alternative: ou bien des réformes, ou bien le cataclysme. D'autres que notre philosophe, en des périodes de l'histoire coloniale plus proches de nous, ont eu, sans plus de succès–et parfois à leur détriment–la même lucidité. Celle de Diderot n'est pas plus en cause ici que la cohérence de sa pensée. On n'en peut dire autant de son plaidoyer en faveur des colons. Le livre XIII de l'*Histoire* se fait en effet l'écho des doléances de ceux-ci à l'encontre de l'administration: absurdité et inefficacité du centralisme versaillais pour des territoires si éloignés et si différents de la France; multiples conflits et égale tyrannie des intendants et des gouverneurs... Pour prévenir l'arbitraire administratif il faudrait, expliquent les éditions de 1770 et 1774, des "lois fixes dont le dépôt fût entièrement confié à des tribunaux", et que ceux-ci fussent

28. Duchet, *Anthropologie et histoire...*, 174. L'auteur montre par ailleurs avec beaucoup de nuances comment l'*Histoire* reflète différents courants d'opinion. Quant à la différence entre le cas de la Guyane et celui de Saint-Domingue, elle était moins évidente pour les lecteurs de Raynal que pour l'Administration.

29. Pas plus qu'il ne *souhaite* voir mettre un terme en France au "despotisme" par une révolution violente, même s'il tend à juger celle-ci inéluctable. Voir Jean Ehrard, *Préface* à l'*Essai sur les règnes de Claude et de Néron*, *O.C.* Hermann, 25: 13-14. Cassandre souhaitait-elle la ruine de Troie?

"composés de magistrats nés dans les colonies".[30] La troisième édition insiste sur la revendication d'un minimum d'auto-gouvernement: "Laissez aux colons assemblés le soin de vous éclairer sur leurs besoins. Qu'ils forment eux-mêmes le code qu'ils penseront convenir à leur situation." (267) Sans doute ce rôle législatif est-il prudemment présenté comme devant être soumis à la sanction de Versailles: "Rien ne paraît plus conforme aux vues d'une politique judicieuse, que d'accorder à ces insulaires le droit de se gouverner eux-mêmes, mais d'une manière subordonnée à l'impulsion de la métropole, à peu près comme une chaloupe obéit à toutes les impulsions du vaisseau qui la remorque." (272-73) Autonomie n'est pas indépendance... Mais quel aurait été le code proposé par les colons? Y avait-il la moindre chance qu'il allât dans le sens d'une réelle humanisation du Code noir, préparant même une abolition progressive de l'esclavage? On peut en douter fortement, et Diderot lui-même, nous l'avons vu, relève la fréquence des libertés prises par les "habitants" par rapport aux dispositions légales qui prétendaient assurer aux esclaves un minimum de protection. Peut-être même a-t-il eu écho des nombreux rappels à l'ordre envoyés du Ministère aux colonies, tout au long du siècle, pour le respect de la loi.[31] En tout cas le portrait qu'il donne de ces créoles dont il propose d'accroître l'influence est peu encourageant: "C'est de l'esclavage des nègres que les créoles tirent peut-être en partie un certain caractère qui les fait paraître bizarres, fantasques, et d'une société peu goûtée en Europe".[32]

Voilà donc un défenseur des Noirs, dont la sincérité n'est pas en cause, qui souhaite renforcer l'autorité de leurs oppresseurs: ce n'est pas le moindre paradoxe de Diderot, du moins à nos yeux. Et nous en venons à nous demander quelle position il aurait prise s'il avait vécu quelques années de plus. Aurait-il suivi Raynal dans sa palinodie de 1785?[33] Cédé, comme tant d'hommes de la Révolution, aux arguments et aux pressions du Club Massiac, ce *lobby* colonialiste qui retardera l'abolition et dont l'influence durable obtiendra en 1802 le rétablissement de l'esclavage et de la traite? Ou bien

---

30. Diderot, *Pensées détachées. Contributions à l'Histoire des deux Indes*, éd. Goggi (Sienne: 1976), 465. Pour l'intégralité du fragment 134, qui correspond au texte donné par l'*Histoire* en 1780, voir 259-74; et pour les variantes, 464-66. La contradiction sur laquelle j'insiste est seulement signalée par Michèle Duchet (*Anthropologie et histoire...*, 135). Diderot prend le parti des colons contre les négociants (sur ce conflit: Gaston-Martin, *Nantes au XVIIIe siècle. L'ère des négriers (1714-1774)* (Paris: Alcan, 1931), 363 et *sq.*): remarquons que si le Ministère l'avait suivi, un nouveau Tanié n'aurait pu siéger dans un tribunal...

31. Duchet, *Anthropologie et histoire...*, 151 et *sq.* Certains viennent de Dubucq (voir note 36).

32. *Pensées détachées...*, 257 (fragment 132). Ce paragraphe appartient déjà aux éditions précédentes.

33. L'*Essai sur l'administration de Saint-Domingue* (1785), où Raynal exprime le point de vue de Malouet, propose d'appuyer les réformes sur les mulâtres, mais abandonne toute idée d'affranchissement des Noirs. Voir Duchet, *Anthropologie et Histoire...*, 176-77.

aurait-il fini par préférer nettement la cause des esclaves à celle des colons? Si ces questions restent à jamais sans réponse, il est du moins possible de comprendre comment la contradiction qui nous frappe échappe en 1780 à un esprit qui n'est pas des moins clairvoyants de son temps. Après avoir vu dans l'histoire contemporaine tant d'exemples d'émancipation de peuples colonisés arrachée seulement par la force, nous ne nous laissons pas aisément convaincre aujourd'hui que même les moins "atroces" (le mot est de Diderot) et les plus "éclairés" des colons puissent se transformer en législateurs raisonnables. Oserions-nous pourtant affirmer que voici trente ou quarante ans nous n'aurions pas plus ou moins partagé l'illusion du philosophe? Plusieurs facteurs contribuent en tout cas à la myopie qui nous étonne: un relativisme inspiré de *L'Esprit des Lois*, qui réclame pour des terres lointaines une législation spécifique; un autre héritage de Montesquieu, le culte de la loi et la priorité donnée à la dénonciation de l'arbitraire et du "despotisme" dans lequel verserait la monarchie française;[34] enfin, et surtout, ses propres relations coloniales. Car celles-ci sont de qualité: l'encyclopédiste Le Romain, ami du baron d'Holbach, ingénieur à la Grenade; des membres encore plus importants de la haute administration comme Malouet et Dubucq. Diderot apprécie en Malouet une "franchise naturelle", "un juge difficile qui se connaît en hommes et en vertus".[35] Il est particulièrement lié à Dubucq, issu d'une grande famille de colons de la Martinique, premier commis au Ministère de la Marine, qui aurait servi de modèle au rigoureux, mais généreux, Monsieur Poultier de *Est-il bon? Est-il méchant?*.[36] Or ce sont là gens de bonne compagnie, des hommes aimables, des esprits ouverts aux idées nouvelles: comment leur fréquentation n'aurait-elle pas donné au philosophe une vision déformée, et plutôt rassurante, de la société coloniale?

Il est temps, après ce voyage aux îles et en Guyane, de revenir sur le continent nord-américain. Si les réflexions de Diderot sur l'esclavage s'appliquent tout particulièrement aux colonies françaises, elles ont évidemment valeur universelle. En serait-il de même des illusions qu'il a pu nourrir sur une évolution positive sur l'esclavage dans le salut qu'il adresse en

---

34. D'où son insistance à réclamer pour les colonies "une législation modérée, frixe et indépendante des volontés particulières". Voir Jean Ehrard, "Diderot et le despotisme", *Diderot. Le XVIIIe siècle en Europe et au Japon* (colloque franco-japonais de Kyoto, 19-23 novembre 1984. Actes recueillis par Hisayasu Nakagawa, 121-26); et "Diderot et la loi civile", *La loi civile, Cahiers de philosophie politique et juridique*, Université de Caen, 12 (1987): 107-19.

35. *Correspondance*, 15: 157 et 161 (octobre 1779).

36. Le nom de Dubucq apparaît dans la *Correspondance* dès le t. 5 (octobre 1765, 144). Diderot l'a rencontré chez les Necker (142) et il ne cessera plus de compter sur sa protection pour le neveu de Sophie, Vallet de Fayolle. Voir à ces deux noms l'index général de la *Correspondance*, t. 16. Et aussi l'anecdote sur Dubucq rapportée dans le compte rendu des *Poésies pastorales* de Léonard, 1771 (*O.C.* Lewinter, 9: 950).

1778 et 1780 à la liberté américaine? Sur le comportement des colons anglais envers leurs esclaves son opinion a varié. En 1773, dans la *Réputation d'Helvétius*, il philosophait sur la dureté du peuple britannique envers les Noirs: "ses nègres sont les plus malheureux des nègres. L'Anglais, ennemi de la tyrannie chez lui, est le despote le plus féroce quand il en est sorti."[37] Le livre XI de l'*Histoire des deux Indes*, il est vrai à propos des îles, présente la réalité sous un jour un peu plus favorable: si le maître anglais est "haï" de ses esclaves, ce n'est pas qu'il les brutalise à l'excès–au contraire précise Raynal, "il n'exige guère des pères et des mères un travail au-dessus de leurs forces"–mais qu'il les considère, avec morgue, "comme des êtres purement physiques".[38] Et le livre XVIII relève, lui, le sort relativement enviable des esclaves continentaux par rapport à celui des insulaires: "mieux nourris et mieux vêtus, moins maltraités et moins accablés de travail". Raynal y note aussi qu'en raison du climat l'"iniquité" de l'esclavage est en Amérique du Nord "d'autant plus criante qu'elle semblait moins nécessaire".[39] Enfin et surtout la seconde édition rapporte avec enthousiasme l'événement extraordinaire qui s'est produit en Pennsylvanie et "doit faire époque dans l'histoire de la religion et de l'humanité". Et Raynal d'ajouter: "Une révolution si frappante devait être l'ouvrage d'un peuple tolérant. Mais n'attendez pas un semblable héroïsme de ces nations qui sont aussi barbares par les vices du luxe, qu'elles l'ont été par ceux de l'ignorance".[40] Les nouveaux Américains de 1776–en qui les Philosophes parisiens voient sans doute autant de Franklin–ont en commun avec les Quakers la tolérance et la frugalité: que ne peut-on espérer d'eux quand on croit pouvoir attendre des colons français des îles un peu d'attention à leur véritable intérêt, un minimum d'humanité? Il n'est pas tendancieux d'interpréter le silence de Diderot comme un signe d'optimisme: non, un peuple libre ne peut durablement en opprimer un autre; la liberté est contagieuse; comme le disait le Quaker de l'abbé Raynal, on ne peut "être libre et tyran tout à la fois".

---

37. *O.C.* Lewinter, 11: 618.

38. *Mélanges* Goggi, 2: 229 et *Histoire*, livre XI, ch. 28 (1775) et 22 (1780). Les *Mélanges* ne retiennent que la seconde idée.

39. "Cinquième édition augmentée de variantes" (reprise de la seconde édition principale), (Maestricht: Dufour et Roux, 1777) t.7, ch. 23: 104.

40. *Histoire...*, 7: 106. L'orateur quaker dont l'*Histoire* résume le propos est Antoine Benezet (voir note 12). Benezet avait mené sa campagne abolitionniste–qui n'était pas sans précédents parmi les Quakers–en 1768-1769. En 1770 les "Amis" américains recommandent de s'abstenir du commerce des esclaves; en 1774 ils se prononcent pour l'émancipation. Mais il ne s'agit pas d'une décision d'Etat: celle-ci n'interviendra en Pennsylvanie qu'en 1780, trois ans après l'exemple donné par le Vermont. La "révolution" célébrée par Raynal n'était donc pas encore effective à la date de la seconde édition des *Deux Indes*, et encore moins lors de la première édition de *L'An deux mille quatre cent quarante...* (précisions dues à l'aimable érudition de M. Yves Benot).

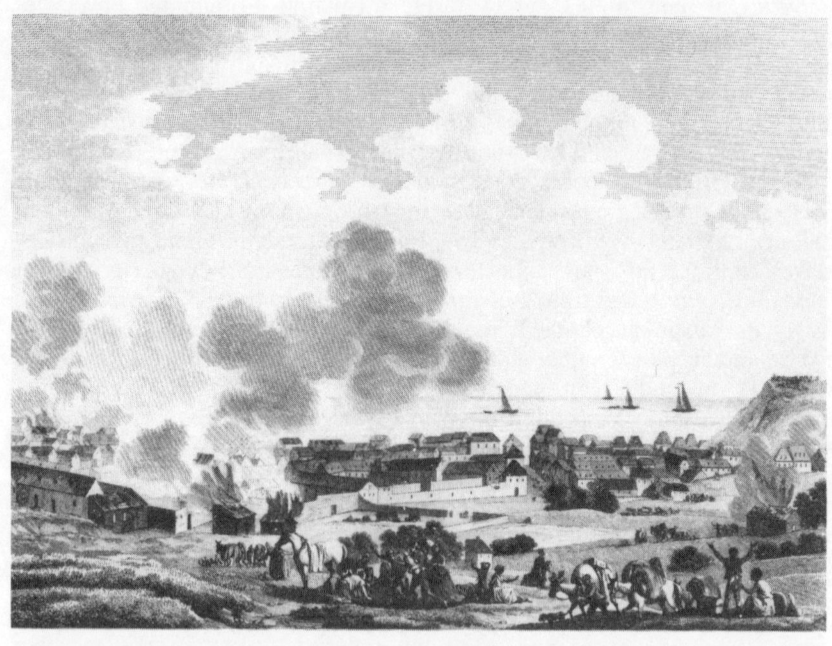

Pierre-Gabriel Berthault (after S.W. Desfontaines), *Incendie du Cap Français*, 1796 (collection of Dr. Fritz Daguillard). Burning of the city of Cap (today, Cap-Haitien) during the fight between Sonthonax, the revolutionary French envoy, allied with the revolted slaves, and the counter-revolutionary forces led by Governor Falband. Sonthonax promised the slaves their freedom; this led to his victory, the burning of the city, and a massive exodus of the white population.

L'aventure américaine des officiers de Rochambeau vue à travers leurs journaux

Jean-Jacques Fiechter

Le but et les limites de cet exposé sont indiqués par son titre. Il n'est pas question de refaire l'histoire de la guerre d'Indépendance des Etats-Unis, d'évaluer le rôle joué par l'intervention française dans ce conflit ou ses répercussions ultérieures sur la Révolution de 1789.

Les excellents travaux du professeur Lee Kennett[1] et du chercheur militaire Gilbert Bodinier[2] ont puissamment contribué ces dernières années à modifier l'approche assez simplificatrice de l'influence du modèle américain sur les prémices de la Révolution française.

Il s'agit donc ici de rappeler en grandes lignes les expériences faites en Amérique par les officiers du corps expéditionnaire de Rochambeau à travers leurs journaux, mémoires ou lettres qui nous sont parvenus.

Les dates limites de cette odyssée vont de l'embarquement des troupes à Brest, en avril 1780, au retour en France des derniers combattants de Rochambeau en juin 1783.

La présence en Amérique pendant trois ans d'une petite armée française de 6 500 officiers, soldats et auxiliaires a modifié profondément les rapports franco-américains et donné une réalité pratique à l'alliance de 1778 entre les deux pays. Les Français vont confronter leur vision romanesque et simpliste de l'Amérique à la diversité d'un pays et d'un peuple encore très hétérogènes. Le choc culturel sera encore plus violent pour bien des Américains, héritiers des préjugés anglais à l'égard des Français, qui les caricaturaient comme efféminés, volages, rabougris et maigres, à force de ne manger que des grenouilles et des escargots. Par sa discipline et sa virilité, le corps

---

1. Lee B. Kennett, *The French Forces in America, 1780-1783* (Westport: Greenwood Press, 1977).

2. Gilbert Bodinier, *Les officiers de l'armée royale, combattants de la guerre d'Indépendance des Etats-Unis, de Yorktown à l'an II* (Château de Vincennes: Service historique de l'armée de terre, 1983).

expéditionnaire se fit un point d'honneur et un plaisir de changer rapidement cette image ridicule de la France.

Seuls nous sont parvenus, et sous des formes variées, les témoignages d'une quarantaine d'officiers, sur les 492 que comptait l'armée de Rochambeau. Nous nous sommes basés tout spécialement sur les journaux personnels écrits au jour le jour et non destinés à être publiés, sans pour autant négliger les mémoires, souvenirs ou récits rédigés ultérieurement par les protagonistes, d'après leurs notes et leurs lectures. Dans aucun cas, il ne s'agit de journaux intimes où l'intéressé écrit pour lui seul tout ce qu'il pense ou ce qu'il fait, sans rien cacher ni embellir, tels les cahiers de Benjamin Constant ou le journal de Gouverneur Morris, mais de comptes rendus de voyage, où sont notés les événements jugés intéressants, destinés à un petit cercle de familiers au retour de son héros en Europe. Peut-être que la crainte d'indiscrétion ou de perte de ce document, dans la promiscuité et les surprises de la vie militaire, a joué un rôle de frein à des notations confidentielles concernant des tiers. Cela n'empêche pas ces journaux de guerre d'être indispensables pour fixer les détails de cette campagne d'Amérique et de donner des indications précieuses sur l'état d'esprit de ses participants. Parmi les principaux documents utilisés figurent les journaux du comte Clermont-Crèvecoeur, de Cromot du Bourg, du lieutenant de Verger, du baron Gaspard de Gallatin, d'un soldat anonyme du régiment du Bourbonnais et surtout du Baron Louis de Closen. Ces journaux ont été complétés par les mémoires et lettres du duc de Lauzun, du comte de Fersen, du comte de Ségur, du comte de Rochambeau, du comte de Deux-Ponts et de bien d'autres.[3] Pour la plupart de ces textes, déjà publiés ou non, les manuscrits originaux ont été consultés, chaque fois que cela a été possible. Quant au petit journal inédit du soldat incorporé dans le régiment du Bourbonnais, retrouvé à la *Library of Congress* sous le nom de Milton Laham, il a le mérite d'être, à ma connaissance, le seul à ne pas avoir été rédigé par un officier et de nous donner, par conséquent, une vision au "ras de guêtres" de cette campagne d'Amérique.

---

3. Voir en plus des textes identifiés dans les notes ci-dessous: Louis-Alexandre Berthier, *Journal de la Campagne d'Amérique (1780-1781)* (Institut Français de Washington: Gilbert Chinard, 1951); François-Jean de Beauvoir Chastellux, *Voyages de M. le Marquis de Chastellux dans l'Amérique Septentrionale dans les années 1780, 1781 et 1782*, 2 vols. (Paris: Prault, 1786); Marie-François-Joseph-Maxime, Cromot du Bourg, baron, *Journal depuis mon départ de France 26 mars 1781 jusqu'au 18 novembre de la même année que l'Armée aux ordres de M. le Cte. de Rochambeau est entrée dans ses quartiers d'Hiver*, Manuscrit original à la Historical Society of Pennsylvania, AM 6360, Philadelphie. Une traduction anglaise a été publiée par Thomas Balch dans le *Magazine of American History*, New York, Vol. 4 (March-June 18-): 205-14, 293-308, 376-85, 441-52, et Vol. 7 (Oct. 1881): 283-95; Guillaume Deux-Ponts, comte de, *Mes Campagnes d'Amérique* (Boston: Massachusetts Historical Society). Le texte français a été publié avec la traduction anglaise par Samuel Abbot Green (Boston: Wiggin and Lunt, 1868); Jean-Baptiste-Donatien de Vimeur Rochambeau, comte de, *Mémoires historiques, militaires et politiques*, 2 vols. (Paris: Fain, 1809).

Ce vaste échantillonnage, dont les auteurs sont français, allemands, suédois ou suisses, est représentatif de la composition largement cosmopolite du corps expéditionnaire sous les ordres de Rochambeau, et ne comporte donc pas d'officier de la marine ou des troupes embarquées sur la flotte de l'amiral de Grasse.

Une question préalable se pose. Quelles sont les motivations de ces troupes envoyées au secours des Insurgents par Louis XVI en mai 1780?

Assimiler cette intervention française à une véritable "croisade de la Liberté", à un élan spontané et généreux pour répondre à l'appel de la jeune république américaine, représente une pure vue de l'esprit. Il s'agissait avant tout de reprendre dans les colonies, le projet mort-né en 1779 d'attaquer l'Angleterre dans son île avec 30 000 hommes. La petite escapade réussie du duc de Lauzun au Sénégal au début de la même année a montré la voie. Mais l'escadre qui s'embarque finalement en avril 1780 à Brest reste très limitée. Cette "expédition particulière", selon son nom de code, porte bien son titre.[4] A peine 5 000 soldats embarqués et 500 officiers, au lieu des 8 000 à 12 000 hommes promis. Il s'agissait d'un premier convoi, qui devait être doublé rapidement. En fait la "deuxième division" resta en rade, ses régiments furent expédiés ailleurs et Rochambeau dut se contenter de ce demi-corps d'armée, entassé dans un désordre indescriptible et sans un seul cheval, le général ayant tristement dû donner l'exemple en laissant les siens à terre.

A l'exception de certains aides-de-camp ou de colonels en second, il ne s'agissait pas là de volontaires. De Rochambeau au dernier soldat du régiment de Soissonnais, ils partaient se battre outre-mer parce que leur unité avait été affectée à l'expédition.

Pour la quasi-totalité d'entre eux, le fait d'avoir été sélectionné relevait de la loterie militaire. L'armée de terre française rénovée et drillée à la prussienne depuis la Guerre de Sept Ans était prête à se battre avec courage et discipline partout où on l'enverrait, que l'ennemi fût anglais, prussien ou turc.

Seule ombre au tableau, la perspective d'une longue traversée en mer n'enthousiasmait personne. Cette "croisière de rêve" s'annonçait pénible. La réalité fut infiniment plus douloureuse, surtout pour les soldats embarqués. A titre d'exemple, le témoignage du jeune grenadier du Bourbonnais, coincé sur le navire amiral "Duc de Bourgogne", avec 1 432 autres malheureux: "quiconque veut fouiller la misère jusqu'au fond, n'a qu'à rester six mois et demi sur mer en qualité de soldat passager: je me flatte après ce temps, qu'il

---

4. Kennett, *French Forces...*, 10.

préférera la plus vile servitude (sans qu'elle soit déshonorante) au charme de la navigation".[5]

Sur l'ensemble des officiers embarqués, bien peu sentaient leur coeur palpiter "au bruit du réveil naissant de la liberté cherchant à secouer le joug du pouvoir arbitraire", comme l'écrit poétiquement 40 ans plus tard le comte de Ségur.[6] Du reste, l'objectif réel de l'expédition n'était connu à bord que de rares initiés. L'escadre croyait voguer vers la Jamaïque alors que le gouvernement anglais, mieux informé par ses espions, savait qu'elle se dirigeait vers l'Amérique septentrionale et envoya une flotte d'appoint pour l'intercepter là. Quand le 17 juin, Rochambeau annonce officiellement le vrai but du corps expéditionnaire, le soulagement est général, non par enthousiasme pour l'indépendance américaine mais par suite "de la mauvaise réputation du climat des îles", comme l'écrivent prosaïquement Gallatin[7] et Closen.[8]

Si combattre pour la liberté des "Insurgents" n'est pas le principal objectif des officiers de Rochambeau, d'autres motivations non idéologiques les stimulent indéniablement. Elles se retrouvent dans tous les Journaux, aussi bien chez les officiers de cour que chez les officiers subalternes:

-un vif désir "d'apprendre bien leur métier", de "compléter leur éducation militaire";[9]

-"la joie parfaite de penser qu'ils vont à la guerre", comme l'écrit Fersen;[10]

-l'espoir de "mériter au coup de fusil" les places qu'ils avaient obtenues par leur situation familiale, selon le comte de Charlus;[11]

---

5. Anonyme, *Journal militaire* inédit d'un soldat du régiment du Bourbonnais, figurant sous Milton Laham Papers, MMC 1907 (Washington, D.C.: Library of Congress, Manuscript Division), 76.

6. Louis-Philippe Ségur, comte de, *Mémoires, ou Souvenirs et Anecdotes*, 3 vols. (Paris: Eymery, 1824-1826). Une édition abrégée est parue chez Fayard en 1910.

7. Gabriel-Gaspard Gallatin, baron de, *Journal* manuscrit en 3 vols. et des feuillets séparés, 80-4405 (Washington, D.C.: Library of Congress, Manuscript Division), partiellement reproduit par Warrington Dawson, "Un Garde Suisse de Louis XVI au service de l'Amérique", *Le Correspondant* (10 août 1931): 321-39 et (10 septembre 1931): 672-92.

8. Louis-Jean-Christophe Closen, baron de, *Journal de Guerre, 1780-1783*. Copie manuscrite de 760 feuillets en 2 vols., *Baron von Closen Journal* (Washington, D.C.: Library of Congress, Manuscript Division).

9. Charles-Joseph-Hyacinthe Du Houx Viomenil, comte de, *Relation de ma vie militaire*, manuscrit de 149 pages, en mains des descendants de M. d'Hennezel d'Ormois (Château de Vincennes: Service historique de l'armée de terre).

10. Axel Fersen, comte de, *Lettres d'Axel de Fersen à son père pendant la Guerre de l'Indépendance d'Amérique*, publiées par le comte F.U. Wrangel (Paris: Firmin-Didot, 1929).

11. Armand-Charles-Augustin de la Croix de Castries Charlus, comte de, *Journal de mon voyage en Amérique (7 mai 1780-27 septembre 1780)* (Paris: Archives Nationales, Marine B 4-183).

-le besoin de se distinguer, d'accélérer leur avancement si lent en temps de paix et surtout le désir de gloire, "fouettés par l'opinion et le préjugé de l'honneur", comme le constate encore Charlus;[12]

-enfin, pour d'autres, l'appel de l'aventure, de nouveaux horizons, ou le goût du risque, quand on a 20 ans et peu d'attaches...

A des degrés divers, ces mêmes motivations se retrouvent à tous les niveaux hiérarchiques, sauf peut-être chez les grands chefs, Rochambeau et l'amiral de Ternay, dont la réputation militaire est faite et le courage maintes fois prouvé.

Choix de Rochambeau

Le choix du comte de Rochambeau pour commander l'expédition s'avère providentiel. Le prince de Montbarrey, ministre de la guerre, l'a proposé, bien qu'il ne fût pas de ses amis et qu'il ne parlât pas un mot d'anglais. A 55 ans, avec 40 ans de service, Rochambeau est un grand professionnel, "exclusivement plein de son métier, qu'il entend à merveille", selon Lauzun.[13] Sa fermeté, la précision de ses ordres, son coup d'oeil militaire, son sang-froid sont incontestés. Ses aides-de-camp l'admirent mais souffrent de sa défiance "désagréable et même insultante" pour son entourage.[14] Fersen constate qu'il se méfie même de ses officiers généraux. Le commissaire des guerres Blanchard confirme qu'il "croit toujours se voir entouré de fripons ou d'imbéciles".[15]

Rochambeau est aimé de ses soldats, qui le savent économe de leur sang. Au très jeune La Fayette, qui ne pense qu'à attaquer l'ennemi, le général confie un grand secret: son plus grand titre de gloire, c'est que "sur 15 000 hommes à peu près qui ont été tués ou blessés sous mes ordres dans les différents grades et les actions les plus meurtrières, je n'ai pas à me reprocher d'en avoir fait tuer un seul pour mon propre compte."[16] Sobre et mesuré en toutes choses, il a selon ses propres termes "pour principe, en guerre comme en morale, qu'il ne faut pas tenter le diable..."[17]

---

12. Charlus, *Journal...*, folio 184 verso.

13. Armand-Louis de Gontaut, duc de Lauzun, *Mémoires du duc de Lauzun, général Biron*, édition établie par Jean-Jacques Fiechter (Paris: Orban, 1986), 230.

14. Fersen, *Lettres*, 113.

15. Claude Blanchard, *Guerre d'Amérique, 1780-1783, Journal de campagne de Claude Blanchard, commissaire des guerres principal au corps auxiliaire français sous le commandement du lieutenant général comte de Rochambeau* (Paris: Dumaine, 1881).

16. Lettre de Rochambeau à La Fayette du 27 août 1781. *Rochambeau's Papers* (Washington, D.C.: Library of Congress, Manuscript Division).

17. Lettre de Rochambeau au gouverneur Trumbull, de Newport, juillet 1780. *Rochambeau's papers*.

Pourtant, d'après Fersen, "c'est un homme très borné", un bon second, un habile général de division, qui a besoin d'être dirigé par un "véritable génie militaire, qui embrasse toutes les parties de la guerre", tel Washington.[18] Tout le secret de la victoire de Yorktown réside là, dans le choix pour chef de la petite armée française d'un homme capable de s'entendre avec le général en chef américain.

Les instructions du prince de Montbarrey étaient précises: "vous serez sous les ordres de monsieur le général Washington, généralissime des troupes du Congrès..., les projets et plans de campagne ou d'expédition particulière seront ordonnés par lui..."[19]

Rochambeau par son âge, son sérieux et son expérience en impose à Washington. Ce dernier rencontre enfin un vrai professionnel de la guerre, qui accepte avec discipline et loyauté sa subordination hiérarchique et qui lui apporte toutes ses connaissances pratiques des grandes campagnes militaires et des sièges des villes, sans chercher à faire valoir sa supériorité manifeste dans ces domaines. Ces deux chefs se ressemblent même sur plus d'un point, grands, forts, excellents cavaliers et surtout partisans de la même discrétion, on devrait dire méfiance, à l'égard de leurs plus proches collaborateurs. Non seulement Rochambeau ne dévoile pas ses véritables intentions à ses aides-de-camp, mais il s'amuse à les tromper, à l'occasion. En écho, cette phrase caractéristique de Washington: "J'ai toujours cru que lorsqu'on ne fait point des siens les premiers dupes d'un subterfuge, celui-ci ne réussit point contre l'ennemi."[20] Les deux généraux prendront un malin plaisir à monter ensemble un chef-d'oeuvre d'intoxication dans le courant de 1781 à l'intention des Anglais.

Il faut se rappeler que les deux précédentes tentatives d'actions combinées entre les forces maritimes françaises et les forces terrestres américaines avaient échoué lamentablement. En août 1778, les Américains du général Sullivan et les navires du vice-amiral d'Estaing n'étaient pas parvenus à déloger les Anglais de Newport. L'année suivante, le siège de Savannah, où la flotte française soutenait le général américain Lincoln, s'était soldé par un sanglant échec, laissant des doutes justifiés sur l'efficacité d'une coopération franco-américaine. Il fallait l'intervention directe d'une armée de terre française pour gagner la guerre d'indépendance. L'arrivée des troupes de Rochambeau en Rhode Island le 12 juillet 1780 concrétisait cet espoir pour Washington, même s'il avait attendu trois fois plus d'hommes et surtout une flotte plus importante. La Fayette était venu lui annoncer la bonne nouvelle par un précédent bateau le 10 mai, mais l'interminable traversée du corps expéditionnaire, embarqué déjà depuis le 12 avril, leur avait fait craindre le

18. Fersen, *Lettres*, 114.
19. Archives historiques de la Guerre: Instructions de Montbarrey à Rochambeau, ref. 3733.
20. Voir Jean Jules Jusserand, *En Amérique jadis et maintenant* (Paris: Hachette, 1918).

pire. Cette bonne nouvelle venait à point pour contrebalancer la capitulation du général américain Lincoln à Charlestown le 12 mai, laissant les Anglais maîtres du Sud du pays, où ils disposaient de 17 000 hommes. Avec sa garnison de 17 000 soldats à New York et les 4 000 en Nouvelle-Ecosse, le général Clinton disposait au total de 38 000 hommes et d'une supériorité navale indéniable pour affronter les 5 000 Français débarqués à Newport, dont plus de 1 000 malades ou handicapés. Les troupes américaines, dont le nombre de citoyens-soldats évoluait sans cesse au gré des saisons et des dangers, passant de 4 000 à 30 000, selon les estimations les plus optimistes, devaient théoriquement faire l'appoint pour rétablir l'équilibre.

Les différents journaux des officiers embarqués avec Rochambeau décrivent en détail la pénible traversée de 72 jours, avec ses privations, ses dangers et ses aventures tragi-comiques. Aux tempêtes succèdent des calmes plats, où les navires se regroupent autour du "Provence", pour écouter la musique du duc de Lauzun leur donner une aubade, et oublier un instant leur misère, l'eau rationnée, rouge de rouille, les biscuits avariés, l'ennui qui les dévore encore plus que les poux, les punaises et les puces, les scorbut et la dysenterie qui les déciment. Ils sont même privés d'un vrai combat naval, avec poursuite, car après quelques échanges de boulets, le chevalier de Ternay renonce à chasser les vaisseaux de guerre anglais qu'ils croisent au large des Bermudes. Il a reçu l'ordre formel de ne pas dévier de sa route d'Amérique et il entend devancer la flotte de l'amiral Graves qui a quitté Plymouth à sa poursuite. Son manque d'aggressivité est largement critiqué par ses propres subalternes comme par les officiers de terre embarqués.

Mais la prudence de Ternay rejoint celle de Rochambeau. Ce dernier, à peine débarqué, s'empresse de renforcer les défenses quasi-inexistantes de Newport. Il est très bien secondé par le duc de Lauzun, auquel il a confié le commandement de la côte "et de tout ce qui était à portée des lieux où l'on pouvait débarquer", afin de rendre la superbe rade inexpugnable...[21]

Il est temps, car le 21 juillet la flotte de l'amiral Graves croise déjà devant Newport, bloquant les issues. Heureusement, comme le constate Lauzun, "pendant tout le cours de cette guerre les Anglais semblent frappés d'aveuglement: ils font toujours ce qu'il ne faut pas faire et se refusent toujours aux avantages les plus clairs et les plus certains".[22] Et il ajoute que si les forces anglaises avaient attaqué immédiatement la Rhode Island sans permettre aux Français de s'y fortifier, "l'escadre et l'armée du roi étaient perdues".[23]

La situation est critique, d'autant plus que la ville n'est plus sûre, les partisans de l'Angleterre, les "Tories", y paraissent encore nombreux. L'accueil

---

21. Lauzun, *Mémoires*, 234.
22. Lauzun, *Mémoires*, 242.
23. Lauzun, *Mémoires*, 234.

glacial des autorités de Newport, le manque d'enthousiasme de la population ont surpris tous les officiers français. Bien vite la discipline de la troupe, consignée hors de la ville et où le moindre maraudage est puni de pendaison, rassure les paysans habitués aux pillages de la soldatesque, tant anglaise qu'américaine, et le charme des nobles officiers logeant chez l'habitant opère des miracles dans la petite société locale.

Washington, cantonné à Morristown, avait prévu une attaque combinée contre New York durant l'été 1780 avec les forces expéditionnaires françaises. L'arrivée tardive de moins de 4 000 hommes en état de se battre et qui réclament au contraire son aide pour défendre leur tête de pont de Newport, oblige le général à changer sa stratégie. Il n'enverra pas de renfort mais fera une descente en direction de New York sur l'Hudson, pour faire croire à Sir Clinton que le plan initial est maintenu. La ruse de Washington va pleinement réussir. Les 6 000 Anglo-Hessois, déjà embarqués sur les transports de l'amiral Arbuthnot le 27 juillet, sont renvoyés quatre jours plus tard à leur cantonnement new-yorkais, pour ne pas dégarnir la ville, en cas d'attaque surprise. L'amiral Graves, qui attendait ces renforts promis pour investir la Rhode Island, renonce et lève le siège. La petite ville de pêcheurs de Providence, dans la baie de Newport, a bien mérité son nom ce jour-là.

Au point de vue militaire la campagne d'été 1780 n'aura pas lieu, d'autant plus que lord Cornwallis, qui commande les troupes anglaises du Sud, vient d'infliger une sérieuse défaite au général américain Gates le 16 août à Camden. Il faut au plus vite définir une nouvelle stratégie et Rochambeau insiste pour rencontrer sans délai Washington, la menace sur Newport étant maintenant écartée. Le rendez-vous est fixé pour le 20 septembre à Hartford, dans le Connecticut, à mi-distance des deux armées, pour permettre à chacun des deux généraux de regagner rapidement leurs camps, en cas de besoin. Fersen accompagne Rochambeau et lui sert d'interprète. La Fayette joue le même rôle auprès de Washington.

Cette première entrevue renforce l'appréciation mutuelle des deux généraux. Malgré l'obstacle de la langue, ils se comprennent à demi-mot, partagent la même prudence, le même sang-froid, et la même stratégie. Avec les forces dont les alliés disposent, des opérations offensives sont impossibles cette année. En priorité, il faut obtenir de la France encore des vaisseaux, des hommes et de l'argent. Rochambeau enverra son fils plaider la cause des Américains à Paris. Dans l'intervalle, les deux armées vont hiverner au mieux dans leurs bases respectives.

Tandis que la petite délégation française regagne sans encombre Newport le 23 septembre, Washington et La Fayette vivent des heures dramatiques. Le général Benedict Arnold, un des vainqueurs de Saratoga, gouverneur de la place forte de West Point, verrou essentiel du blocus des Anglais dans New York, a accepté les offres de lord Clinton. Non seulement il livrera West Point aux Britanniques, mais il organisera l'enlèvement du général Washington et de son état-major. Après les deux graves défaites américaines de 1780, si l'armée des Insurgents était décapitée, une paix négociée s'imposerait d'elle-même, et, commente Fersen, "nous aurions eu la honte de n'être arrivés ici que pour être spectateurs de la ruine entière de nos alliés."[24]

Comme souvent dans les plus habiles combinaisons, un grain de sable, en l'occurence l'arrestation par hasard du major André, l'officier anglo-suisse qui portait sur lui les instructions de Clinton et les plans détaillés d'Arnold, déjoue le piège. Arnold réussira à s'enfuir, le major André sera pendu comme espion: Washington appliquera fermement le jugement de la cour martiale, pour faire un exemple. Selon les propres termes de La Fayette "sa naissance très distinguée servira d'épouvantail aux espions de mauvaise compagnie..."[25] Les officiers français, habitués aux ruses de guerre, sont consternés. Fersen estime que "c'est dommage de pendre un jeune homme de vingt-quatre ans qui a beaucoup de talents".[26] Closen note que "vivant, le major André avait l'estime et l'attachement de toute l'armée, et sa mort l'a fait regretter de tout l'univers impartial".[27] Le mot de la fin revient à La Fayette: le malheureux André "s'est conduit d'une manière si franche, si noble, si délicate, que je n'ai pu m'empêcher de le regretter infiniment".[28]

L'hiver 1780-1781 sera terrible pour les Américains, "arrivés au dernier terme de leur misère", selon Washington. Sans un secours puissant "maintenant ou jamais" de la France, ils sont perdus.[29] Vergennes, qui estime déjà bien lourds les 150 millions de livres de dépenses extraordinaires de la campagne précédente, envoie néanmoins une rallonge immédiate de six millions en espèces et promet une aide maritime pour l'automne.

En attendant, il faut faire patienter l'armée continentale, qui menace de se disloquer totalement, à l'exemple du contingent de Pennsylvanie, révolté depuis le 1er janvier 1871. Comme le note Closen, seule l'intervention personnelle de Washington et son appel à leur patriotisme a permis d'apaiser les mutins. "Le manque absolu de paiements, la mauvaise nourriture, et point d'habillement, joints à ce que le Congrès ne leur permet pas de quitter les drapeaux, quand même leur capitulation serait finie d'une ou deux années, sont les raisons qui les ont poussés à cette extrémité. En Europe, on le serait à moins".[30]

---

24. Fersen, *Lettres*, 84.

25. La Fayette, *Lettre au chevalier de La Luzerne, West-Point, 25 septembre 1780*, publiée dans la *Revue de la Révolution* (1885), t.5.

26. Fersen, *Lettres*, 85.

27. Closen, *Journal*, 3 octobre 1780, 93.

28. Marie-Joseph-Paul-Yves-Roch-Gilbert Du Motier La Fayette, marquis de, *Mémoires, correspondance et manuscrits du général de La Fayette publiés par sa famille*, 6 vols. (Paris: H. Fournier, 1837-38), 1: 376.

29. Washington, *Instructions au colonel Laurens*, 9 avril 1781.

30. Closen, *Journal*, 12 janvier 1781, 118.

Washington obtient du Congrès quelques fonds pour verser un premier accompte aux troupes révoltées et ne les punit pas, car elles ont repoussé les offres de deux émissaires du général Clinton, envoyés pour les rallier à la cause anglaise. Il se contente de faire pendre ceux-ci, mais quand le contingent du New Jersey essaye à son tour de se mutiner, le 20 janvier, Washington le soumet par la force et fait fusiller les meneurs, pour éviter la contagion. Cela n'empêchera pas ces mêmes troupes, en septembre 1781, à la veille du siège de Yorktown, de refuser de marcher si on ne leur payait pas leurs arriérés de solde. Selon Closen, lorsque le général Washington en informa Rochambeau, ce dernier partagea chrétiennement avec lui ses maigres fonds et lui remit 50 000 livres en argent qui furent distribuées immédiatement aux malheureux soldats pour leur remonter le moral et les décider à s'embarquer.[31]

Vues initiales des officiers

Les opinions des officiers français sur les milices américaines sont souvent très critiques. "Il n'y existe aucune espèce de discipline, chacun veut bien servir comme officier mais ne veut pas être soldat, l'ivrognerie les met souvent hors d'état de faire leurs devoirs, les officiers sont généralement d'une ignorance et d'une extrême vanité, les troupes presque nues, mal payées, composées de vieillards, de nègres et d'enfants," etc.[32]

Verger nuance ce sombre tableau:

> Les milices donnent quelques exemples de bravoure, mais c'est lorsqu'elles ont la supériorité du nombre, ou la possession de quelque défilé où l'ennemi doit passer, et où ils puissent tirer à couvert... On a vu des milices faire des actions que les troupes de vétérans se glorifieraient d'avoir faites. Mais c'est lorsque l'éloquence persuasive de leurs chefs les met dans une ardeur enthousiaste, de laquelle il faut tout de suite profiter. [...] Les troupes continentales américaines sont très aguerries et assez bien disciplinées, très rompues aux fatigués que les soldats soutiennent sans beaucoup se plaindre, pourvu que leurs officiers leur donnent l'exemple...[33]

Cette vision assez méprisante se modifiera avec le temps. Si les milices continuent à être médiocres, les troupes continentales, mieux équipées, mieux

---

31. Closen, *Journal*, 7 septembre 1781, 311.

32. Rousseau de Fayolle et Preudhomme de Borre, cités par Bodinier, *Les officiers...*, 327-28.

33. Jean-Baptiste-Antoine de Verger, *Journal des faits les plus importants arrivés aux troupes françaises aux ordres de Monsieur le comte de Rochambeau*, manuscript dans la Anne S.K. Brown Military Collection (Providence, R.I.: Brown University), 207. Nous avons utilisé la copie d'époque figurant au Musée cantonal de Porrentruy, en Suisse.

habillées et mieux payées grâce aux secours français et au butin de Yorktown, surprendront le comte de Ségur, qui trouve en débarquant en juin 1782, "une armée disciplinée, où tout offrait l'image de l'ordre, de la raison, de l'instruction et de l'expérience".[34]

Les troupes américaines ne répondent pas encore à cette image en juillet 1781, quand les soldats de Rochambeau les rejoignent à Philipsburg, sur la rive gauche de l'Hudson, après un mois de marche sous un soleil de plomb.

A peine réunis, Washington et Rochambeau ont monté une superbe entreprise d'intoxication à l'intention du général Clinton, grâce à des lettres "confidentielles", qu'ils feront astucieusement intercepter, et à la construction de fours à pain à Chatham, aux portes de New York, indices d'un long siège prévu. La manoeuvre réussira pleinement. Le commandant en chef anglais, persuadé que l'armée franco-américaine allait attaquer l'île de Manhattan, y conserve sa flotte de soutien. A Yorktown, en Virginie, le général Cornwallis attendra en vain les navires promis pour rallier New York avec ses 7 000 hommes.

Dans l'intervalle, le piège s'est refermé sur lui. En août, la flotte de Barras a quitté Newport avec l'artillerie de siège et celle de l'amiral de Grasse, les Antilles, pour bloquer la baie de Chesapeake. Pendant ce temps, les troupes françaises ont repris leur marche vers le Sud. Le 4 septembre, après une courte halte, selon Gallatin, pour "faire mettre leurs guêtres blanches et poudrer les cheveux des soldats",[35] elles défilent en grand ordre à Philadelphie, devant le Congrès réuni là. Tous les officiers soulignent l'accueil enthousiaste de la population, qui a pavoisé la ville aux couleurs de la France et des Etats-Unis. Ils sont fiers de l'admiration des charmantes Philadelphiennes, ravies de voir "des troupes aussi belles et d'entendre une aussi bonne musique",[36] comme le note Closen, qui caracole avec l'état-major de Rochambeau et les hussards de Lauzun à la tête des troupes. Il faut dire qu'elles ont grande allure dans leurs splendides uniformes, en particulier les grenadiers du régiment des Soissonnais, aux bonnets ornés de plumes blanches et roses.

Ce défilé prélude à celui de la victoire de Yorktown, le 19 octobre, après un siège de 20 jours rondement mené, qui a entraîné la capitulation de Cornwallis, et de ses 7 000 hommes, affamés, décimés et sans munitions. Les pertes françaises ont été très réduites: une soixantaine de tués et 200 blessés.

La scène grandiose de la reddition a été maintes fois décrite dans les Journaux, montrant la garnison anglaise en grand uniforme défilant avec une tristesse mêlée de morgue entre les deux lignes formées par leur vainqueurs au garde-à-vous. Closen est le seul à y ajouter une petite note humoristique: le comte de Barras, qui remplace l'amiral de Grasse, cloué par la goutte sur

34. Ségur, *Souvenirs*, 118.
35. Gallatin, *Journal*, 54.
36. Closen, *Journal*, 3 septembre 1781, 299-300.

"la Ville de Paris", "est un excellent marin mais rien moins qu'un bon écuyer... Pendant cette cérémonie, son cheval s'étendant pour pisser, il s'écria: Seigneur Dieu, mon cheval coule bas."[37]

Les craintes du brave navigateur furent aussi mal fondées que celles des stratèges qui s'attendaient à voir l'Angleterre reprendre vigoureusement la guerre, après cette défaite humiliante. Pour une fois, l'optimisme congénital de La Fayette est justifié. Comme il l'écrit le lendemain de la victoire au ministre Maurepas: "La pièce est jouée, monsieur le Comte, et le cinquième acte vient de finir..."[38]

Images plus profondes de la société américaine

Rochambeau et son armée resteront encore plus d'une année en Amérique, donnant ainsi à ses officiers l'occasion de mieux connaître ce vaste pays et ses habitants. Pour la troupe les règles de non-fraternisation restent aussi strictes qu'auparavant. Quand les deux armées s'étaient rejointes à Philipsburg, les états-majors avaient veillé à ce que les deux camps soient séparés par une vallée et une rivière, "seules les patrouilles communiquant les unes avec les autres", selon Closen.[39] Les officiers des deux états-majors, qui ont de fréquents contacts mutuels et qui nouent de bonnes relations, forment l'exception. Clermont-Crèvecoeur relève que "jamais on ne voyait un officier français avec un Américain. On était en assez bonne intelligence mais on ne vivait point ensemble. C'est, je crois, ce qui a pu nous arriver de plus heureux. Leur caractère étant si différent du nôtre, les querelles s'en seraient bien vite mêlées."[40]

L'origine sociale des officiers français joue certainement son rôle. A peine cinq pour cent d'entre eux ne sont pas nobles et en dehors des questions de service, ils ont peu de points communs avec leurs homologues américains qui étaient souvent des cordonniers, des bouchers et surtout des aubergistes. Sans se l'avouer, ils les snobent et se sentent effectivement beaucoup plus proches des officiers anglais, qui partagent leurs manières et leur éducation, que de leurs alliés américains. Après la capitulation de Yorktown, Verger et Closen décrivent en détail "les marques prévenantes de l'armée française vis-à-vis des officiers anglais et hessois...qui donnèrent beaucoup de jalousie aux officiers

---

37. Closen, *Journal*, 19 septembre 1781, 386.

38. La Fayette, *Mémoires*, 1: 470, 20 octobre 1781.

39. Closen, *Journal*, 7 juillet 1781, 233.

40. Jean-François-Louis Crèvecoeur, comte de Clermont, *Journal de la guerre d'Amérique pendant les années 1780-1783* (Providence: Rhode Island Historical Society), 64. Traduction anglaise dans Howard C. Rice, Jr. et Anne S. K. Brown, *The American Campaigns of Rochambeau's Army* (Princeton & Providence: Princeton Univ. Press & Brown Univ. Press, 1972).

américains".[41] Rochambeau et Lauzun montrent l'exemple, invitant à plusieurs reprises les officiers supérieurs anglais et allemands à dîner dans leur camp. Rochambeau prête même 150 000 livres à Lord Cornwallis sur sa cassette militaire pour lui permettre de régler certaines dépenses sur place. A peine arrivé à New York, le général anglais remboursa la somme en y joignant 100 bonnes bouteilles et du fromage de Chester. Cornwallis, dans son rapport au général Clinton du 20 octobre 1781, cité intégralement par Verger, rend un vibrant hommage aux officiers français dont la générosité et la sensibilité à l'égard de leurs adversaires malheureux "sont réellement au-dessus de tout ce qu'on peut exprimer".[42] Cette façon chevaleresque de traiter les ennemis indigne certains Américains, qui n'oublient pas les atrocités commises par les Anglais et les Tories combattant pour eux. Closen ou Verger trouvent tout naturel de voir le duc de Lauzun trinquer avec le colonel Tarleton et échanger des souvenirs de guerre. Pourtant Verger a été personnellement témoin des horreurs commises par les dragons de Tarleton à Jamestown, en Virginie. Il a vu, attaché à une porte, le cadavre mutilé d'une jeune femme enceinte, le ventre ouvert d'un coup de sabre, le bébé massacré et l'inscription "damné rebelle, tu n'enfanteras plus".[43] Les milices américaines n'étaient pas en reste et cette façon cruelle de faire une guerre de partisans ou de traiter les prisonniers a profondément choqué les officiers français qui n'y étaient pas habitués.

Ce même malaise se ressent au niveau des relations entre le corps expéditionnaire et leurs fournisseurs américains, à qui ils reprochent de leur avoir "tout vendu au poids de l'or" comme l'écrit le baron de Montesquieu, de les voler, de les ruiner.[44] L'armée paye pour tout: nourriture, fourrage, chevaux, même les terrains sur lesquels ils établissent leurs camps. Le pillage est sévèrement puni, les dégâts éventuels remboursés au plus juste, Rochambeau y veille, mais il se plaint aussi de ses chers alliés, et, en particulier de "l'avidité et de la cupidité démesurés de commerçants", même "les plus patriotiques" qui ne visent qu'à s'enrichir rapidement.[45] Les aubergistes les rançonnent. Sur ce point aussi les avis convergent et quand Closen ou Du Bourg bénéficient d'une hospitalité désintéressée en cours de route, ils le notent soigneusement. Par contre ces mêmes officiers ne tarissent pas d'éloges sur les familles de la bonne bourgeoisie qui les reçoivent à Newport, à Boston, à Philadelphie, ou durant leurs quartiers d'hiver à Williamsburg. Ils y ont trouvé un accueil généreux, des manières raffinées, des hommes intéressants et cultivés, des familles heureuses et surtout des

41. Closen, *Journal*, 321; Verger, *Journal*, 93.
42. Verger, *Journal*, 93-104, lettre de Cornwallis.
43. Verger, *Journal*, 61-62.
44. Lettre de Montesquieu, Newport, 16 octobre 1780, Voir Bodinier, *Les officiers...*, 326.
45. Rochambeau, *Rochambeau's Papers* (Newport, 1780).

jeunes femmes, généralement jolies, modestes et vives, musiciennes et adorant danser.

La liberté et la confiance laissées aux jeunes filles avant le mariage, et en particulier la pratique du "bondelage" (bundling), les ont tous frappés. Ils ont consacré de longs développements à cette coutume essentiellement campagnarde, qui consistait à autoriser des amoureux, même non-fiancés, à passer ensemble des heures et parfois des nuits seuls dans une chambre, couchés tout habillés, mais sans chaussures, sur un lit à causer, à s'embrasser sur la bouche et à "se prodiguer de tendres caresses...hormis celles que le mariage a seul le droit de permettre", comme l'écrit joliment Clermont-Crèvecoeur. Tout cela nécessite une grande maîtrise de soi, de part et d'autre et une certaine froideur de tempérament, si l'on ne veut pas être roué de coups par la maisonnée ameutée par les cris de la pucelle effarouchée. Le Français conclut: "Le bondelage n'est fait que pour les Américains."[46]

Si les jeunes filles mènent souvent une vie assez libre avant le mariage, dès qu'elles sont mariées, elles deviennent des épouses modèles. En France, c'est alors l'inverse. Il est vrai que certaines femmes américaines ont eu des aventures extra-conjugales avec les officiers de Rochambeau, mais ces derniers gardent une discrétion de bon aloi sur ce sujet délicat. "Honni soit qui mal y pense", ajoute Closen.[47]

Malgré la réputation de séduction des Français, deux faits sont à noter. Aucun des officiers n'a épousé une Américaine, et, durant leur long séjour aux Etats-Unis, aucun n'a fait l'objet d'une plainte ou poursuite pour inconduite ou abandon de petits bâtards...

Quant à la prostitution, elle existe aussi en Amérique, surtout dans les villes. Clermont-Crèvecoeur s'interroge sur la cause "du grand nombre de prostituées dans un pays si neuf, où le vice ne devrait pas être profondément enraciné".[48] Il en voit la raison dans cette liberté accordée aux jeunes filles, qui peuvent parfois tomber victimes de leur tempérament ou d'individus sans scrupules qui les séduisent et ne les épousent pas ensuite.

La bonne tenue des officiers, logés chez l'habitant, est plus méritoire que celle des soldats, cantonnés à l'écart des villes et soumis à une discipline et à une ségrégation sévère. Selon l'abbé Robin, les seigneurs de la cour "ont les premiers donné l'exemple de la simplicité et de la vie frugale; ils se sont montrés affables, populaires, comme s'ils n'avaient jamais vécu qu'avec des hommes égaux".[49] Nul doute que les officiers, stimulés par les ordres stricts de Rochambeau, aient mis un point d'honneur, une coquetterie même, à

46. Crèvecoeur, *Journal*, 38, 39.
47. Closen, *Journal*, 404.
48. Crèvecoeur, *Journal*, 38.
49. Abbé Robin, *Nouveau Voyage dans l'Amérique Septentrionale, en l'année 1781 et Campagne de l'Armée de M. le comte de Rochambeau* (Philadelphie et Paris: Moutard, 1782).

s'adapter à la société américaine. La quasi-totalité de ces militaires de carrière, habitués à parler à leurs soldats, à traiter courtoisement leurs intendants et leurs fermiers, à entretenir des relations souvent cordiales avec leurs domestiques, font naturellement preuve de savoir-vivre et de politesse, à défaut de réelle sympathie, envers leurs interlocuteurs américains. Ceux-ci prennent généralement pour du bon argent la condescendance un peu protectrice de leurs alliés, et les plus susceptibles imputent aux difficultés de traduction les éventuelles traces d'arrogance qui les heurtent. A l'exception de La Fayette, du comte de Ségur et de quelques autres, qui communient dans un même amour passionné pour l'Amérique et les Américains, la grande majorité des officiers du corps expéditionnaire ne se font guère d'illusions sur leurs alliés. A la fin du séjour, Fersen, pourtant assez pondéré dans ses jugements, avoue à son père qu'il regrette vivement le départ de Rochambeau, "le seul homme capable de nous commander ici et de maintenir cette parfaite harmonie qui a régné entre deux nations si différentes par leurs moeurs et leur langage, et qui, au fond, ne s'aiment pas". Et il conclut: "Nos alliés ne se sont pas toujours bien conduits vis-à-vis de nous, et le temps que nous avons passé avec eux nous a appris à ne pas les aimer ni à les estimer".[50] Le régime démocratique égalitaire, tant admiré dans les salons parisiens, dont les officiers français ont pu voir le fonctionnement et les limites, ne convient, selon la plupart d'entre eux, qu'à un pays neuf comme l'Amérique. Ils reconnaissent, avec Clermont-Crèvecoeur, que là "un serrurier, un savetier, un marchand peut devenir membre du Congrès... Il entrera dans le militaire comme capitaine, comme colonel et même comme général, s'il a les connaissances requises à l'état qu'il embrasse". Mais cette égalité juridique a ses limites dans l'inégalité des richesses. "Quoique les Américains se regardent comme égaux entre eux, ils ont toujours une certaine déférence pour ceux qui sont riches; ces derniers ne vivent qu'entre eux".[51]

Le marquis de Chastellux, observateur bienveillant et lucide de l'Amérique, ajoute: "La richesse établit toujours des différences marquées et d'autant plus grandes qu'il n'en existe pas d'autres. Or, partout où cette inégalité existera, la véritable force sera toujours du côté de la propriété".[52]

Les officiers de Rochambeau savaient qu'ils débarquaient au pays de la tolérance religieuse, mais ils ont été surpris à Newport de trouver tant d'églises, de temples et même une synagogue. L'abbé Robin observe avec une pointe d'envie que dans ces lieux de culte "règne un silence, un ordre, un respect qu'on ne trouve plus depuis longtemps dans la plupart de nos églises catholiques".[53] Les esprits moins pieux regrettent que le dimanche soit observé

---

50. Fersen, *Lettres*, 136, Boston, 30 novembre 1782.
51. Crèvecoeur, *Journal*, 48.
52. Lettre de Chastellux à Madison, 12 janvier 1783; Bodinier, *Les officiers...*, 343-44.
53. Robin, *Nouveau Voyage*, 11.

avec une telle sévérité. Tout est fermé le jour du Seigneur et les cérémonies religieuses sont si lugubres qu'on se croirait à un enterrement. D'autres déplorent enfin le fanatisme engendré par la multiplication des sectes. Selon Montesquieu, "les sectes sont elles-mêmes intolérantes et jalouses l'une de l'autre".[54]

A Newport, les officiers ont aussi rencontré leurs premiers Indiens, à la fin août 1780. Le comte de Charlus, Verger, Closen et bien d'autres ont dessiné et décrit "ces sauvages qui se peignent tout en rouge", aux corps huilés et malodorants, venus apporter à Rochambeau l'alliance de leurs diverses tribus iroquoises.[55] Tous les récits s'accordent à les trouver un peu trop civilisés pour de vrais sauvages, sauf dans le feu de leurs danses guerrières. De la curiosité, certes, mais pas de sympathie. Seul Rochambeau, en bon diplomate, prend au sérieux ces alliés dévoués de la France malheureuse au Canada. Il organise un grand défilé et un festin en leur honneur, les comble de petits cadeaux, et leur fournit même un aumônier, selon leur demande, car ces Indiens sont restés bons catholiques.

Aux Etats-Unis, les officiers ont aussi été confrontés au phénomène de l'esclavage, sans en paraître particulièrement choqués. Ils relèvent la grande différence existant à ce sujet entre le Nord et le Sud, le fait que les milices américaines comptent des compagnies entières de nègres, et qu'en Amérique les esclaves sont mieux traités que dans les îles sucrières, sauf peut-être en Virginie, où, selon Closen, "un chien courant mène très souvent une vie plus heureuse et est beaucoup mieux nourri que les pauvres nègres ou mulâtres". Mais il ajoute qu'ils sont "voleurs comme des pies, ou fidèles comme de l'or".[56] Son brave Peter, un Noir qu'il a acheté pour son service, né de parents libres du Connecticut, tombe dans cette catégorie honnête. Closen en profite pour constater que les esclaves libérés sont souvent plus misérables et malheureux que ceux restés sous de bons maîtres. Si certains Français condamnent l'esclavage pour des raisons humanitaires, la majorité des officiers s'en accomodent fort bien. Déjà à Newport, Rochambeau et les cadres de son armée achètent des Noirs comme domestiques. Mais la grande razzia prendra place après la victoire de Yorktown. Comme le note sans complexe Clermont-Crèvecoeur: "les nègres non réclamés par des maîtres en trouvèrent de nouveaux parmi les Français, et nous avons fait une véritable moisson de

54. Charles-Louis de Secondat, Montesquieu, baron de, Lettres publiées par Octave Beuve, "Un Petit-Fils de Montesquieu, soldat de l'Indépendance Américaine", dans *Revue Historique de la Révolution Française et de l'Empire*, 5 (janv.-juin 1914): 504-24.

55. Charlus, *Journal*, folio 321; Verger, *Journal*, 240-41; Closen, *Journal*, 84-85; Montesquieu, *Lettres*, 242.

56. Closen, *Journal*, 2: 56-57.

domestiques. Ceux d'entre nous qui n'avaient pas de serviteur furent bien heureux d'en trouver un, bon marché..."[57]

Les quelques dizaines d'officiers dont nous avons étudié les journaux et les lettres consacrent tous de longs développements à décrire les magnifiques paysages, les bourgades et les villes de ce grand pays neuf, sa flore et sa faune pittoresque. Mais dans le cadre de cette présentation il nous est impossible d'évoquer cet aspect touristique et scientifique de leurs récits, qui mériterait à lui seul une étude approfondie.

La vision qui se dégage de ce survol de l'aventure américaine des officiers de l'armée de Rochambeau peut paraître paradoxale, voire caricaturale. Les témoignages des partisans enthousiastes des Etats-Unis, amplifiés dès leur retour en France par les nombreux admirateurs restés sur place, ont occulté les critiques et les réserves de ceux qui n'étaient pas revenus fascinés par l'expérience américaine. Pour beaucoup d'entre eux la Révolution est venue ensuite bouleverser bien des perspectives, et colorier leurs souvenirs au gré de leur propre évolution. Ce n'est pas ternir la gloire des Français qui ont puisé en Amérique l'amour de la liberté que de constater objectivement que pour la grande majorité d'entre eux l'aventure américaine a représenté une longue promenade militaire, instructive et utile pour leur carrière, glorieuse et sans grand risque, en un mot, la dernière "guerre en dentelle" du XVIIIe siècle. Ni pour les officiers, ni pour la troupe, elle n'a été une vraie cure de démocratie. Chacun a réagi à sa manière, les futurs "Américains" de 1789 trouvant ample matière à leur enthousiasme égalitaire et libéral, les "Aristocrates", à leurs préjugés nationaux ou de caste.

Au plan politique, la France a certes réussi une action de "relations publiques" remarquable. L'armée brave et disciplinée de Rochambeau a détruit, en trois ans de présence en Amérique, trois siècles de préjugés, selon le bel hommage que lui a rendu Washington. Pourtant, avec le recul historique, le prix peut en paraître élevé. Le poids immense des frais de guerre français, évalués à un milliard et demi de dollars, qui furent financés en bonne partie par des emprunts, sera un des éléments déterminants de la convocation des Etats généraux en 1789. Payer la publicité avec de l'argent emprunté est toujours dangereux.

Finalement, au plan militaire, si les Etats-Unis ont gagné leur indépendance à Yorktown, la France, elle, a perdu tout espoir de suprématie navale à la bataille de Saintes en 1782. Dans cette perspective globale, l'expédition d'Amérique reste un brillant échec, mais de cela, ni les officiers de l'armée de Rochambeau ni personne en France ne se rendit compte alors...

57. Crèvecoeur, *Journal*, 64.

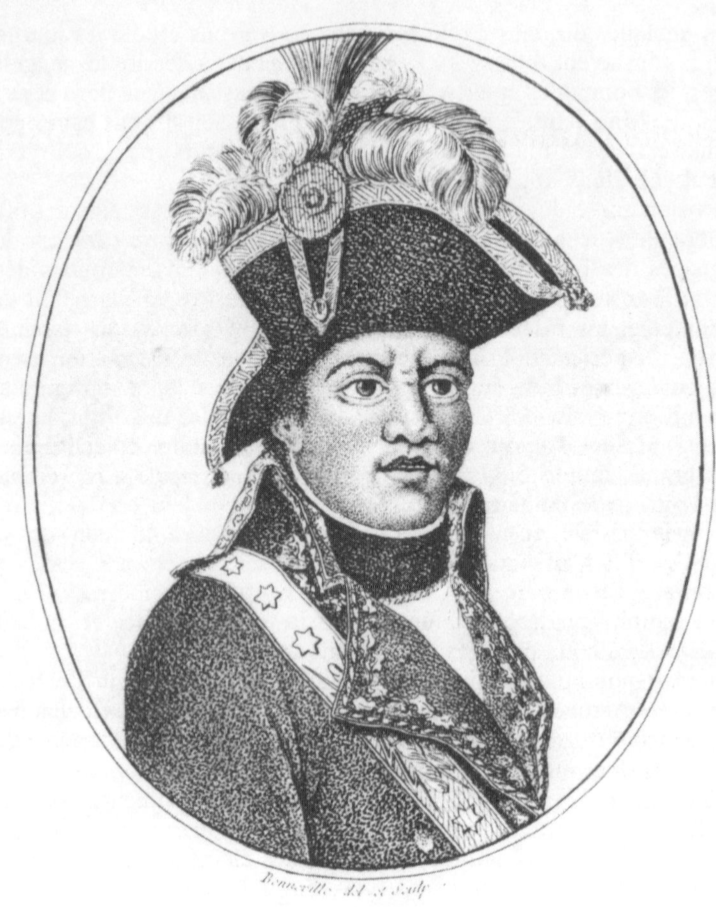

TOUSSAINT LOUVERTURE

Général en Chef à St. Domingue

François Bonneville, *Toussaint Louverture* (collection of Dr. Fritz Daguillard). This portrait is one of a series of two hundred portraits of famous figures of the French Revolution published by the artist from 1793 to 1802.

Images de l'Amérique dans la conscience lyonnaise de 1770 à 1800

Louis Trenard

La région lyonnaise, en raison de ses activités économiques et de son rayonnement culturel, s'est montrée attentive, en tout temps, au monde entier. Au Siècle des Lumières, ses négociants sont en relation avec les autres continents; elle abrite des voyageurs passionnés d'aventure, des savants curieux d'ethnologie et d'histoire. Dans la conscience des Lyonnais, quelle que soit leur situation sociale, les événements survenus en Amérique septentrionale en 1776 occupèrent une grande place, inculquèrent des valeurs nouvelles, suggérèrent des comportements.

La participation à la croisade libératrice

Le très jeune marquis de La Fayette traverse l'Océan et se joint aux Insurgents, Beaumarchais les aide matériellement, Franklin obtient à Paris en 1778, un secours financier et l'intervention d'un corps expéditionnaire; ces événements réactivent le mythe américain né dans les milieux éclairés, entretenu par des récits de voyageurs.[1] La narration d'une longue traversée périlleuse, la description de Charlestown, de Philadelphie, de la Caroline ou de la Virginie, l'évocation des moeurs, des sectes, des concepts de liberté ou de patriotisme... suscitent dans le royaume troublé par l'agitation parlementaire, par les projets de réforme, par les assemblées provinciales, un intérêt considérable.[2]

La presse périodique française augmente en nombre; même si l'on estime qu'elle reflète les préjugés et les idées régnantes, qu'elle ne modifie pas

1. Gérard Defamie, *Le mythe américain à la veille de la Révolution française* (Université Charles de Gaulle: Thèse de 3ème cycle, 1973). Résumé, *Information Historique* (mars-avril 1974), 59-64.

2. Eugène Griselle, "Un voyage en Amérique au temps de la guerre d'indépendance", *Revue du XVIIIe siècle*, No. 1 (jan.-juin 1918): 52-73.

profondément les sentiments, elle contribue à assurer une inclination réciproque entre Américains et Français et à fortifier une anglophobie latente. Dès la fin de la Guerre de Sept Ans, en ce rêve américain, s'allient les images d'une nature généreuse se nourrissant de "bons sauvages" à la Rousseau, et les vertus des colons quakers, philanthropes et amis de la liberté dont Voltaire faisait des modèles du bonheur humain.[3] Dès 1775, la *Gazette de France* met en honneur le terme d'insurgent; l'année suivante, Vergennes favorise la création d'un journal, les *Affaires de l'Angleterre et de l'Amérique*, qui relate les opérations militaires, insère la Déclaration d'indépendance, exalte le courage des soldats-citoyens. Le *Courrier de L'Europe* publié d'abord à Londres par Serre de Latour, rédigé par Brissot de Warville et le comte de Montlosier, puis imprimé à Boulogne-sur-Mer avec l'indulgente complicité de Vergennes, diffuse un message politique dès 1776. Les *Affiches provinciales* transmettent des échos de cette guerre libératrice.[4]

Le mirage américain, reflété dans de nombreuses brochures, explique l'envoi du corps expéditionnaire, commandé par Rochambeau, que les amiraux d'Estaing et de Grasse parviennent à acheminer à Newport. La victoire de la *Belle-Poule*, le 17 juin 1778, au large de Roscoff, sur la frégate anglaise l'*Arethusa*, provoque l'enthousiasme; l'américanomanie s'exprime dans les coiffures des élégantes "à la Belle-Poule". La valeur de notre marine, réorganisée par Choiseul et ses successeurs, se confirme avec le succès de l'escadre sous les ordres de d'Orivilliers et de la Motte-Picquet.[5] Mais la levée du corps expéditionnaire de 6 000 hommes pour suppléer les volontaires et aider les Insurgents, battus à Savannah, mérite attention.

La région lyonnaise contribua largement à la formation de ce contingent. Les deux tiers des soldats qui le composent sont des engagés; Choiseul, Monteynard, le comte de Saint-Germain avaient amélioré la qualité du recrutement: des agents du roi remplacent les racoleurs pour recruter, dans les quinze départements militaires, des volontaires; les pratiques abusives du racolage, dénoncées par Voltaire, sont interdites; des engagés dans ces "campagnes de la liberté" peuvent devenir bas-officiers, c'est-à-dire des sous-officiers, et même adjudants, grade créé par Saint-Germain permettant aux roturiers d'accéder à l'épaulette. Ce n'est qu'en 1781 que le comte de Ségur décide d'exiger quatre quartiers de noblesse pour devenir officier. En revanche, ce ministre supprime les châtiments corporels et il se préoccupe du bien-être des hommes, leur assurant à chacun un lit, alors qu'ils couchaient

3. Pierre Albert, *La France, les Etats-Unis et leurs presses* (Paris: Centre Georges Pompidou, 1977).

4. Louis Trenard, "Les échos dans la presse périodique," *Cahiers d'Histoire littéraire comparée*, no. 5-6 (1980-1981): 51-78.

5. Jacques Launay, *La croisade européenne pour l'indépendance des Etats-Unis* (Paris: Albin-Michel, 1988).

auparavant par trois. La carrière militaire ainsi rénovée peut attirer des jeunes par ses perspectives d'avancement, à tout le moins d'une vie assurée.

Le transport des quatre régiments d'infanterie, d'un élément de cavalerie, d'un bataillon d'artillerie est effectué par une escadre commandée par le chevalier de Ternay; elle quitte Brest au début du mois de mai 1780 et arrive à Newport le 11 juillet. Elle comprend des Bressans, des Dombistes, des Bugistes venus des villages. Ambérieu-en-Bugey et Ambronay en fournissent chacun trois; Vaux-en-Bugey, deux, comme Tenay; de nombreuses communautés n'ont qu'un engagé.[6] 24 soldats bugistes sont originaires de la région voisine du grenier à sel de Langieu, appelée à cette époque Bas-Bugey, actuellement Plaine de l'Ain. Ils sont, pour la plupart, cultivateurs, vignerons, artisans. Le plus âgé a 50 ans et a servi pendant 30 ans dans le régiment Soissonnais, dans la milice, dans Champagne-Cavalerie. Le plus jeune a moins de 20 ans. Les deux tiers de l'effectif ont moins de 30 ans; ils sont dans la force de l'âge; quelques-uns ont fait campagne et ont un entraînement militaire certain. Le contingent bugiste qui sert dans les unités Soissonnais, Boulonnais, Gâtinais, Hainaut, Saintonge, Auxonne, subit des pertes: un tiers ne revient pas, victimes des combats, des blessures, des maladies, d'épuisement; un certain nombre, dont la trace est perdue, a pu rester en Amérique.[7]

Ces volontaires, qui ont vécu des moments pénibles, provoqué parfois des drames familiaux, ont contribué à la victoire de Yorktown en Virginie à l'automne de 1781; le port a été bloqué par l'amiral de Grasse, dans la baie de Chesapeake; la ville assiégée se rend le 19 octobre. L'Anglais O'Hara, au nom de Cornwallis, offre son épée à Rochambeau au lieu de s'adresser à Washington! Le 25 novembre 1781, Louis XVI envoie une lettre de félicitations au marquis de la Tour-Dupin de Gouvernet, lieutenant-général et commandant en chef dans la province de Bourgogne englobant les Pays de l'Ain. Le roi tient à proclamer ses intentions pacifiques: "Le succès de mes armes ne me flattera jamais que comme étant un acheminement à la Paix", mais il justifie son intervention en Amérique par la légitimité des revendications des Insurgents. Il s'agit d'une guerre juste. Aussi les soldats bressans, bugistes, lyonnais ont-ils recueilli l'enthousiasme des populations dans les villes et dans les villages: on chante, on joue de la musique, on danse...

Louis XVI dont les armées ont vaincu les Anglais sur terre et sur mer, demande par cette lettre du 25 novembre 1781 de célébrer un *Te Deum* dans toutes les églises en présence des corps constitués. A Bourg-en-Bresse, les

6. *Les combattants français de la guerre d'Amérique 1776-1783*, Recueil publié par les soins du ministère des Affaires étrangères (Paris, 1903).

7. Général Vautray, "Le Bugey et l'indépendance des Etats-Unis d'Amérique", *Le Bugey*, No. 69 (1982): 359-70.

officiers municipaux fixent la cérémonie l'avant-veille de Noël. A Notre-Dame de Bourg, le curé Peret, syndic général du clergé, officie tandis que la foule des fidèles se presse dans le nef derrière les personnalités de la petite province de Bresse. L'office terminé, la fête naît dans les rues; la foule se rassemble place d'Armes devant l'Hôtel de Ville bâti depuis peu. Une partie se dirige, par la rue de Crèvecoeur vers le bastion Montrevel; l'hôtel de ville et l'hôtel de la province s'illuminent.

Durant deux nuits, la capitale de la Bresse offre, à ses 8 000 habitants, un spectacle nocturne. On se presse, bourgeois, artisans et paysans, qui malgré le froid, sont venus de la campagne. Sur le bastion, on a entassé du bois et, sur un signe du maire, un valet embrase le feu de joie. Le vin coule des tonneaux mis en perce, on danse...[8]

Le même enthousiasme reparaît en 1783 lors de la signature du Traité de Versailles, mettant fin au conflit. Parmi les festivités prévues à Lyon, le collège de la Trinité présente un dialogue en vers sur la Révolution américaine et une dissertation situe les rapports du cosmopolitisme et du patriotisme: "Nous rendons justice aux ennemis de la patrie. Apprendre à nos élèves à les estimer, c'est prévenir l'antipathie mutuelle qui germe dans les coeurs avec les premiers mouvements du patriotisme et ne laisser à l'ardeur qui dévore les jeunes âmes que le choix des moyens nobles et légitimes pour servir la patrie."[9]

Cette liesse se comprend. En 1763, les Français avaient été chassés des Indes et de l'Amérique du Nord par les Anglais. Même si les Français ne se rendirent pas immédiatement compte de l'ampleur des pertes subies au traité de Paris, ils souhaitaient prendre leur revanche sur l'humiliante défaite. Choiseul et Vergennes ne s'engagent donc pas en 1778 aux côtés des Insurgents pour créer une république, ni pour reprendre le Canada, ni pour faire des conquêtes sur le continent américain; ils veulent battre l'Angleterre et modifier l'équilibre européen au profit de la France.

Cette rivalité, voire cette anglophobie explique-t-elle l'engagement des soldats lyonnais? Ce patriotisme, cette riposte à l'Angleterre qui a tant de fois paralysé les entreprises françaises, a vraisemblablement pesé dans certaines décisions individuelles mais, pour le paysan ou pour l'artisan lyonnais, ces considérations restaient abstraites et loin des soucis quotidiens. Il en est de même du libéralisme, même si ces adeptes ont été souvent formés par les théoriciens anglais: "Je suis bien aise", écrit Manon Phlipon à Sophie Cannet, "de penser comme toi sur l'importance de cette révolution ; je la vois avec intérêt et je souhaite la liberté de l'Amérique comme une juste vengeance du

---

8. Alain Gros, "L'engagement de la Bresse dans la Révolution américaine", *Visages de l'Ain*, no. 163 (mai 1979): 14-20.

9. Ordonnance de police concernant le bon ordre...à l'occasion des réjouissances de la paix (Lyon, 1783). *Exercice sur la rivalité de la France et de l'Angleterre* (Lyon: Delaroche, 1783).

droit naturel violé de tant de manières dans ce continent malheureux et si peu fait pour l'être".[10] Le goût du risque, de l'aventure, de l'inconnu a certainement entraîné des jeunes Lyonnais et là, les images de cette Amérique diffusées par les gazettes, par les philosophes, par les voyageurs, parvenaient dans les milieux modestes par des intermédiaires culturels, au cours de veillées villageoises.

Selon Robert Palmer, sur les 30 000 Français qui combattirent en Amérique, une douzaine de milliers y demeurèrent.[11] A la veille d'embarquer ses soldats en 1782, pour les Antilles, le comte de Ségur doit les surveiller: "la perspective du bonheur que la liberté offrait aux soldats dans le pays avait inspiré, à un grand nombre d'entre eux, le désir de quitter leurs drapeaux et de rester en Amérique". Dans une lettre, il parle de "la rage de la désertion".[12] Ce comportement des soldats laisse penser que, pour eux, l'Amérique était paradisiaque.

Faut-il penser que c'est la misère qui incite les ruraux de la région lyonnaise à tenter l'aventure? L'explication semble simple et logique. Mais il ne faut pas oublier que la conscience de la pauvreté est délicate à déceler. A l'automne 1791, la levée des trois premiers bataillons de l'Ain par l'Assemblée constituante révèle un empressement exceptionnel: 4 698 engagés s'inscrivent sur les registres alors qu'il en fallait 1 722. Or, une idée de l'aisance est donnée à cette date par le classememt des citoyens en actifs ou passifs; ceux qui paient la valeur locale de trois journées de travail ont le droit de vote. Dans le royaume 15,8% de la population totale sont actifs; dans l'Ain 13%, dans la Saône-et-Loire 15,2%, dans le Rhône-et-Loire 15,5%, dans l'Isère 18%, dans le Jura 19%. La région lyonnaise se situe dans la moyenne nationale.[13] Quand les biens nationaux provenant des biens de l'Eglise et des émigrés sont mis en vente, des paysans achètent ces biens et quand l'Assemblée constituante entreprend une enquête sur la mendicité en 1791, beaucoup de villages répondent qu'ils ne connaissent pas de mendiants. Il est vrai que la communauté éprouve une certaine gêne à avouer qu'elle abrite des mendiants souvent confondus avec les vagabonds. Toujours est-il que l'appauvrissement qui s'amorce en 1788 n'explique pas, à lui-même, le désir d'évasion des Lyonnais.

---

10. *Lettres de Mme Roland*, éd. Claude Perroud, Nouv. série, 2 vols. (Paris: Impr. Nat., 1913), 2: 144, (4 oct. 1777).

11. Robert Palmer, *The Age of Democratic Revolution, 1760-1800* (Princeton: Princeton University Press, 1959), 247.

12. Louis-Philippe Ségur, comte de, *Mémoires, Souvenirs, Anecdotes...*, 2 vols. (Paris: Firmin-Didot, 1859), 1: 223; *Extraits des lettres écrites de l'Amérique* (Paris: Mélanges publiés par la Société des Bibliophiles français, 1903), 178.

13. Jean-Michel Levy, *La formation de la première armée de la Révolution française; l'effort militaire et la levée d'hommes dans le département de l'Ain en 1791* (Thèse, Sorbonne, 1969). Résumé, *Information Historique* (mars-avril 1973): 68-74.

Faut-il attribuer ces sentiments complexes, mêlant patriotisme et jalousie à l'égard de l'Angleterre, à la situation de Lyon? L'anglophobie est réelle dans la capitale de la soierie et l'emprise de la ville atteint toute la région par le système de la proto-industrialisation. D'autre part, cet ensemble de provinces est frontière avec la Savoie si longtemps associée aux ambitions des Habsbourg, avec la Franche-Comté annexée seulement sous le règle de Louis XIV.

Le vif sentiment d'appartenance au royaume de France est corroboré non seulement par la quantité des engagés dans la croisade libératrice en 1780 mais aussi par la qualité des chefs qui commencent leur carrière par cette campagne. Les opérations militaires de la Guerre d'indépendance ont été parfois comparées à une guerre révolutionnaire dans la mesure où les milices ont pris le pas sur les armées régulières, ont véhiculé les idées de liberté et d'égalité. Certes, il y eut des actions de guerillas, des représailles contre les loyalistes mais il ne faut pas voir dans ces milices les précurseurs des soldats de l'An II. La Guerre d'indépendance obéit, avant tout, aux règles classiques de l'art militaire du XVIIIe siècle. La défaite britannique résulte d'opérations savamment montées, comme à Yorktown.[14]

Cette guerre fut l'école de nombreux chefs militaires qui s'illustrèrent pendant un quart de siècle. Le marquis de Rostaing, châtelain de Sausselange, grand bailli du Forez, combat aux côtés du marquis de La Fayette, son voisin de Chavagnac; il est blessé à Yorktown; à son tour, maréchal de camp, il est surnommé "le La Fayette forézien", il siège à l'Assemblée provinciale, il est élu par le Tiers Etat aux Etats généraux et il prend place parmi les "patriotes", dans le sens politique du terme.[15] Le futur baron de l'Empire, Claude Dallemagne, né dans le Bugey belleysan, après ses études au Collège de Belley, s'engage en 1773 au régiment de Hainaut-Infanterie; nommé caporal en 1773, il est volontaire pour partir aux Amériques et s'embarque à Toulon, sur la flotte du comte d'Estaing en avril 1778; il participe à une opération manquée sur Rhode Island, rejoint le marquis de Bouillé aux Antilles françaises, prend part à la conquête des Iles du Levant des Petites Antilles, débarque sur le continent, se distingue à l'assaut de la citadelle de Savannah; il est promu sergent en octobre 1779. Après avoir conquis tous les grades en campagne, il meurt en 1813, général de division, chevalier de Saint-Louis et commandeur de la Légion d'Honneur.[16]

---

14. Claude Fohlen, *La Révolution américaine et l'Europe* (Actes du colloque international de Paris-Toulouse, organisé par Claude Fohlen et Jacques Godichot) (Paris: C.N.R.S., 1979), 15; Lee Kennett, "The American Revolution as a model of Revolutionary War", *La Révolution Américaine...*, 579-93.

15. Jean Cohas, *Saint-Germain-Laval pendant la Révolution française* (Roanne: Imprimerie Soucher, 1912), 36.

16. Albert Dallemagne, "Vie et campagnes du général Dallemagne (1754-1813)", *Le Bugey*, no. 55 (1968): 3-40.

Parmi les membres des professions libérales qui s'engagèrent et bénéficièrent de l'aventure américaine, Jean-François Coste est un médecin du Haut-Bugey formé à Belley et à Lyon. Affecté en 1775 comme premier médecin de l'Hôpital militaire de Calais, il est désigné, en 1780, par le Ministre de la Guerre comme le premier médecin du corps de Rochambeau. Il s'embarque en avril et dès son arrivée à Newport, doit s'occuper de l'hospitalisation de 800 soldats et de l'organisation d'un service médico-chirurgical. Ses travaux amenèrent le Collège William and Mary de Williamsburg à lui décerner le titre de docteur en médecine; Washington lui témoigne lui-même sa reconnaissance. Il poursuit une brillante carrière dans le service de Santé des Armées sous la Révolution et l'Empire.[17]

Dernier exemple de chef militaire formé par la campagne d'Amérique: Anne Joseph Marie de Moyria. Il appartient à la branche de Maillat d'une ancienne, puissante et illustre famille de noblesse bugiste. Né en 1745, il entre à l'Ecole militaire; enseigne en 1761 au régiment de Briqueville, il participe à la campagne d'Allemagne durant la Guerre de Sept Ans. Son régiment prend le nom de Soissonnais et tient garnison dans différentes places du royaume; il est capitaine en 1778. Désigné pour l'Amérique, il s'embarque avec le corps du comte de Rochambeau, il se fait remarquer pour sa bravoure à Yorktown. A son retour en France, il est nommé major du régiment de la Couronne en 1784. Le marquis de Lameth, mestre de camp, commandant le régiment, assure dans son rapport que "le chevalier de Moyria a été obligé d'épuiser le peu de fortune qu'il avait pour se soutenir au service et pour remplir les dépenses indispensables qu'ont occasionnées neuf campagnes". Il est promu colonel en 1791.[18]

Le rêve américain

Vergennes, un homme d'état des plus réalistes, n'avait pas été séduit par le rêve de la Nouvelle Arcadie américaine conçu par Rousseau, Voltaire, Dupont de Nemours, mais il cherchait un avantage pour la France. Cependant, le mythe qui avait favorisé l'engagement des soldats lyonnais dans la croisade se trouve transformé par cette intervention sur le continent américain. Ce "monde sauvage", décrit et inventorié par les voyageurs, qui présentait la triple originalité de n'être ni européen, ni chrétien, ni national, sans lois, sans gouvernement, sans histoire, est, après 1783, perçu comme un monde

---

17. Général J. des Cilleuls, "Jean-François Coste (1741-1918)" *Revue historique des Armées*, no. 1 (1977).

18. Service historique de l'Armée de terre, XB 53 et 58YB 410.

incarnant les idées des philosophes et des physiocrates; Franklin en est le vivant symbole.[19]

Il est difficile de mesurer l'impact populaire de ce séjour en Amérique septentrionale. D'après l'historien américain Forrest MacDonald, les régions françaises où se déchaînèrent en 1789 les révoltes les plus violentes contre la féodalité sont celles qui fournirent les régiments de l'armée de Rochambeau. Ces soldats avaient passé vingt-huit mois en Amérique, visité neuf états, du Massachusetts jusqu'à la Virginie, vécu au contact d'une société agricole presque entièrement libre de toute entrave seigneuriale, où il n'existaït aucun des abus contre lesquels ils luttaient à leur retour. Là encore, l'hypothèse est séduisante et il est vraisemblable que des soldats des campagnes lyonnaises aient été influencés par leur expérience américaine mais Samuel Scott, après avoir suivi la biographie des soldats revenus dans des régions touchées par les troubles agraires en 1789, ne découvre aucune corrélation entre les combattants de Rochambeau et les révoltes ou les désertions. Les soldats étaient partis sans motivation idéologique; à leur retour, des possibilités de carrière s'ouvraient à eux; ils étaient dispersés et semblaient peu soucieux de déclencher des troubles agraires ou des mutineries dans l'armée royale.[20]

Le comportement des officiers vétérans d'Amérique reste également ambigu dans la région lyonnaise. Ils ont accepté la phase libérale de l'Assemblée constituante et de l'Assemblée législative; ils ont partagé l'idéal des Rolandins mais, depuis la fuite du roi, ils éprouvent de l'inquiétude. Avaient-ils acquis leurs idées libérales en Amérique ou s'étaient-ils engagés parce qu'ils partageaient cet idéal de liberté?[21] On a remarqué que beaucoup de ces officiers étaient affiliés à la Franc-Maçonnerie et il est vrai que les loges lyonnaises participèrent à l'enthousiasme que déclenche la résistance américaine. Le Sud-Est fournit presque le tiers des volontaires engagés aux côtés des Insurgents: des régiments portent les noms de Forez, de Lyonnais, de Beaujolais. En 1785, la loge lyonnaise le *Patriotisme* reçoit triomphalement La Fayette. Venant de ses terres d'Auvergne, il se rendait à Berlin; il dîna chez l'archevêque, rencontra Mathon de la Cour, le philanthrope, s'intéressa au commerce de Lyon avec le Nouveau Monde. Le *Journal de Lyon* en profita

---

19. François Furet, "De l'homme sauvage à l'homme historique: l'expérience américaine dans la culture française", *La Révolution américaine...*, 91-108.

20. Jacques Godechot, "Les combattants de la guerre d'indépendance aux Etats-Unis et les troubles agraires en France, de 1789-1792," *Annales historiques de la Révolution Française*, vol. 28 (1956): 294; Samuel F. Scott, "The soldiers of Rochambeau's Expeditionary Corps: from the American Revolution to the French Revolution", *La Révolution américaine...*, 565-78.

21. Gilbert Bodinier, *Les officiers de l'armée royale combattants de la guerre d'Indépendance des Etats-Unis, de Yorktown à l'an II* (Château de Vincennes: Service historique de l'armée de terre, 1983); "Etude du comportement des officiers qui ont combattu en Amérique pendant la Révolution", Actes du 102e Congrès National des Sociétés Savantes (Limoges: Comité des travaux historiques et scientifiques, 1977), 2: 107-22.

pour célébrer les vertus des "Fils de la Liberté". Leur cause rassemblait un goût littéraire pour la simplification patriarcale, un sentiment d'anglophobie attisé par la concurrence commerciale, l'adhésion aux principes libéraux proclamés par le Congrès en 1776.[22]

S'il est délicat d'attribuer tel ou tel comportement d'officier, de libéral, de philanthrope, à l'expérience américaine, il est certain qu'elle renouvela les images de l'Amérique et provoque un intense mouvement intellectuel. Ainsi, l'astronome Jérôme Le François de Lalande fonde, en 1776, avec l'aide de Mme Helvétius, la loge des "Neuf-Soeurs", qui reçoit Franklin en 1779 et Paul Jones, un héros de la guerre navale contre l'Angleterre en 1780. A Bourg-en-Bresse, la Société d'Emulation, fondée par Thomas Riboud en 1783, constitue un foyer de réflexions. Cet avocat bressan, installé à Lyon, voit dès 1778, dans l'insurrection américaine, le symbole de l'homme s'affranchissant de ses chaînes, se dégageant de ses préjugés; cette libération lui paraît le résultat des oeuvres et des combats de nos philosophes. Il examine avec attention "la forme de l'administration de la nouvelle république américaine"; le Congrès est l'émanation de la nation; dans ce régime, chaque citoyen possède une parcelle de pouvoir; "ce sont autant de petites républiques qui correspondent par divers échelons à la masse générale". La division territoriale en districts permet l'existence de cette démocratie authentique. Comme tous les penseurs des Lumières, Thomas Riboud estime qu'il faut réviser la géographie administrative du royaume, créer des circonscriptions rationnelles équivalentes. Aux Etats-Unis, observe-t-il, sur chaque territoire vit une communauté; sept habitants, quelle que soit leur profession ont le droit de demander une assemblée publique de tous les membres du district. C'est une façon exemplaire d'exercer une démocratie directe.

Dans ses *Notes philosophiques et littéraires*, Riboud, émule de Condorcet, admire cette administration américaine. Le peuple est intéressé aux affaires directes et y prend part. "Il y a nécessairement chaque année plusieurs de ces assemblées et tout homme, de la première comme de la dernière classe, paysan, marchand, journalier, gentilhomme, magistrat a le droit de voter et de dire son opinion sur les affaires publiques." Chaque citoyen assume donc un rôle consultatif, peut même proposer des plans de réforme, donner des conseils aux représentants. Riboud prête une attention particulière à cette vie de la cité outre-Atlantique, car chacun y participe en citoyen actif, utilisant pleinement ses droits. Il transpose, par la pensée, ce système en Bresse: chaque habitant aurait un rôle à jouer dans le fonctionnement administratif de la province, pourrait s'opposer à un projet qui lui paraîtrait injuste. Riboud souhaite que tous les habitants de la province soient associés aux décisions et que celles-ci ne soient pas l'oeuvre d'oligarchies. Dans cette nouvelle

---

22. *Journal de Lyon* (6 juillet 1785): 218-22.

république d'Amérique, les mandataires transmettent les propositions de leurs électeurs au gouvernement. "La correspondance du citoyen avec la tête de l'Etat est parfaite et le bien peut partir et être indiqué par l'homme le plus inconnu".[23]

Riboud exprime les mêmes propos devant l'assemblée du Tiers Etat de Bresse en cette année 1781 et dans son discours inaugural de la *Société d'Emulation de Bourg* en 1783. Pour cet optimiste, tout particulier peut faire beaucoup de bien commun si l'on n'étouffe pas sa voix. Mais si cette liberté de parole doit exister, elle doit se mériter. "Tant que le peuple usera souvent de sa faculté de s'assembler, il sera vraiment libre".[24] A cette date, Riboud est subdélégué de l'intendant de Dijon. En 1784, dans son *Discours à l'Assemblée générale du Tiers Etat de Bresse*, il accorde une large place à la guerre qui s'achève par la paix de Versailles; il se félicite de la modération de Louis XVI, du rétablissement de notre marine, de l'indépendance américaine et de l'accroissement du commerce qui en résultera pour la France et en particulier pour la région lyonnaise.

Dans son discours lu à la séance de la *Société d'Emulation*, le fondateur énumère les savants qui prouvent que la nature n'a point refusé aux Bressans les dons de l'esprit et de l'intelligence; il n'oublie pas deux contemporains qui ont milité en faveur de l'indépendance américaine: Antoine Marie Cerisier et Joseph Mandrillon. Cerisier, né en 1749, est le fils d'un épicier de Châtillon-lès-Dombes, il fait ses études au college des Jésuites de Bourg, voyage en Angleterre et en Hollande: il apprécie les qualités de travail et de tempérance des Hollandais et publie, en 1777, à Utrecht, *Tableau de l'histoire générale des Provinces-Unies*, ouvrage qu'il dédie aux Etats-Unis d'Amérique, ce qui irrite les publicistes britanniques. Une polémique s'engage: Lalande et Mirabeau le soutiennent.

Cerisier publie alors *Le destin de l'Amérique* qu'il affirme être traduit de l'anglais puis *Remarques sur les erreurs de l'Histoire philosophique et politique de Raynal par rapport aux affaires de l'Amérique septentrionale*, édité à Amsterdam en 1785. A son retour en Dombes, il reçoit une pension de Louis XVI pour son rôle joué dans la préparation de l'alliance nouée entre la Hollande et la France qui a isolé l'Angleterre. Il correspond avec Washington, John Adams, La Fayette, Mirabeau... Il est élu député suppléant aux Etats généraux, fonde la *Gazette Universelle*. Ses presses sont brisées le 10 août

---

23. Louis Trenard, "Un provincial éclairé: Thomas Riboud, émule de Concorcet", *Condorcet Studies* (University of Maryland), 1983, 147-70. Arch. dépt. Ain, E 755: Notes philosophiques et littéraires, ms.

24. Thomas P. Riboud, *Discours lu à la première scéance de la Société d'Emulation de Bourg-en-Bresse, le 24 février 1783, sur l'utilité de cet établissement* (Lyon: Faucheux, 1783), 13. (Préface d'Alain Gros, 1983).

1792; il est jeté dans un cachot, traduit devant le tribunal révolutionnaire de Lyon; la chute de Robespierre le délivre.

Joseph Mandrillon, né à Bourg en 1743, dans une famille modeste, devenu négociant, est fasciné par le Nouveau Monde, par les espaces immenses, les animaux inconnus en Europe. A son retour, il s'installe à Amsterdam, ouvre un comptoir, réalise des affaires fructueuses. Attiré par les idées nouvelles, il collabore en 1777 à la *Gazette littéraire d'Amsterdam*; dès cette époque il emploie l'expression "révolution américaine" car il est conscient de l'importance de l'événement; plus qu'une guerre pour une question de territoire, c'est la notion de droit qui est en cause. En 1782, il traduit le *Voyageur américain ou Observations sur l'état actuel de la culture, le commerce des colonies britanniques en Amérique*, ouvrage écrit par un Anglais en 1769. Il accorde une très grande importance au commerce des colonies britanniques et il ajoute un *Précis sur l'Amérique septentrionale et la République des 13 Etats-Unis*. Mandrillon dresse le portrait du négociant, homme du juste milieu, actif, économe; alors que le *Voyageur américain* se préoccupe de rentabilité, méprise les Indiens, ignore les Noirs, le *Précis* manifeste une certaine sympathie pour les Indiens. Il espère que la France supplantera l'Angleterre dans les relations commerciales avec le Nouveau Monde. Pour lui, la Révolution américaine marque l'avènement d'un commerce libéré des entraves.

Mandrillon pense que la communauté de langue et de religion conduiront l'Angleterre et les Etats-Unis à reprendre leurs échanges lorsque la guerre s'achèvera. Il ne se limite pas à ces remarques d'ordre économique; il dépeint les paysages, se réjouit de la quiétude qui règne dans les villes américaines, il admire la nature, évoque le "bon sauvage", décrit d'une façon lyrique les castors et leur organisation. "Cet animal possède des dons secourables de la société sans en éprouver comme nous les vices et les malheurs"; il plaint ces rongeurs traqués par les chasseurs pour leur fourrure.

La proclamation de l'indépendance l'enthousiasme: "Tous les coeurs sensibles et bons doivent désirer que l'Europe voie cette révolution sans jalousie et sans crainte et que, la considérant comme un décret éternel et inviolable, elle s'empresse d'y donner les mains en sacrifiant des prétentions imaginaires que la force lui a données et que la force peut lui enlever de même". Il récuse l'emploi de la violence pour contraindre un peuple, dénonce le fanatisme, vante le régime de la Pennsylvanie où il constate que la liberté de conscience favorise la prospérité. L'urbanisme de la capitale Philadelphie le séduit; Voltaire a déjà célébré "La ville des frères" dans l'*Essai sur les Moeurs*. Mandrillon reprend: "Tout, dans Philadelphie, porte l'empreinte du travail et de l'industrie et l'on n'y a rien épargné pour faciliter le commerce".

Notre Bressan admire les quais, les magasins vastes et bien disposés, les rues...[25]

Membre de la *Société d'Emulation*, Mandrillon correspond avec ses confrères bressans et leur envoie ses ouvrages. En 1784, le *voyageur américain...* devient le *Spectateur américain* qui condamne la façon dont les Espagnols et les Anglais ont conquis le Nouveau Monde; il rejette toute agression et, comme Franklin, il réclame les bonnes moeurs, prône le bien-être qui s'oppose au luxe et à la misère; cette aisance ne peut s'acquérir que par le travail et le vertu. Tolérant, il se proclame partisan de l'intégration des Indiens; ils doivent devenir des citoyens. "Heureux le peuple qui, faisant chérir son gouvernement aux indigènes, leur fera quitter leurs retraites pour concourir avec eux à l'accroissement de la population du Nouveau Monde et à la gloire de briser ses fers". Il faut condamner l'esclavage, "attentat horrible à la dignité de l'homme", dénoncer l'infâme commerce des nègres. Une ère nouvelle commence: les traités d'amitié entre la France et les Etats-Unis d'une part, entre la France et la Hollande d'autre part, annoncent un âge d'or. "D'après la confiance que les traités actuels seront purs et inaltérables, je bénis votre auguste nom, monarque intéressant, bon Louis XVI! Puissiez-vous, pendant une longue suite d'années, jouir du fruit de votre sagesse n'avoir, auprès du trône, que des ministres dignes de vous; dans votre empire, que des sujets dans la prospérité".[26]

Mandrillon publie beaucoup dans ces années: à Paris, en 1784, *Recherches philosophiques sur la découverte de l'Amérique*; en 1788, *Fragments de littérature et de politique*; à Bruxelles en 1789, *Voeux patriotiques*. Il admire Necker, se lie avec Mirabeau, ce qui lui vaut d'être condamné à mort et exécuté le 7 janvier 1794.

Le modèle américain

Lyon constitue un autre foyer où se renouvellent, à la suite de la Guerre d'indépendance, les images de l'Amérique. Des réseaux se créent dans le cadre de la sociabilité culturelle, caractéristique de l'époque, pour répandre ce qu'on a appelé la franklinomanie. Les Académies, comme les Sociétés savantes, comme les Salons, participent à cette diffusion des connaissances sur l'Amérique. Devant l'intérêt porté aux titres littéraires qui tendent à occulter les titres de la noblesse, Benjamin Franklin, membre de l'Académie des Sciences, est chargé, en 1776, de mettre au point un projet de périodique

25. Warren J. Wolfe, "An Admirer of the Early American Republic: J. Mandrillon, 'Patriot of the World'", *Laurels* (Soc. Américaine de la Légion d'honneur) (The American Society of the French Legion of Honor), Vol. 55, no. 1 (Spring 1984): 31-40.

26. Alain Gros, "L'Engagement de la Bresse dans la Révolution américaine", *Visages de l'Ain*, no. 163 (mai 1979): 18-23.

contenant les correspondances de savants et d'artistes, projet formulé par Claude Pahin de la Blancherie, ami de Manon Phlipon.[27] C'est encore Franklin qui est affecté à la Commission d'enquête sur les guérisons opérées par le magnétisme; il siège aux côtés du médecin Guillotin, de l'astronome Bailly, du chimiste Lavoisier...En ces années de crise, les uns adoptent les doctrines illuministes de Swedenborg et de Louis de Saint-Martin; d'autres, selon Ségur, "s'empressant autour du baquet de Mesmer, croyaient à l'efficacité universelle du magnétisme, étaient persuadés de l'infaillibilité des oracles du somnambulisme".[28]

La mode de Mesmer et de Deslon, son disciple, ameute une foule de beaux esprits. Selon Meister, le Comité des souscripteurs, présidé par Chastellux, comprend La Fayette, Noailles, Bergasse, plus de 300 adeptes dont William Temple, Franklin et Brissot.[29] Ce dernier avoue que le magnétisme sert à rassembler les libéraux autour de Nicolas Bergasse; il confie à Roland de la Platière qu'il n'accepterait d'entrer dans une Académie qu'à Boston, Philadelphie ou Londres "parce que là, on n'enchaînera pas mes idées".[30] Brissot rejoint Condorcet, Chastellux, La Fayette, Buffon, La Rochefoucauld... dans l'*American Society* de Philadelphie... Tout cet entourage est celui des Rolandins lyonnais.

Franklin, affilié aux Sociétés savantes de Lyon, vénérable de la *Loge des Neuf-Soeurs*, est mêlé au mouvement académique français. L'abbé Raynal passant à Lyon, venant de Genève où il surveille, en 1780, l'édition de son *Histoire philosophique des Deux Indes*, propose un prix en 1783 sur la question: "La découverte de l'Amérique a-t-elle été utile ou nuisible au genre humain? S'il en résulte des biens, quels sont les moyens de les conserver et de les accroître? Si elle a produit des maux, quels sont les moyens d'y remédier?" Le *Journal encyclopédique* annonce le concours: "L'Académie ne fixe aucunement l'étendue des mémoires et se contente d'inviter les auteurs à les écrire en français ou en latin".[31]

Seize mémoires parviennent à l'Académie; elle prolonge le concours jusqu'en 1785, onze nouveaux mémoires s'ajoutent mais le jury les considère comme insuffisants et, pendant plusieurs années, la docte assemblée se préoccupe des bienfaits ou des méfaits de la découverte réalisée par

---

27. François Metra, *Correspondance secrète*, 1787 (13 juin 1774, 21 janvier 1777, 15 mai 1779, 25 novembre 1780) (Genève: Slatkine Reprints, 1967).

28. Comte de Ségur, *Mémoires*.... 1,96.

29. Jakob Heinrich Meister, *Correspondance littéraire philosophique et critique*, 16 vols. (Paris: Garnier Fr., 1877-82), 13: 510 (avril 1784) et 14: 20-25 (août 1784).

30. Jacques-Pierre Brissot de Warville, *Mémoires*, éd. Claude Perroud, 2 vols. (Paris: A. Picard, 1911), 2: 54; *Correspondance et papiers*, éd. Claude Perroud (Paris: A. Picard, 1912), 143.

31. *Journal encyclopédique*, t.50 (novembre 1780): 475; t.59 (1er janvier 1785): 45; t.60 (nov. 1785): 146. Nouvel appel t.62 (décembre 1786): 349.

Christophe Colomb.[32] Joseph Mandrillon réédite son *Voyageur américain* et le fait suivre de *Recherches philosophiques sur la découverte du Nouveau Monde* qui est une réponse à la question de l'abbé Raynal. Après avoir décrit chacun des Etats en puisant amplement dans l'*Histoire des Deux Indes*, Mandrillon formule une mise en garde: la corruption des moeurs européennes favorise l'essor et la puissance de l'Amérique; elle parviendra à subjuguer ses anciens maîtres.

Dans ce milieu lyonnais admiratif de Franklin, enthousiasmé par la révolution américaine, Charles Mathon de la Cour, homme des Lumières, Vénérable de la *Loge du Parfait Silence*, apparaît comme un des guides de l'opinion publique. Il publie *La Science du bonhomme Richard*, recueil des proverbes insérés par Franklin dans ses almanachs, nouvel évangile très accessible; le texte est volontiers réédité avec des additifs. Mathon de la Cour lui associe le *Testament de Fortuné Ricard, maître d'arithmétique* et la *Science populaire de Claudius*. La *Science du bonhomme Richard* est également publiée avec des textes choisis du "compagnon de Simon de Nantua". Ces éditions gardent leur caractère populaire revêtu dès l'origine dans les almanachs; elles amorcent, avec leurs illustrations, la création d'un personnage légendaire, un vieillard aux longs cheveux, le bonhomme Richard se confond avec Franklin lui-même, image de la sagesse et de l'expérience.

Mathon de la Cour diffuse ce modèle américain par ses discours maçonniques, philanthropiques, académiques, par ses brochures, par son périodique, le *Journal de Lyon*. En 1786, il reproduit dans plusieurs numéros, en quelque 45 pages, une série de lettres adressées par Savary, fils d'un ancien agent de change de Lyon, à des amis lyonnais. Savary, après avoir tenté fortune dans des entreprises d'assèchement des marais de Bourgoin puis dans le commerce à Paris, part aux Etats-Unis vers 1782. Il achète des terres sur les rives de l'Ohio et cherche, selon le rêve américain à la mode, à y établir une sorte de vaste colonie agricole. Il se propose de transmettre à son ami, "une idée du gouvernement, du commerce et du génie du peuple américain". Il garantit sa sincérité:

> Personne ne connaît mieux que vous quel était mon enthousiasme pour la cause américaine dans sa scission avec l'Angleterre... Cet intérêt tient à mon caractère un peu romanesque et, quand la question était encore indécise, j'imaginais voir un continent immense se dégageant plus tard que les autres parties de la terre, des eaux de la mer, présentant une terre libre, vierge et fertile aux mains qui venaient la cultiver; un peuple dont l'origine était respectable et attendrissante par un purisme et un zèle

32. René Rémond, "La morale de Franklin et l'opinion française..." *Revue d'Histoire Moderne et Contemporaine*, t.7 (juillet-septembre 1960): 196-201.

de religion persécutée; ces nouveaux colons adoucissant ou contentant d'un côté la barbarie des sauvages et, de l'autre, luttant contre la tyrannie européenne. Je voyais ce peuple entre ces deux fléaux, défendre ces biens essentiels, sa vie et sa propriété et surtout sa liberté qui seule rend ces deux autres biens si précieux.

Ce correspondant décrit son installation dans les forêts, la construction de sa cabane et l'aménagement d'un lit à vingt-deux places, il essaie de recruter des colons et se plaint de la rareté du whisky, il doit boire de l'eau fraîche. Il pense, comme l'écrit Turgot, que l'Amérique pourrait être le laboratoire où l'on expérimenterait des programmes sociaux qui seraient applicables en Europe; cette république devient "l'espoir du genre humain". La profession de foi de ce Lyonnais reste optimiste, même s'il reconnaît que le nouvel Etat a adopté les lois anglaises qui sont atteintes de l'antique barbarie féodale. Les sciences progressent, l'esprit de tolérance se répand, les souverains pratiquent une politique modérée pour éviter l'exode de leurs sujets.[33]

Malgré les difficultés que connaît la France, l'intérêt pour le Nouveau Monde demeure. Il se révèle par des faits de langage: dans la *Complainte historique* sur le triste événement arrivé dans la ville de Lyon au mois d'août 1786, les révoltés sont appelés les insurgents. Les mémoires continuent de fleurir: de Mathon de la Cour,[34] d'un anonyme qui est en réalité François-Jean de Chastellux,[35] de Louis Genty...[36]

Les débats académiques se prolongent. En 1790, l'Académie de Lyon propose, comme prix d'éloquence, l'éloge de Franklin qui vient de mourir et, comme dissertation: "Quelle a été l'influence de la découverte de l'Amérique sur les moeurs, la politique, le commerce de l'Europe?"[37] L'Académie reçoit de nouveaux essais: de Carle,[38] de Paul Jones.[39] La question de l'esclavage et la traite des nègres introduit une nouvelle dimension. Dans son ouvrage *La Cause des esclaves nègres*[40] qui s'apparente à l'*Histoire des Deux Indes*, le

---

33. *Journal de Lyon ou Annonce et Variétés littéraires*, 19 mars 1786. L. Trenard, "La presse lyonnaise et son utilisation politique" dans *Les pratiques politiques en province* (Université de Montpellier, 1987), 175-97.

34. Charles-Joseph Mathon de la Cour, *Discours sur les meilleurs moyens de faire naître et d'encourager la patriotisme dans une monarchie...* (Paris: Cuchet et Gattey, 1787, 1788).

35. François-Jean de Chastellux, *Discours sur les avantages ou les désavantages qui résultent pour l'Europe de la Découverte de l'Amérique* (Londres et Paris: Prault, 1787).

36. Abbé Louis Genty, *L'influence de la découverte de l'Amérique sur le bonheur du genre humain* (Paris: Nyon l'aîné, 1787, 1788).

37. *Courier de Lyon*, 2 septembre 1790.

38. Henri Carle, *La découverte de l'Amérique a-t-elle été utile ou nuisible au genre humain?* (Paris: Moutard, 1790).

39. Paul Jones, *Défenseur de la Liberté américaine. A tous bons Lyonnais* (Paris, octobre 1790).

40. Benjamin Frossard, *La Cause des esclaves nègres*, 2 vols. (Lyon: Delaroche, 1788).

pasteur Benjamin Frossard rapporte des faits qui alarmèrent les âmes sensibles. Son livre paraît encore une réponse à la question posée par Raynal sur les inconvénients et les avantages de la découverte de l'Amérique. Toujours intéressé par cette critique, Mathon de la Cour commente l'essai de Frossard. Il évoque les méfaits de la traite: "On ravit à des hommes le plus précieux des biens, la liberté et on brise les liens les plus sacrés de la nature". On voit des esclaves déportés qui contemplent la progéniture de leurs maîtres "en versant des torrents de larmes" parce que ces enfants leur rappellent les leurs. Pour recruter ces esclaves, les marchands déclenchent des guerres entre les tribus guinéennes; à leur tour, les planteurs agissent en "véritables despotes"; des sociétés comme celle des Quakers de Pennsylvanie "s'efforcent d'atténuer ces horreurs"...[41]

Le prix offert par l'abbé Raynal attire encore une cinquantaine de candidats. L'abbé Louis Jacquet examine, en 1791, les dissertations et constate que, depuis la création du prix, le ton a changé. "On commence à rougir d'une conquête longtemps célébrée avec emphase"; on s'interroge sur la portée de la pénétration européenne, sur le trafic des esclaves, sur ce "commerce illicite et barbare". Plusieurs textes insistent sur la cruauté des conquérants; d'autres déclarent qu'il est difficile de mettre en balance les pertes humaines et les richesses comme la cochenille ou la pomme de terre. Cependant, la prospection de ce continent a renouvelé l'esprit des Européens et permet d'étudier "les formes primitives de l'homme tel qu'il sortit des mains du Créateur"; la découverte de cet univers nouveau favorise l'extension du commerce et par suite, augmente l'étendue de la civilisation, ainsi que l'expose le marquis de Chastellux dans son *Discours sur les avantages ou les désavantages...*. L'Afrique n'était qu'un repaire de brigands; l'Asie, l'apanage des tyrans; "l'anarchie féodale déchirait l'Europe et la préparait au despotisme"; peuplée de mécontents, elle était "le pays de la mode et des révolutions"; or, "le dernier degré de la civilisation est de devenir plus humain, plus compatissant, plus généreux et on le devient à force de se communiquer".

Le Nouveau Monde affermit aussi les idées relatives à la liberté; les Suisses et les Bataves avaient procédé à quelques tentatives, mais l'Europe croyait que "la liberté ne convenait qu'aux plus petits Etats et que les grands empires étaient essentiellement voués à l'esclavage. La patrie de Franklin prouve que l'on peut instaurer partout une liberté aussi loin de la licence que de l'esclavage". L'Amérique renseigne aussi l'Ancien Monde sur les effets du luxe. Quoique nuisible à bien des égards, le luxe stimule l'industrie et l'art, à condition de détruire "le goût dépravé et ruineux des productions étrangères". Le seul point noir est que ce continent idyllique souffre de la dépopulation mais il ne faut pas désespérer; les progrès s'affirment sur toute la planète:

---

41. Louis Trenard, *Lyon, de l'Encyclopédie au préromantisme* (Paris: PUF, 1958), 282.

l'Europe et l'Amérique montrent que "la civilisation sans liberté ne fait que des esclaves et la liberté sans la civilisation des sauvages".[42]

Ce bilan de plusieurs années de réflexions dressé par l'académicien lyonnais révèle que l'information transmise par les récits de voyages s'est étendue au domaine de la philosophie; elle alimente deux pôles de méditation: pour les uns, l'Amérique sert de modèle, elle incarne les principes des philosophes français et anglais; ce qui se passe au delà de l'Atlantique peut se répéter en Europe; pour les autres, chaque pays possède ses valeurs particulières, ses lois propres; le succès de la République américaine ne prouve rien, si ce n'est que le monde est divers. "Ce serait une grande chimère", écrit Necker, en 1792, dans *Du Pouvoir exécutif dans les grands Etats*, "d'imaginer que la liberté, l'égalité et toutes nos institutions nouvelles nous assimileront aux Américains".[43]

En réalité, en cette phase de la Révolution française, l'image de l'Amérique exemplaire demeure dans le groupe lyonnais gravitant autour des Roland, de Brissot, de Servan, de Lanthenas...

L'ouvrage de Brissot et d'Etienne Clavière, *De la France et des Etats-Unis ou De l'importance de la Révolution d'Amérique pour le bonheur de la France*, publié à Londres en 1787, les guide dans leur action politique et sociale. Ainsi en est-il de la Maison Philanthropique de Lyon · et du programme de prévoyance sociale des Brissotins.[44] Parmi les images que rapportent les voyageurs des Etats-Unis, plusieurs concernent leurs mesures humanitaires en faveur des pauvres, des malades, des prisonniers, des fous. Crèvecoeur admire, en 1787, la bienveillance de ces républicains. "Dans presque toutes les grandes villes, il y a des hôpitaux pour les malades et les matelots ainsi que des écoles gratuites pour l'éducation des enfants pauvres et des orphelins; les prisons sont construites avec beaucoup de soin, dans des endroits isolés et bien aérés".[45] Brissot s'étonne, en 1788, de la qualité de la prison de Philadelphie où l'on s'efforce de réadapter les malfaiteurs à la vie sociale en leur apprenant un métier et en les rétribuant. L'hôpital psychiatrique traite ses patients avec humanité, sans oublier de les soigner, au lieu de les exposer, comme à Bicêtre, à la curiosité du public. "Il est donc une terre", s'exclame-t-il, "où l'âme d'un directeur d'hôpital n'est pas une âme de bronze!"[46]

---

42. Louis Jacquet, *Coup d'oeil sur les 4 concours qui ont eu lieu à l'Académie pour le prix offert par l'Abbé Raynal* (Lyon: Bruyset, 1791).

43. Durand Echeverria, "L'Amérique devant l'opinion française, 1734-1870", *Revue d'Histoire Moderne et Contemporaine*, t. 9 (janvier-mars 1962): 51-62.

44. *Lettres de Mme Roland*, 2: 729-31.

45. Saint-John de Crèvecoeur, *Lettres d'un cultivateur américain...depuis l'année 1770 jusqu'à 1786*, 3 vols. (Paris: Cuchet, 1787), 3: 452-53.

46. Jacques-Pierre Brissot de Warville, *Nouveau Voyage dans les Etats-Unis de l'Amérique septentrionale fait en 1783* (Paris: Buisson, 1791), 1: 301-08, 2: 161-66.

La séduction de la jeune république conduit le groupe d'amis des Roland non seulement à s'inspirer des institutions nouvelles mais aussi à envisager la création, en Amérique, de cette cité idéale que la France tarde à fonder. Les voyages en Amérique se multiplient; certains disciples de Rousseau souhaitent même s'établir aux Etats-Unis, parfois par lassitude de la vie française. "J'abhore, au plus profond de mon âme", écrit Manon Roland à son mari, en janvier 1782, "un Etat et des moeurs où l'homme vertueux peut être entraîné à se mesurer avec l'être vil, souvent indigné de sa colère. L'affreux gouvernement que celui qui laisse en balance des choses aussi inégales! M. Lanthenas est tout justifié à mes yeux de fuir en Pennsylvanie. Je voudrais être avec toi dans les déserts". En effet, François Lanthenas que le couple Roland a logé à Lyon, songe, dès 1785, à profiter de ses relations dans la province de New York, pour s'y installer. Le bruit courut même que Roland allait l'accompagner. En 1788, lors de la réunion de l'Assemblée des notables, Mme Roland écrit à Bosc: "Attendons et voyons, bénissons l'Amérique et pleurons sur les rives du fleuve de Babylone".[47]

Quand Brissot retourne aux Etats-Unis, Roland lui écrit, le 20 mars 1789: "Je vous ai tenu fidèle compagnie, Monsieur, dans votre voyage d'Amérique et, Crèvecoeur à la main, j'ai souvent envié votre sort. Combien de fois me suis-je écrié: Et moi aussi, si j'avais 20 ans de moins".[48] Les rêveries du *Cultivateur américain* lui paraissent un substitut à l'agitation révolutionnaire. Les Roland, Brissot, Bosc, Lanthenas, Servan et un Quaker anglais qui séjourne alors en France, M. Pigott, font "un étrange rêve d'évasion né des fantasmes de ces têtes exaltées remplies d'illusions rousseauistes et de mirage américain". Ils veulent créer une petite république rurale en France et, si l'événement le permet, en Amérique où elle serait un ultime refuge. "On achèterait ensemble un bien national et l'on vivrait en communauté; on attirerait des paysans et des artisans, on créerait des manufactures, une imprimerie" et une bibliothèque pour répandre l'instruction, un café et un club patriotique pour l'initiation civique. "On échapperait ainsi à la corruption des villes, on offrirait au pays un modèle de vertu et de prospérité, on formerait des citoyens et des apôtres de la liberté..."[49]

Le rêve américain demeure. Madame Roland avoue à Brissot ses sentiments à l'égard des Etats-Unis: "Si mon excellent ami [son mari] eût eu quelques années de moins, l'Amérique nous aurait déjà reçus en son sein. Nous regrettons moins cette terre promise depuis que nous espérons une patrie. La Révolution, toute imparfaite qu'elle soit, a changé la face de la France; elle développe un caractère et nous n'en avions pas". Elle rêve

47. *Lettres de Mme Roland*, 1: 180, 380, 412, 531; 2: 17, 689.
48. Brissot, *Correspondance et papiers*, 220.
49. Guy Chaussinand-Nogardet, *Madame Roland. Une femme en révolution* (Paris: Seuil, 1985), 88-89.

toujours avec ses amis d'acheter un domaine ecclésiastique que la nation met en vente dans la région lyonnaise pour y vivre une vie rustique à l'américaine, en philosophant et en répandant les Lumières autour d'eux à la manière des fermiers américains décrits par Crèvecoeur.[50]

Un de leurs compatriotes du Beaujolais, Riche-Dupin, le frère du mathématicien, le baron de Prosny, achète à une Compagnie américaine, la Compagnie du Scioto, à un prix modique, quelques terres situées sur un affluent de l'Ohio et s'y rend en 1790. Après un séjour à Philadelphie, il franchit les Alleghanys mais quand il parvient à Buffalo Creek, il apprend que les Indiens contrôlent les territoires du Scioto et scalpent les colons novices qui leur tombent sous la main. Il s'embarque sur un bateau qui descend l'Ohio et qui l'amène à Gallipolis, établissement français où il compte rester mais ses tribulations se poursuivent encore quelques années. Il rentre dans la région lyonnaise, ruiné, en 1810![51]

Malgré de telles déconvenues, le rêve perdure. En octobre 1793, emprisonnée à Sainte-Pélagie, l'Egérie de la Gironde écrit à Edme Mentelle qu'elle appelle "dear Jany", à propos de son fils installé au Massachusetts: "Lorsque vous parlez d'Amérique, vous chatouillez mes oreilles, c'est bien là que j'ambitionnerais de me transporter si je redevenais libre, mais je n'espère point en recouvrer la faculté".[52]

Modèle, mirage, rêve... La République américaine devient, au moment de la Terreur, un refuge. Rassemblés autour de la librairie de Moreau de Saint-Méry à Philadelphie en 1795, un petit groupe de Constituants se rappellent les jours patriotiques d'antan. Hommes des Lumières, modérés, ils ont rêvé de l'Amérique, terre de liberté. Brillat-Savarin, Talleyrand, Dupont de Nemours, Volney..., tous ont éprouvé la franklinomanie en 1790. A l'initiative de La Fayette, ils ont participé aux débats élaborant la Déclaration des Droits... Les uns ont été déçus par l'expérience de la monarchie constitutionnelle, les autres ont été menacés par les Montagnards de la Convention. Tous éprouvent la joie d'avoir échappé à la guillotine et ils rapporteront de leur séjour de nouvelles images des Etats-Unis, selon leur tempérament, leurs convictions, leurs aventures.

L'avocat Brillat-Savarin, député du Tiers-Etat, maire de sa ville natale, Belley, se réfugie à New York avec son ami Jean-Antoine Rostaing quand la Société populaire le dénonce comme modéré et comme fédéraliste. Vivant de leçons de français et de musique, il s'accommode fort bien de son exil,

50. *Lettres de Mme Roland*, 2: 77-80.

51. Robert Pinet, "Un enfant du Beaujolais, le frère du baron de Prosny, va aux Etats-Unis en 1790", *Bulletin de l'Académie de Villefranche-en-Beaujolais* (1970): 112-20, 107-15; (1973-1974): 23-28; (1975): 25-31; (1979-1980): 51-59.

52. *Lettres de Mme Roland*, 2: 526-27.

chassant la dinde sauvage dans le Connecticut, appréciant la saveur inédite des jeunes Américaines et la simplicité candide des jeunes Quakeresses. Vantant leurs institutions libérales, il rapporte la conversation d'un fermier américain heureux de son sort:

> Tout ce qui vous entoure et que vous avez vu chez moi sort de mes propriétés. Ces bas, mes filles les ont tricotés; mes souliers, mes habits proviennent de mes troupeaux; ils contribuent aussi, avec mon jardin et ma basse-cour, à me fournir une nourriture simple et substantielle... Les impôts, ici ne sont presque rien... Le Congrès favorise de tout son pouvoir notre industrie naissante... Tout nous vient de la liberté que nous avons conquise et fondée sur de bonnes lois.[53]

Pour Brillat-Savarin, après un exil de trois ans, la République américaine demeure un modèle.

---

53. Jean-Anthelme Brillat-Savarin, *Physiologie du goût* (1826), éd. Jean-François Revel (Paris: Flammarion, 1982), 90; Arnold Whitbridge, "Brillat-Savarin in America", *The Franco-American Review* (1936), trad. *Le Bugey*, Belley, no. 31 (1937): 433-49.

Raynal and His View of Trade as Destroying the European Ethos

Daniel Price

In 1773 the Academy of Marseilles offered a prize for the best essay in response to the question, "What has always been the effect of trade upon the spirit and mores of peoples?" This may strike one as unusual when one reflects that Marseilles was a leading port of France and of the Mediterranean. Why would the members of the Academy pose such a question about an interest so vital to the success of their city? Yet it is even more unusual that the prize was awarded to an essay which answered that the overall effect had been one of disaster. At the end of the essay, the author even suggested that the ships be burned and the harbor filled in.[1]

French Trade

The prize and the essay were part of a larger discussion. For during the eighteenth century, the French had greatly expanded their commercial activities. From the time of Louis XV's accession to the Revolution, the total volume of trade quadrupled,[2] and much of this was due to the growth of maritime commerce. Of principal importance was the trade with the Antilles and Louisiana. The great ships delivered their cargoes of sugar, tobacco, indigo and coffee to eager French markets. And the plantations of the Indies demanded in turn a large subsidiary trade in slaves. Shipments of furs and fish from Canada were important too, though less so after the Seven Years War.

The major port was Bordeaux from which over 3 000 vessels sailed annually for the Americas and whose amount of trade grew from 40 million

---

1. André Liquier, "Quelle a été dans tous les temps l'influence du commerce sur l'esprit et sur l'esprit et les moeurs des peuples" (Marseilles: Brebion, 1778).

2. John Lough, *An Introduction to Eighteenth-Century France* (New York: David McKay and Co., 1961), 71.

livres in 1720 to over 250 million by 1780.[3] In his travels through pre-Revolutionary France, Arthur Young observed that Bordeaux was much superior to any English port.[4] The commerce of the city stimulated the local industry and supported the surrounding shipyards, refineries, and distilleries. There were other significant ports too. Each year Nantes sent over 150 ships in the Atlantic shipping lanes. Le Havre had a growing position in the slave trade after the Seven Years War, and Marseilles commanded the traffic of trade with the Levant.[5] Thus trade came to play an increasingly important role in the economy of France.[6]

The growth of trade did not pass unnoticed. Its impact upon the economy and upon society as a whole was the subject of much debate among the intellectuals. The physiocrats, for example, attacked the kind of mercantilism and protectionism identified with the policies of Colbert. In their presentation of what we today call political economy, they argued for free trade and an end to government regulation. Other commentators focussed more on the social consequences of trade. They asked which virtues–and vices–did an increasingly commercial economy favor.

The discussion in France about the social consequences of trade took an added impetus from the reviews of Bernard Mandeville's *The Fable of the Beehive* in the 1720s. Mandeville had claimed that private greed, specifically the acquisitiveness of the commercial class, was a public benefit in terms of its long-range effects. For these so-called vices actually promoted the wealth of the nation as a whole and that in turn paid for the nation's civilization and its military strength.[7] In 1734 this argument was seconded and expanded by Jean-François Melon in his *Essai politique sur le commerce* and by Voltaire's *Le Mondain*. In general, both claimed that a free economy promoted the national wealth and spending on luxury items, created jobs for the poor in

---

3. Henri Sée, *La France économique et sociale au XVIIIe siècle* (Paris: Armand Colin, 1927), 116.

4. See "Overseas Commerce and European Manufacture," *New Cambridge Modern History*, 14 vols. (Cambridge: Cambridge Univ. Press, 1965), 7: 35.

5. Sée, 118.

6. The rise in trade and commercial interests affected other nations too, notably England. Here the lines of discussion were drawn between court and country. Court stood for a commercial influence which sought the expansion of credit, a national bank, standing and professional armies, and support of the established church. The landed gentry saw this policy development as a potential threat to English liberties of which they were the guardians. See John G.A. Pocock's *The Machiavellian Moment: Florentine Political Thought and the Atlantic Republican Tradition* (Princeton: Princeton Univ. Press, 1975), 462-67; and his article, "Virtue and Commerce in the Eighteenth Century," *Journal of Interdisciplinary History*, 3, 1: 119-34.

7. On Mandeville, see Isaac Kramnick, *Bolingbroke and His Circle* (Cambridge, Mass.: Harvard Univ. Press, 1968), ch. 5.

addition to giving them an incentive for industriousness.[8] Though they did not clearly distinguish between luxury and simple commerce, each of them considered commerce as a kind of irrigation for the overall economy.

The new lines of thinking did not, of course, win universal acceptance. Besides the preachers who railed against the corrupting influence of wealth and luxury,[9] Rousseau added his dissent. In his "Essay on the Sciences and the Arts" (1750), he denied that trade promoted virtue. In fact quite the opposite was true. While the ancients had been concerned only with virtue, the people of his day spoke only of money, and this undercut any possible concern for the common good.[10] In a later essay, he brought up another key issue about trade. Did trade circulate wealth and help towards a greater distribution of wealth? From a little different perspective, did it raise the general standard of living? Rousseau did not think so. "The peasant is without a shirt precisely because the other must have ruffles...We must have liqueurs on our tables and that is why the peasant drinks only water. We must have flour to powder our wigs, and that is why the poor have no bread."[11] Resources are limited therefore, and Rousseau had noted how concentrated they were among the rich, and trade only made the rich richer.

In *The Spirit of the Laws*, Montesquieu was ambivalent about trade. He readily conceded that it led to a gentility of manners and that commercial relations fostered the conditions of peace. At the same time, he was afraid that trade corrupted morals and fostered avarice. In any case, it was more suited for a republic than a monarchy. Trade, especially a great deal of trade, brought a large amount of influence to bear on the decisions of state. Thus, the political role of the merchant was more consistent with his role in the economy of the republic which was dominated by commercial enterprises.[12] No doubt he was thinking here of the positions of merchants in the republics of Holland and Venice. Moreover, privilege and the consequent influence at court were better suited to the arrangements of a monarchy. It would seem that the President would not allow the merchants to form such a party of privilege and influence at court.

---

8. On Melon and Voltaire and their contributions to the trade debate, see the unpublished dissertation by Ellen Ross, "The Debate on Luxury in 18th-century France" (Univ. of Chicago, 1975), 86-92.

9. See M. Daniel Price's dissertation, "Jesuit Preachers in Paris, 1729-1762" (Univ. of Chicago, 1981).

10. Jean-Jacques Rousseau, *Discours sur les sciences et les arts, Oeuvres Complètes*, 3 vols. (Paris: Gallimard, 1964), 3: 7, 30.

11. Rousseau, "Dernière réponse," *O.C.*, 3: 79. Ross discusses both these essays in her dissertation, 121-23 and 124.

12. Montesquieu, *The Spirit of the Laws*, transl. by Thomas Nugent (New York: The Hafner Press, 1949), Books 20 and 23.

Raynal and *The History*

An important and representative voice in the trade debate was the Abbé Raynal and his multivolume *Political and Philosophical History of the Settlement and Trade of Europe in the Two Indies*. The work was important because it gave a detailed analysis of the impact of trade upon Europe. He discussed how trade affects political structures, which virtues and vices it promotes and how it reveals the nature of man. The work was representative because it sold very well, and there were almost immediate translations into English, Dutch, German, Spanish and Italian. Evidently it touched some resonance among enlightened opinion throughout Europe.[13]

The author of *The History* had an interesting and checkered career in his own right. Guillaume-Thomas Raynal, born in 1713, educated by the Jesuits, entered that order, and as a seminarian taught in Clermont and Toulouse. Sometime after his ordination as a priest, he left the Jesuits and moved to Paris, where he made a living as a ghost writer for members of the *Parlement*. From 1750-1754, he edited *Le Mercure*.[14] His first book was about the Dutch Stadhouderat and his second about the English Parliament. In the first he appeared as an opponent of despotism, while in the second he championed absolute monarchy, though neither was a masterpiece of scholarly exposition.[15] For a number of years he attended the famous dinner parties of Baron d'Holbach, where he acquired the nickname of *inquisitif*. During this period he was reading voraciously and gathering notes on a topic which absorbed him completely for several years–the involvement of Europe in colonial activities. In 1770 Raynal published the first edition of six volumes, and it was an immediate success. As a result, Raynal undertook the prodigious task of a new and expanded version which was ready four years later. Like the first, the second was published at Geneva and done so anonymously, although the identity of the author was always taken for granted. Once again the work was a success and this time was placed on the *Index*. Once again Raynal set about to prepare a new and substantially revised edition.

For some reason, the Abbé published the third edition (1781) under his own name. Indeed, his picture was on the flyleaf. This step was too much for the Parisian guardians of morals. The Attorney General, Louis Séguier, condemned the book as an open attack on religion and privilege which, in fact,

---

13. See Anatole Feugère, *Un précurseur de la Révolution, l'abbé Raynal (1713-1796); documents inédits* (Angoulême: Imprimerie Ouvrière, 1922).

14. Feugère numbers the pre-Revolution editions at more than 70, p. iii. A contemporary of Raynal and editor of the *Correspondance littéraire*, J.H. Meister, called it the most important work since *The Spirit of the Laws* (see Feugère, 403).

15. Such is the opinion of Robert Shackleton in "Raynal," *Encyclopedia Britannica* (1968 edition), 18: 1195.

it was.[16] The *Parlement* agreed, ordering the book to be burned and the author imprisoned. Rather than face the Bastille, Raynal fled into exile, first to Holland and then to the court of Frederick the Great. In 1784 he was allowed to return to France on condition that he not reside in Paris. Eventually the aged Abbé, now 73, settled in Marseilles. At the eve of the Revolution, he greeted the calling of the Estates General with enthusiasm, though he refused to be nominated as a representative. Two years later his initial enthusiasm had considerably cooled. Called to Paris in 1791 to be recognized by the National Assembly, he felt compelled to issue a public letter in which he attacked the license of the Revolution and the violation of property rights.[17] He was condemned by the Assembly and sentenced to the guillotine, though spared because of age.

There is some problem of authorship for the multivolume work. As with many works of the eighteenth century, the final text was the product of many hands but with one single editor. Diderot has long been presumed to have been a contributor, although the exact amount has been the subject of some controversy.[18] Raynal did write to Diderot in a letter that Diderot's rhetoric would help to compensate for his own everlasting calculations.[19] Antoine Jussieu, a noted botanist of the period, contributed over fifty articles on horticulture, and there is a record of his corrections which he sent to Raynal.[20] Alexandre Deleyre wrote large portions of the last book of the second edition.[21] Others contributed too but were not paid for their work, and some

---

16. Anthony Louis Séguier, "Speech to Parlement," from a contemporary and anonymous translation from the French (London, 1781).

17. Guillaume-Thomas-François, Abbé de Raynal, "Lettre à l'Assemblée Nationale" (Paris, 1791).

18. Virgil Topazio in "Diderot's Supposed Contribution to Raynal's Work," *Symposium*, 12 (Spring-Fall 1958): 103-17, challenges the general opinion. He uses circumstantial evidence such as the absence of Raynal's name from Diderot's correspondence with Melchior Grimm and Sophie Volland in the years immediately prior to the first edition. When Grimm sharply criticized the third edition eleven years later, Diderot made a spirited defense of the work. Topazio thinks it unlikely that Grimm would have attacked the work so, if he had known that it was the work of his friend. Moreover, he cannot imagine Diderot defending himself so spiritedly. On the other hand, Michèle Duchet argues from stylistic similarities that the pieces from the Fonds Vandeul are the work of Diderot and so substantiates the supposition that Diderot contributed significantly to Raynal's work, in "Diderot, collaborateur de Raynal: A propos des 'Fragments Imprimés' du Fonds Vandeul," *Revue d'Histoire littéraire de la France* 60 (1960): 531. How the printed sheets of the Fonds Vandeul correspond with the published work of Raynal's third edition has been worked out by Hans Wolpe in *Raynal et sa machine de guerre* (Stanford: Stanford Univ. Press, 1957), 186-252.

19. Arthur Wilson, *Diderot* (New York: Oxford Univ. Press, 1972), 687.

20. Cecil P. Courtney, "Antoine-Laurent de Jussieu, collaborateur de l'Abbé Raynal" *RHLF*, 63 (1963): 217-27.

21. Franco Venturi, "Un Encyclopedista: Alexandre Deleyre," *Rivista Storica Italiana* 77, 4 (Sept. 1965): 791-824.

sections were just plagiarisms of slightly reworked material.[22] However, one may still consider the opus as a whole as the work of Raynal since he was the common editor and had final say about what went into the published work.

Raynal's multivolume work has some resemblance to the *Encyclopedia* of his friend and dinner companion, Denis Diderot. It contains a wealth of information about foreign places, their peoples and their plants. For example, from the section on the Indies, the reader may learn of that area's camphor plants–where and how they are grown, the shape and color of the leaves, how the oil is extracted when pressed, what kind of fragrance it gives off when burned.[23] Moreover, there is information about the weather of these foreign places–when the climate changes, how much rainfall the place receives, the direction of the sea breezes, the best time for visiting.[24] It is indeed as if one were reading a travelogue. He characterizes the peoples of each nation with wit, if not always with affection. So the French are a people who pass quickly from pain to pleasure and vice versa. They are womanly in their follies and in their delights, and each week brings them a new hero.[25]

Reading through all of this is sometimes like ploughing through an encyclopedia. Yet what holds the work together and keeps the reader's attention are the narrative threads. There is an overarching framework within which Raynal has inserted the observations and descriptions of an incurable bibliophile. That framework is precisely the history of European colonization, and it is the narrative which makes the work more readable than the *Encyclopedia*. One is led to turn the page to continue the story to the next episode. He describes the discovery of each land, the first contact with the natives, the establishment of forts, trading posts, and colonies. Then he goes on to give the developments, whether they be wars with the natives or with other European nations. History itself becomes the medium of his message. He gives no abstract, theoretical analysis of trade and settlement. Rather he narrates the actual events, first in Asia and then in the Americas, of Europe's involvement in these colonial enterprises. And from these events he draws his conclusions.

---

22. Feugère, 201-35.

23. Guillaume-Thomas-François Raynal, *A Philosophical and Political History of the Settlements and Trade of the Europeans in the East and West Indies*, as translated from the third French edition by J.O. Justamond, 8 vols. (London: W. Strahan, 1783), 1: 282. (Hereafter *History*)

24. E.g. on the Cape of Good Hope, *History*, 1: 313; or Cartegena, 3: 60.

25. *History*, 4: 90.

The Positive Effects of Trade in the First and Second Editions

Trade, in its most basic meaning, is the exchange of goods and services between one society and another. There is a sharing from the surplus of one society to supply what is lacking in the other.[26] Raynal, though, is not so interested in the basic or economic details of trade as in the effects of trade upon society.[27] One of the primary effects is political. For trade promotes liberty. "Men are never so sensible of freedom as in commercial intercourse."[28] To be prosperous, the trader must have freedom, first to come and go within his own country, and then in the host country to examine the markets and to arrange the best sale of his goods. He must be without restraints. In this way free trade invigorates the political make-up of a society and serves the cause of liberty. The natural liberty of man must be exercised in civil and political societies. No man must be dependent upon a religious or civil authority for his freedom, and the trader's need of freedom shows this.[29] From the same line of argument, he declares that trade promotes the cause of peace. Since war disrupts the flow of trade and decreases a nation's prosperity, it is to the commercial advantage of the nations that they refrain from war.[30]

Trade brings social benefits because it keeps peoples in contact with one another and softens prejudices about one's own culture. The growth of toleration shows up specifically in the area of religion. Raynal attributes the decline of superstition and the role of Christianity on society to the commercial contact of Europe with other societies. Throughout the eighteenth century, many intellectuals had pointed to China as a counter example for the organizing of society without a system of superstition or privilege. Here Raynal was following the lead of Voltaire and Leibniz among others.[31] He remarks how the Chinese do not have a cultic priesthood which imposes an irrational creed. For a code of conduct, the Chinese have only guidelines of the reasonable Confucius, which can be summed up in the aphorism, "Do unto others." One of the most attractive features of this society for Raynal and others is the rule by a meritocracy; and the meritocracy achieves its position

---

26. *History*, 3: 221, 234.

27. The contrast with the article on commerce for the *Encyclopedia* is remarkable. There, Forbonnais, a physiocrat, is concerned with government regulation of trade, with the relationship between trade and agriculture and the questions about the impact of trade upon population growth. "Commerce," *Encyclopedia*, translated from the French by Nelly Hoyt and Thomas Cassirer (New York: Bobbs-Merril, 1965), 46-88.

28. *History*, 3: 188.

29. *History*, 3: 189, 191, 220; 4: 195.

30. *History*, 3: 239.

31. *History*, 8: 367. See Voltaire's *Philosophical Dictionary*, "Chinese Catechism," or the articles by Donald Lach, "Leibniz and China," *Journal of the History of Ideas*, 6,4 (Oct. 1945): 436-55, or his "The Sinophilism of Christian Wolff (1679-1754)," *JHI*, 14, 1 (Oct. 1953): 561-74.

through education.[32] In making these observations about China, Raynal is in effect passing judgement upon his contemporary France and showing up its weaknesses by unfavorable contrast with the Chinese.

Another benefit of foreign trade stems from its stimulation of the domestic economy. Trade makes work for those at home: ships have to be built, ports developed, and guns cast. Items for trade have to be manufactured such as cloth, brandy and products of luxury.[33] Holland provides the best example for the Abbé of how the overseas trade has improved the domestic scene, and as a result the Dutch economy is well integrated.[34] Yet caution is needed since Portugal was ruined by her commercial enterprise.

The Portuguese decline occurred because too many of her people went abroad and not enough stayed home to develop the domestic supports of a thriving trade. Thus the Abbé warns that a nation must have a sufficient agricultural base, and only then can it begin to manufacture items for trade.[35] If the economy is prosperous, the population will be supported, and a large population increases the wealth of the country.[36]

Trade also benefits society in other ways, for it stimulates new scientific discoveries and tools. The astrolabe and compass and the contribution of Prince Henry's School of navigation would be important examples of the indirect benefits to mankind. In reflecting on these advantages he remarks rather prosaically: "Trade has improved the construction of ships, navigation, geography, astronomy, medicine, natural history, and some other forms of knowledge, and these advantages have not been attended with any known inconvenience."[37]

Trade not only benefits society as a whole, but also calls forth the best of human resources from individuals. From this perspective the trader becomes for his society a kind of ideal figure who displays the best qualities of that society and evokes them in other members. He functions somewhat like the knight for feudal society and the landed aristocrat for a privileged one. Among the virtues of the trader are industriousness, thrift, honesty, and ingenuity.

Raynal gives counsel to the trader. He calls upon him to be honest in consideration of the larger picture.[38] The trader himself may not be directly harmed by a petty crime of deception, but the good name of merchants and the whole network of exchanges will be damaged. Moreover, there is the brotherhood of man to be considered, and one would not deceive one's

---

32. *History*, 1: 156-70.
33. *History*, 8: 179, 180, 189.
34. *History*, 1: 390.
35. *History*, 1: 224.
36. *History*, 1: 224; 3: 192.
37. *History*, 8: 367.
38. *History*, 8: 190.

brother. He even goes so far as to say that the trader should take a loss rather than be deceitful. Riches are to take a backseat to honor. He further calls upon the trader to be generous with alms as an antidote to the intoxication of gold.

At one point the Abbé becomes positively rhapsodic about the talents necessary for the trader. He must be more innovative than a Newton or a Galileo. They have merely discovered the laws of a static universe, whereas the trader must observe and master the laws of men–and these are infinitely more diverse. He must be attentive to the fluctuations of the market, know when men will buy and sell, be aware of how the climate has affected the crops, have information about which shipping lanes are open or closed by natural disaster or by war. With the simple stroke of the pen, the trader can affect events in the four corners of the world. Seen in this light, he is as powerful as a monarch and needs the genius of a Newton to master all of the complexities just to turn a profit.[39]

Thus Raynal sees many benefits which trade brings to society. Yet more than that, he considers trade to be the mainspring of civilization. It is a prime mover in advancing a society from barbarism to civilization. As an example, he reminds the reader that it has been primarily trade which has propelled European society from the age of darkness into the age of light, from superstition and privilege to reason and cultivation.[40] And the converse is true for him, that is, without trade people are barbarians. In this vein he observes that Sparta and Egypt, two societies without extensive trade, did not make any notable contributions to mankind.[41] So trade develops mankind. "By nature all the continents are not self-contained. They can and have survived apart from each other, but they can be improved by a sharing and a developing of the world."[42] He asks the reader to imagine all the ships of the world as they cross the several seas. "They are stitching the world together. Like flying bridges in a thousand channels, they help mankind come together and further the brotherhood of man."[43] With great satisfaction he sums up how the deity must observe this scene with contentment.

The Third Edition of *The History*: The Negative Effects of Trade

All of these positive features about trade are in Raynal's second edition of *The History*. They are retained in the third. Indeed, at the beginning of the third, Raynal again uses his imagination. He invites the reader to ascend with

39. *History*, 8: 190-98.
40. *History*, 8: 369.
41. *History*, 8: 36.
42. *History*, 1: 190.
43. *History*, 8: 189.

him above the clouds to a point from which they can observe all of Europe at one glance. He then asks the reader some questions about the progress of Europe–who has dug these canals, built these cities, clothed and civilized these peoples? And the answer of all enlightened men, he graciously tells the reader, can only be commerce.[44]

As optimistic as this sounds, it is deceptive because in this edition Raynal describes what are for him more powerful negative effects of trade. Though it benefits society and has become its very mainspring, it also brings about its corruption and eventual dissolution. For those engaged in trade lose their loyalties, become avaricious, indulge in indolence, and increasingly promote and live off slavery.

A major disadvantage for traders is that they become rootless. Those who spend so much time at sea do not have the opportunity to develop loyalty to one nation, and that is the immediate loss of the nation's industrious citizens, nor time to raise a family, and so promote the population and ultimately the wealth of the nation. "If celibacy is bad for society, then these men have increased its ranks, for they do not develop family ties, cultivate the nation, or establish a progeny for the country. They are a new species of 'anomalous savage'."[45] When men leave their native societies, they become a law unto themselves. One has seen the results of such a law in colonizations and avarice. The sentiments of humanity grow weaker the more distant one is from his native land.[46]

Trade with Asia and the Americas has led to avarice, and he shows how this is true for each of the empires. Both the Spanish and the Portuguese abandoned their native lands and allowed them to become unproductive as their peoples have run off in search of the shiny metals. They have despoiled their own lands while despoiling the natives of what was rightfully theirs.[47] In Portugal he observes an increased separation of the classes, while conceding that the Portuguese may have had some excuse. After all, they were without an example to follow, since at the beginning of the sixteenth century the experience of this kind of trade and colonization was a new one for all of Europe.[48] However, the Spanish have wasted so much of their enormous wealth from the mines of Peru and Mexico that they now are poorer than when they began their colonies.[49] In the peroration to the Dutch, he castigates them for having lost their original spirit of common sacrifice and the building

44. *History*, 1: 3.

45. *History*, 8: 370. Another theme is that frequently the colonists are those who are unfit for labor at home. 5: 3.

46. *History*, 4: 359.

47. *History*, 8: 368.

48. *History*, 1: 223.

49. *History*, 3: 200; 4: 195.

of a common nation. There was a time, he reminds them, when they could boldly say to any enemy, "If you invade us, we will open the dikes and destroy both of us." Now, however, they no longer have that kind of courage because they are afraid of destroying the wealth which they have accumulated from their colonies and their commerce. Their attachment to gold now replaces their attachment to that liberty which has made them great. "Opulence lulls your lethargy, and you prepare chains for your posterity... Enervated by your riches, you will not have the courage to defend them."[50] In closing the section on North America, he offers some general advice about avarice to the thirteen colonies. "Dread the influence of gold for with luxury comes corruption and a contempt of the law." He further counsels the newly formed confederation to dread the unequal distribution of wealth.[51] Certainly this is odd advice for one who favored trade, as in the second edition.

The European trade with Asia and the Americas led the nations of Europe to impose their domination upon these areas. Without any consultation, they have claimed these areas as their own territories and treated them as a part of their own lands. Even more, they have subjected the native population to their own will and made them dependent upon the mother country. Quite simply, to take the land is theft, and to deprive its people of their liberty constitutes despotism.[52] At this point, Raynal invites the various colonizing nations to "judge for themselves what name they deserve. They are like a beast if they have made a slave of others. They are strangers to any idea of equity."[53] So, for example, he reminds the Dutch about their colonial operations. "You have landed among the Hottentots, not to better them but to deprive them of liberty and to force their labor." He puts the argument in the mouth of a native chieftain. "On what grounds or what pretense do you sow our lands? How would you behave if we did the same to you?"[54]

To speak of avarice affords him the opportunity to attack slavery. This practice is immoral, says Raynal, because it deprives a person of freedom and dignity,[55] adding, as an eighteenth-century psychologist, that it degrades the master as much as the slave.[56] He further points out the hypocrisy which he

---

50. *History*, 7: 563.

51. *History*, 4: 195.

52. *History*, 4: 192.

53. *History*, 4: 195. Along this line, he asks by what right have the French transferred the Louisiana territories to the Spanish. The citizens of France of that colony were not consulted, and this is despotism (7: 66).

54. *History*, 3: 313.

55. *History*, 5: 304. "Let us hasten then to substitute the light of reason and the sentiments of nature for the blind ferociousness of our ancestors. Let us break the bonds of so many victims to our mercenary principles. We should be obliged to give up a commerce which is founded only upon injustice and the object of which is luxury." (304)

56. *History*, 8: 371.

found among many intellectuals of his own day. While they railed against the abuses of serfdom, they have been slow to attack those of slavery which was before their eyes. He surmises that it strikes too close to home and may affect their attachment to luxuries. One of the curious things about the treatment of slavery in this edition is how he attributes a different form and use of slavery to each of the different European nations. So the Portuguese use it as an instrument of debauchery, the Spanish as a companion of indolence. The Dutch are victims of their own avarice. The English treat their slaves as some lower form of animal nature and do not speak directly to them nor look at them directly. The French, on the other hand, are merely haughty toward their slaves. He then underlines how neither the Catholic nor Protestant religion has done very much for the slaves themselves or for the abolition of the system.

Raynal knows the arguments which are used to continue slavery–that it is the right of the stronger, that it has always been a part of human society, that some men are born for slavery and some to be masters, that slaves are the legitimate booty of war. He counters each of these propositions with the more basic rights of liberty and dignity. There is no way in which an individual or a nation can deprive anyone of those rights.[57] He then makes a rather elliptical remark about a future black Spartacus arising in the West Indies, a remark of which Toussaint L'Ouverture was rather fond.[58]

He concludes the section on slavery with some practical suggestions on how to eliminate it. Among them he includes the idea of compensation by the government. Yet another possibility would call for the slaves' continued labor on the plantations or in the mines for a period of five years with pay. This would allow for the necessary adjustments of the economy to be worked out.

Just from the economic point of view, the colonies have not paid off. They have simply led to greater and more expensive commitments. They burden the mother country with increased military expenditures for soldiers and forts. Moreover, a strong navy is needed to protect the ships and the colonies and to prevent them from trading with other countries. At the same time, they require an expensive administration and network of communication. He says that of all the colonies, perhaps only Bengal and the Sugar Islands of the West Indies have repaid the initial investments.[59] Even a Mandeville could understand an argument against the colonial enterprises presented on such terms.

In the overall picture, the destruction which trade brings far outweighs the benefits. Furthermore, the European contact with the native populations had

---

57. For the section on slavery, see *History*, 5: 267-304.

58. David Brian Davis, *The Problem of Slavery in the Age of Revolution* (Ithaca: Cornell Univ. Press, 1975), 108.

59. *History*, 1: 224; 3: 214.

poisoned those peoples. Writing of the effect of empire in India, he states: "We have carried our discord to all parts of the world, our rapaciousness has inspired them with hatred, fear, contempt, and they look upon us as conquerors, usurpers, and oppressors. Our example has increased national vices."[60] The recent history of man's inhumanity to man has resulted from trade, and in this sense, trade has even replaced religion as the bane of the human community.[61] Avarice and domination have superseded superstition and dogmatism.

In the third edition, the Abbé has drawn a dialectic, though not an explicit one. Trade does develop society. It is even the mainspring of civilization. But within its wake it seems to bring about the destruction of the society which it has helped to create. Evidently, this became obvious to Raynal only with the writing of the third edition, for it is only here that he sharpens the negative features of trade sufficiently to speak of a dialectic. He resolves the tension between the creative and destructive forces of trade by introducing a cycle or a pattern.

Throughout the work, Raynal reminds the reader that, like a haunting melody, there is a pattern that recurs in all human affairs. He observed it in the arts. A certain level of perfection is achieved, say in the writing of drama, and then one may expect only inferior works.[62] He sees it demonstrated by history. "All nations follow a regular cycle of misfortune and prosperity, of liberty and slavery, of morals and corruption, of knowledge and ignorance, of splendor and weakness. The law of nature requires that all societies should gravitate to despotism and dissolution, that empires arise and be annihilated, and this law will not be suspended for any one of them."[63] As surely as the Roman Empire collapsed, so will the British Empire fall into ruin someday.[64] Even in the short span of 300 years treated in *The History*, he has narrated the rise and fall of two such empires, the Spanish and the Portuguese–and the Dutch are without vitality. From this perspective he calmly draws out the conclusion. "As each society is destined to move from barbarism to civilization, so each civilization moves towards barbarism."[65]

In writing of the cycle he uses several images. One is of the individual lifespan. As a person grows from birth to vigor to senescence and finally death, so is the pattern of empires and nations. "Ye nations, what are you in the hands of nature but the sport of her laws. You are dust in motion and the

60. *History*, 3: 217.
61. *History*, 8: 358.
62. *History*, 8: 317.
63. *History*, 8: 20.
64. *History*, 8: 368.
65. *History*, 8: 18. In his *Diderot: de l'athéisme à l'anticolonialisme* (Paris: Maspero, 1970), Yves Benot writes of Diderot's "oscillation between the advantages and disadvantages of trade," (180). I think it is more correct to speak of a dialectic.

motion will reduce your achievements to death."[66] Another image is that of the sea. The pattern of the waves builds up gradually to break upon the shore, and then slowly ebb away to gather momentum for the next assault. So he pictures the rise and fall and rise again of nations and empires.[67]

Certainly Raynal is not alone among eighteenth-century intellectuals to perceive a cycle in human events. Gibbon observes one in writing about ancient Rome, while among the French, Montesquieu, Voltaire and Turgot all refer to patterns in history.[68] Raynal may be singled out, however, in making the connection between the cycle and trade. For trade becomes the mainspring or the motor of the cycle itself–at least insofar as the cycle is shown to be affecting eighteenth-century Europe.[69] He understands the civilization of his day as created in large measure by trade and at the same time in an even larger measure as corrupted by trade.

From the preceding analysis, one may appreciate Raynal's position within the eighteenth-century debates about trade and its impact upon society. One may see how he takes an increasingly moralistic and pessimistic view of trade. In the first two editions, he has underlined how it promotes freedom, contributes to the domestic economy, and stimulates scientific knowledge and accompanying tools. All of these are present in the second edition, but in the following one there is a development of the negative features–the increased attention to colonization, to slavery, and to avarice, and the introduction of the resolution of these two opposite tendencies into a fatalistic cycle. One may say that Raynal knows the advantages of trade just as Mandeville and his disciples do, but is increasingly conscious of the debilitating, even fatal consequences, and thus he lines up more and more with a Rousseauan perspective. One is tempted to ascribe the evolution of his thought to particular political events of these years, 1774-1780, e.g. the fall of Turgot, or the great increase of national debt due to the American wars. Perhaps, though, the evolution of this

---

66. *History*, 8: 311.

67. *History*, 4: 138.

68. See Henry Vyverberg, *Historical Pessimism in the French Enlightenment* (Cambridge, Mass.: Harvard Univ. Press, 1958), 99-155, for a discussion of different theories of decline and rise of empires. Turgot saw progress accumulating from the various declines; see Ronald Meek, *Social Science and Ignoble Savage* (Cambridge: Cambridge Univ. Press, 1976), 71-76.

69. I hesitate to say that he makes trade into the universal corrupter of society. It is clear that trade has brought about the ruin of his society, but he does not spend enough time on other societies and their decline to say that trade always and inevitably brings society to ruin. When speaking of the advantages of trade, he speaks more generically, so that one may say that, for the Abbé, trade always does develop society. In the above-cited work, Meek notes that in the 1750s there emerged a fourfold universal development of societies, that each society goes through four stages to arrive at advanced development: hunter, herdsman, farmer, trader. This is not explicit in the work of Raynal, however.

thought was the simple fruit of his continued meditation upon the history which he had recorded.

Raynal, Paine et la Révolution américaine

Claude Fohlen

S'il est un ouvrage qui connut un grand succès dans les années qui précédèrent la Révolution, c'est bien l'*Histoire philosophique et politique des Etablissemens et du Commerce des Européens dans les deux Indes*, de l'abbé Raynal.

> Son nom, associé à celui des Voltaire, des Rousseau, des Montesquieu, fut un moment sur toutes les bouches, et son *Histoire philosophique*, le seul de ses livres qui ne soit pas oublié aujourd'hui, était alors dans toutes les mains; mais le temps, qui emporte les fausses renommés, n'a pas fait grâce à la gloire usurpée de l'abbé Raynal. L'*Histoire philosophique* a depuis longtemps cessé d'être lue: elle n'est plus consultée que comme dictionnaire.[1]

Quel que soit l'oubli dans lequel est tombé Raynal depuis plus d'un siècle, l'intérêt essentiel de son oeuvre est qu'elle est contemporaine de la Révolution américaine et que cet apôtre de l'anti-colonialisme a vécu, de loin et en simple spectateur, la cause à laquelle il s'était voué. Entre la première édition de l'*Histoire philosophique*, parue en 1770, et l'édition "définitive", en 1780, les Etats-Unis sont nés. Chance unique pour l'historien, d'autant plus précieuse que la parution de l'édition de 1781 entraîna une réplique violente du plus célèbre pamphlétaire du temps, Tom Paine.

Il est utile de situer d'abord l'*Histoire philosophique* dans l'existence de Raynal. Né en 1711, à Lapanouse, dans le Rouergue, élevé chez les Jésuites, il se destina à la prêtrise, exerça d'abord à Pézenas, dont il semble avoir épuisé assez vite les charmes, avant de "monter" à Paris en 1747 et d'être attaché à la paroisse de Saint-Sulpice. C'est alors que débute vraiment sa vie

---

1. Joseph-François Michaud, *Bibliographie universelle ancienne et moderne*, art. Raynal, 45 vols. (Paris-Leipzig, 1843), 35: 260.

active. Pauvre, il entreprit de se faire quelques ressources en prêchant, mais fut gêné par un accent méridional qui ne le quitta jamais. "Jé né prèchais pas mal", disait-il, "mais j'avais un assent dé tous les diables". Il gagna quelque argent en administrant les sacrements à des protestants, ce qui lui valut d'être chassé de Saint-Sulpice. Grâce à des appuis, car il était intrigant et avait un sens développé des relations personnelles et de ses intérêts particuliers, il devint rédacteur au Mercure de France.

Commence alors une carrière littéraire, marquée par la publication d'une longue série de titres: *Histoire du Stathoudérat* (1748), *Mémorial de Paris*, de l'abbé Antonini, augmenté (1749), *Anecdotes littéraires* (1750), *Anecdotes historiques, militaires et politiques de l'Europe* (1753), reprises en 1762 sous le titre *Mémoires politiques de l'Europe*, sans parler de nombreux ouvrages mineurs ou extraits des précédents sous une présentation différente. En 1770, paraissent à Amsterdam les quatre volumes de l'*Histoire philosophique et politique...*, sans nom d'auteur. Cette somme, dont l'attribution à Raynal ne fit pas de doute alors, assura, à tort ou à raison, sa célébrité. Plusieurs éditions, toujours anonymes, parurent dans les années suivantes, d'abord en six, puis en sept volumes, avant l'édition, dite Pellet, cette fois avec nom d'auteur et portrait, publiée à Genève en 1781, sous deux formes différentes, l'une en dix volumes in-8°, l'autre en quatre in-4°. Le flot des éditions continua dans les années suivantes, au point qu'Anatole Feugère, auteur d'une thèse sur Raynal,[2] en mentionne trente "officielles" entre 1770 et 1787, et estime à 70 le nombre total d'éditions en y incluant les éditions "pirates", plus nombreuses que les autres.

Au nombre de ces éditions "pirates" figure un ouvrage, *Révolution de l'Amérique*, qui est, en réalité, la reproduction du livre 18 (et parfois du livre 17) de l'*Histoire philosophique...* consacré aux colonies britanniques d'Amérique du Nord. Plusieurs versions en furent publiées en 1781, simultanément à Londres, Dublin, La Haye, Philadelphie et Amsterdam.[3] Il semble bien qu'un éditeur anglais ait eu vent–comment?–de la nouvelle version de ces chapitres et ait voulu en profiter pour s'enrichir. On lit, en tête de l'édition de Londres, dans un Avertissement de l'Editeur:

> L'*Histoire philosophique...* par M. l'abbé Raynal, est certainement un des plus beaux ouvrages ayant paru depuis la renaissance des lettres, est peut-

2. Anatole Feugère, *Un précurseur de la Révolution, l'abbé Raynal (1713-1796); documents inédits* (Angoulême: Imprimerie ouvrière, 1922).

3. L'édition d'Amsterdam, "chez la compagnie des Libraires, 1781" porte le titre de *Tableau et Révolution des Colonies Angloises dans l'Amérique septentrionale*, par Guillaume-Thomas Raynal, et comprend deux volumes, de 173 et 170 p. Ils reprennent les livres 17 et 18 de l'*Histoire philosophique...*, tandis que les autres se limitent en général au livre 18, considéré, à tort, comme le seul consacré à l'Amérique du Nord.

> être le plus instructif de ceux que nous connoissons. C'est une production dont on n'avoit point de modèle; et qui pourroit bien en servir un jour. Le public souhaitoit avec impatience ce Supplément attendu depuis si longtemps, qui devait traiter des démêlés de la Grande-Bretagne et de ses colonies.
>
> L'Editeur, dans le cours de ses voyages, a eu le singulier bonheur de se procurer une copie de cet excellent Traité, qui n'a pas encore paru dans l'étranger. Il se flatte que l'illustre historien aura quelque indulgence pour un homme, qu'aucune considération n'auroit pu engager à donner, sans son aveu, cet écrit au public, s'il n'eût été intimement persuadé que les raisonnements solides dont il est rempli, pourront, dans ce moment de crise, être de quelque service à cette patrie qu'il aime et chérit avec une ardeur, qui ne le cède qu'à cette flamme d'un ordre supérieur, dont brûle l'écrivain philanthrope, pour la liberté et pour le bonheur de toutes les nations de la terre. L'éditeur ne donne pas seulement ce brillant morceau tel qu'il a été composé en Français; il en publie aussi la traduction en Anglais...[4]

Cette édition de Londres fut ensuite reproduite à Philadelphie, comme nous l'apprend Thomas Paine:

> On a réimprimé à Philadelphie, et dans d'autres parties du continent, une traduction faite à Londres d'un ouvrage original écrit en français par l'abbé Raynal, dans lequel il traite de la révolution de l'Amérique septentrionale...L'éditeur de Londres a intitulé l'ouvrage qu'il publie *La Révolution de l'Amérique*, par l'abbé Raynal: et les imprimeurs américains ont suivi cet exemple. Mais j'ai pensé, et je ne crois pas m'être trompé dans mes conjectures, que ce morceau, qui seroit mieux intitulé *Réflexions sur la révolution*, avoit été dérobé à l'imprimeur de l'abbé Raynal...[5]

C'est la publication de cette édition américaine qui détermina Thomas Paine à répondre à Raynal dans une longue lettre. Elle constitue, avec le texte qui vient d'être cité et d'autres pièces relatives à la condamnation de l'*Histoire Philosophique...* par le Parlement de Paris, le tome 10 de l'édition de Neuchâtel et Genève, en 1784, sous le titre *Recueil de diverses pièces servant de Supplément à l'Histoire philosophique et politique...*

---

4. *Révolution de l'Amérique*, par M. L'abbé Raynal, Auteur de l'*Histoire Philosophique et Politique des Etablissements et du Commerce des Européens dans les Deux Indes*, Ouvrage qui peut servir de Supplément à la ditte Histoire Philosophique, etc. (Londres: Lockier Davis, Holbourn, 1781).

5. Voir *The Writings of Thomas Paine*, collected and edited by Moncure Daniel Conway, 4 vols. (New York: Putnam, 1894), 2:67-131.

Telles sont quelques-unes des péripéties de la publication de cette oeuvre et des réactions qu'elle entraîna. Ainsi se confirme, en tout cas, l'écho que rencontra chez les contemporains, en France et ailleurs, un ouvrage considéré comme révolutionnaire en son temps. Etait-il réellement révolutionnaire en ce qui concerne l'Amérique? Et pourquoi Paine a-t-il réagi si vivement?

L'Amérique dans les livres 17 et 18 de l'*Histoire philosophique*

Il est bon de commencer par donner quelques informations sur la place de l'Amérique dans la composition de l'ouvrage. Dans toutes les éditions, elle en forme les volumes 17 et 18. Pour des raisons inconnues, Raynal a, en effet, divisé les colonies britanniques en deux tranches. Ainsi le livre 17 s'intitule "Colonies anglaises de la Baie d'Hudson, du Canada, de l'Ile Saint-Jean, de Terre Neuve, de la Nouvelle Ecosse, de la Nouvelle Angleterre, de la Nouvelle-York, de la Nouvelle Jersey", alors que le livre 18 a pour titre: "Colonies anglaises fondées dans la Pennsylvanie, dans le Maryland, dans la Virginie, dans les Carolines, dans la Géorgie et dans la Floride. Considérations sur tous ces établissements".

On aurait pu s'attendre, en raison de l'hostilité viscérale de Raynal à l'esclavage, à une distinction entre les colonies esclavagistes et les autres. Pas du tout, puisque la Pennsylvanie, la plus hostile à l'esclavage car dominée par les Quakers, figure dans le second groupe. On aurait pu s'attendre à une distinction entre colonies françaises d'Amérique du Nord, qui figurent dans les livres 15 et 16, et colonies anglaises. Pas du tout, car il est également question des Français du Canada dans le livre 17. On aurait surtout pu s'attendre à une nouvelle distribution à la suite de la Révolution américaine. Or rien n'avait changé sur ce point. Raynal n'a pas modifé son plan, si bien que les Etats-Unis, écartelés entre les livres 17 et 18, ne sont jamais présentés dans leur ensemble. L'ouvrage est, on le sait depuis longtemps, une compilation hâtive et brouillonne dont Raynal escomptait de grands profits pour rémunérer ses collaborateurs anonymes.

Il existe cependant de grandes différences entre l'édition originale de 1770 et les éditions postérieures à 1780, en particulier l'édition Pellet, à laquelle se réfèrent en général les érudits. Dans l'édition de 1770, les diverses parties sont présentées "en vrac", sans subdivisions, dans un désordre apparent qui en rend l'utilisation fastidieuse. Dans les éditions plus récentes apparaissent des mentions marginales qui correspondent à des chapitres.

Les chapitres sur l'Amérique sont plus étoffés dans les éditions les plus récentes, avec des informations statistiques qui ont été renouvelées et souvent des passages entiers insérés entre des paragraphes anciens simplement reproduits. Il y a eu, de la part de ou des auteurs un effort sérieux d'actualisation, portant en particulier sur les chapitres 1 à 37 du livre 18.

La nouveauté essentielle est, bien sûr, l'adjonction de quinze nouveaux chapitres au livre 18, tous consacrés à la Révolution américaine: chapitres 38 à 45, rupture avec l'Angleterre; 46 à 51, opérations militaires; 52, quelle idée il faut se former des 13 provinces confédérées. Ces quinze nouveaux chapitres représentent, en volume, un apport nouveau d'environ 60% pour l'ensemble du livre 18. C'est dire que chacun d'entre eux est plus fourni que ceux de la version de 1770, et que leur texte est original, à l'exception du quinzième qui incorpore une péroraison déjà présente dans l'édition de 1770. Même là, l'auteur a fait, en quelque sorte, du rapetassage.

Au-delà de ces questions de forme, qui sont essentielles pour comprendre l'économie de l'oeuvre, que trouve-t-on pour le fond? D'abord, une véritable encyclopédie sur les colonies américaines: description de chacune d'entre elles, avec son cadre physique, sa population, sa composition religieuse, ses productions, le tout accompagné de statistiques pour lesquelles Raynal semble avoir un penchant presque maniaque. Puis un tableau de la flore, de la faune, des plantes exploitées, des moeurs, de la monnaie, du commerce et de l'industrie. Raynal a compilé une documentation considérable et très précise, qui le range davantage du côté des économistes comme Boulainvilliers ou des naturalistes comme Buffon que des philosophes. Ce faisant, il répondait à la curiosité des lecteurs de son temps, qui ont beaucoup apprécié ce côté encyclopédique. Dans les chapitres nouveaux de l'édition de 1780, deux traits frappent le lecteur. D'une part, Raynal demeure au ras des faits, aussi bien dans l'examen des causes de la révolution que dans la relation des événements militaires. De l'autre, il s'arrête en 1778, au moment de l'alliance française, comme si cet événement marquait pour lui le terme d'une époque.

En même temps, il ne peut s'empêcher de se laisser aller à son penchant naturel pour la rhétorique et de pourfendre ses trois bêtes noires, l'esclavage, la religion et le despotisme. Pour l'esclavage, la condamnation la plus sévère avait été exprimée dans les livres précédents, concernant les Antilles: "L'Espagnol en [des esclaves] fait les compagnons de son indolence; les Portugais les instruments de leur débauche; les Hollandais les victimes de leur avarice; les Anglais les regardent comme un bétail humain... Aux yeux de l'Anglais, ce sont des êtres purement physiques, qu'il ne faut pas user ou détruire sans nécessité; mais jamais il ne se familiarise avec eux, jamais il ne leur sourit, jamais il ne leur parle."[6] Dans le livre 18, il s'en prend particulièrement à la pratique des engagés ou travailleurs sous contrat. "Embarqués sans être en état de payer leur passage, ces malheureux sont à la disposition de leur conducteur, qui les vend à qui bon lui semble. Cette espèce d'esclavage est plus ou moins long, mais il ne peut jamais durer plus

6. Raynal, *Histoire philosophique...*, livre 11, ch. 25.

de huit années..."[7] Et de rappeler l'inscription que Dante avait gravée à la porte de l'enfer: "Voi ch'entrate, lasciate ormai ogni speranza".[8]

La religion fait l'objet d'un chapitre entier, le septième du livre 17, consacré au fanatisme en Nouvelle-Angleterre, avec l'exemple, longuement développé, des sorcières de Salem, une occasion inespérée pour Raynal de se laisser aller à ses penchants anti-religieux, et de nombreuses mentions ailleurs. Le livre 18 s'ouvre sur un long passage sur les anabaptistes, suivi, à propos de la Pennsylvanie, d'un développement sur la religion des Quakers, qui, eux, ne sont guère portés vers le fanatisme. A part les sorcières de Salem, qui appartiennent au XVIIe siècle, les colonies américaines ne confortent guère les positions de Raynal, très sensible à l'importance du phénomène religieux dans les colonies britanniques.

Pour ce qui est du despotisme, l'étude des origines de la révolution lui fournit facilement l'exemple de la tyrannie de Londres, opposée à la simplicité des Américains. C'est l'occasion d'une belle envolée rhétorique:

> C'est la vile ambition de commander qui prête son bras au despotisme et consent à être esclave pour dominer (*sic*), à livrer un peuple pour partager ses dépouilles, à renoncer à l'honneur pour obtenir des honneurs et des titres...Tous ces vices, fruits d'une société opulente et voluptueuse, d'une société vieillie et parvenue à son dernier terme, n'appartiennent point à des peuples agriculteurs et nouveaux. Les Américains demeurèrent unis. L'exécution d'un bill (fermeture du port de Boston, 1774) qu'ils appelaient inhumain, barbare et meurtrier ne fit que les affermir dans la résolution de soutenir leurs droits avec plus d'accord et de constance.[9]

La Révolution américaine justifie la haine de Raynal contre le despotisme et, étrange coïncidence, il trouve cette fois un étrange allié en la personne des ministres du culte.

> C'était sans doute un spectacle intéressant pour la philosophie de voir que dans les temples, aux pieds des autels, où tant de fois la superstition a béni les chaînes des peuples, où tant de fois les prêtres ont flatté les tyrans, la liberté élevait sa voix pour défendre les privilèges d'une nation opprimée.

---

7. Raynal, *Histoire philosophique...*, Livre 18, ch. 32.
8. Citation incorrecte, car Dante avait écrit (*Inferno*, III, 9): "Lasciate ogni speranza voi ch'entrate".
9. Raynal, *Histoire philosophique*, livre 18, ch. 41.

La religion, au service de la liberté, voici ce que Raynal découvre dans la Révolution américaine, qui bouscule ses idées sur l'origine des révolutions. C'est le noeud même du conflit qui l'oppose à Paine.

La réplique de Paine

Ce dernier lui répliqua vertement dans une longue *Lettre adressée à l'abbé Raynal sur les Affaires de l'Amérique septentrionale, où l'on relève les erreurs dans lesquelles cet auteur est tombé en rendant compte de la révolution de l'Amérique*[10] qui, on l'a vu, fut incorporée dans les dernières éditions de l'*Histoire philosophique....* Les critiques de Paine portent à la fois sur la méthode et sur le fond, car Raynal s'est souvent trompé dans l'exposé des faits et dans l'interprétation de leurs causes et des principes qui les produisirent.

Paine reproche d'abord à l'abbé de l'avoir plagié, en insérant des passages de son *Sens commun*, sans jamais le citer. Il en donne de nombreux exemples, entre autres la distinction entre la société et le gouvernement, par laquelle commence sa brochure. Là, Paine, sans le savoir, se trouvait en excellente compagnie, puisque Raynal avait véritablement pillé ses contemporains sans jamais les citer. Il lui reproche aussi de se laisser aller à des digressions sans rapports avec le sujet.

> Dans la plupart de ses ouvrages, l'abbé Raynal...me paroit s'écarter trop souvent de son sujet; il les surcharge d'une inutile variété: on peut les comparer à quelque paysage agréable et désert, au travers duquel on n'a pratiquement aucune route; tous les obstacles flattent également la vue, aucun ne la fixe et ne l'attire; on s'y plaît, on aime à s'y égarer, mais il est difficile d'en trouver l'issue.[11]

Ce disant, Paine ne fait que traduire l'impression générale des lecteurs de Raynal.

Mais il va plus loin, lorsqu'il lui reproche de ne pas établir les faits d'une façon scrupuleuse et de négliger ainsi un des devoirs essentiels de l'historien.

> Il établit les faits avec froideur et négligence, sans instruction, sans intérêt pour le lecteur; beaucoup sont erronés; beaucoup sont obscurs et défectueux... Il précipite sa narration en homme qui brûle d'être

10. Thomas Paine, *Letter Addressed to the Abbé Raynal on the affairs of North America* (Philadelphia, 1791), Traductions de l'anglais publiées à Amsterdam et à Bruxelles, 1783.

11. *Lettre sur les affaires...*, 3.

> débarrassé d'une tâche fastidieuse; on sent qu'il lui tarde de s'exercer dans le champ plus vaste de l'éloquence et de l'imagination.[12]

Cette critique rejoint la précédente: Raynal est plus à l'aise dans le discours et les généralités que dans l'exposé méticuleux des faits. Pour Paine, qui a vécu cette révolution, qui y a participé, c'est une déficience majeure.

Les critiques factuelles portent d'une part sur l'interprétation de la révolution, de l'autre sur un certain nombre de points précis. D'après Raynal, les ingrédients caractéristiques ne se trouvaient pas réunis en Amérique pour l'éclosion d'une révolution.

> De toutes les causes énergétiques qui produisoient tant de révolutions sur le globe, aucune n'existoit dans le Nord de l'Amérique. Ni la religion ni les loix n'y avoient été outragées, le sang des martyrs ou des citoyens n'y avoit pas ruisselé sur les échafauds. On n'y avoit pas insulté aux moeurs... Tout se réduisoit à savoir si la métropole avoit ou n'avoit pas le droit de mettre directement ou indirectement un léger impôt sur les colonies.

Anathème, pense Paine, qui se déchaîne contre ce passage, en dénonçant les inexactitudes de l'auteur. Le sang n'avait pas coulé? Et le massacre de Boston en 1770 qui avait fait trois morts et deux blessés?[13] Ce que reproche surtout Paine, c'est d'être infidèle à la chronologie: Raynal se place dans les conditions de 1763-1764, où effectivement les dissentiments avec Londres se réduisaient à des questions de taxation, et non pas en 1770-1774, lorsque les conditions s'étaient complètement modifiées et étaient devenues favorables à l'éclatement d'une révolution. Il s'agit de la causalité en histoire, et là Paine marque certainement un point. Raynal a rapetassé les développements sur l'Amérique du Nord, selon une méthode qui lui était chère, sans reprendre en profondeur les choses.

Les critiques ponctuelles portent sur des aspects très divers. D'abord, sur les événements militaires, en particulier sur les batailles de Trenton et Princeton (1776-1777), auxquelles Paine consacre de longs développements, en critiquant la façon dont Raynal les avait présentées et minimisées. Pour Paine, c'est un moment essentiel de la lutte, une preuve de la ténacité et du génie stratégique des Américains et de Washington. Son patriotisme a visiblement été blessé par la façon cavalière dont le sujet a été traité et esquivé. Une autre critique porte sur la façon quelque peu dédaigneuse dont Raynal présente l'émission de papier-monnaie et ses effets sur la vie des Américains. Discussion technique sur laquelle il n'y a pas lieu de s'attarder,

---

12. *Lettre sur les affaires...*, 26-27.

13. La diatribe est bien résumée dans Bernard Vincent, *Thomas Paine, La religion de la liberté* (Paris: Aubier, 1987), 139-44.

sauf à relever, chez l'un comme chez l'autre, l'importance des facteurs économiques. La critique majeure de Paine porte sur le rôle attribué par Raynal à l'alliance française dans la politique américaine. Ce dernier soutient que le Congrès américain a rejeté les offres de conciliation de lord North du 17 février 1778 parce qu'entre-temps il avait eu connaissance de l'alliance française. Dans une minutieuse démonstration, Paine arrive à la conclusion que le rejet des propositions britanniques est antérieur à l'arrivée de l'annonce de l'alliance française. Question de détail, dira-t-on. Que non pas. Admettre l'interprétation de Raynal eût été sous-estimer le patriotisme américain. Paine a raison: Raynal a péché par inexactitude chronologique, sans se rendre compte des conséquences auprès des Américains.

Allant plus loin, Paine s'en prend à l'interprétation générale de l'alliance franco-américaine donnée par Raynal, d'après qui "le bonheur de l'humanité n'y a point de part".

> Il n'y eut peut-être jamais d'alliance établie sur des fondements plus vastes que celle qui réunit l'Amérique et la France... Alliance non pas conclue par les besoins d'un jour, mais établie sur des fondements plus justes et plus solides. Les deux peuples y trouvoient des avantages égaux; et par la manière ouverte et affectueuse avec laquelle ils ont vécu depuis entr'eux, elle devient non seulement un traité politique entre deux gouvernements, mais encore un lien moral entre les deux nations. A présent, nos armes sont unies comme nos intérêts; et nos coeurs, aussi bien que notre prospérité, demandent la continuation de cette union.[14]

On ne pouvait rendre hommage plus sincère à l'alliance française dans la bouche d'un Américain. Il est dommage que Raynal n'ait pas jugé utile de répondre à son tour à son contradicteur.

La lettre de Paine est le complément indispensable des développements sur la Révolution américaine dans la mesure où elle en révèle les qualités et surtout les défauts. En dépit du titre qu'il a choisi, Raynal n'est pas un historien: les rapports de causalité lui échappent, par manque d'intérêt pour le détail, par défaut d'application à la chronologie, par goût inné des tirades et des idées polémiques. Il excelle, par contre, dans la description politique, géographique, physique et surtout économique de l'Amérique. Il est curieux que cet anti-colonialiste presque professionnel n'ait pas mieux compris la portée des événements auxquels il assistait. On peut invoquer en sa faveur des arguments: d'une part, il ne travailla que par ouï-dire, sans connaissance du terrain, à la différence de ces nombreux voyageurs que fascina le contact physique avec le Nouveau Monde; de l'autre, il termina son ouvrage avant la

---

14. *Lettre sur les affaires...*, 75-77.

confirmation de l'indépendance en 1783, et ne modifia plus son texte. Ainsi l'édition d'Avignon, de 1786, reproduit celle de Genève, antérieure de six ans, sans effort d'actualisation.

A la différence de certains de ses contemporains, comme Crèvecoeur qui avait, lui, une expérience personnelle du pays, il n'a pas entrevu la formation d'une nation américaine:

> On y voit, tantôt réunies, tantôt éparses, des familles des diverses contrées de l'Europe. Ces colons, en quelque endroit que le hasard ou le choix les ait fixés, conservent avec une prédilection indestructible la langue, les préjugés et les habitudes de leur patrie. Des écoles et des églises séparées les empêchent de se confondre avec le peuple hospitalier qui leur ouvrit un refuge. Toujours étrangers à cette nation par le culte, les moeurs et peut-être par les sentiments, ils couvent des germes de dissension qui peuvent un jour causer la ruine et le bouleversement des colonies.[15]

En réalité, il ne croit pas à l'avenir du continent américain:

> On ne détermineroit pas sans témérité quelle pourra être un jour la population des Etats-Unis. Ce calcul, assez généralement difficile, devient impraticable pour une région dont les terres dégénèrent très rapidement, et où la mesure des travaux et des avances n'est pas celle de la reproduction. Si dix millions d'habitans trouvent jamais une subsistance assurée dans ces provinces, ce sera beaucoup...[16]

Il partage les vues pessimistes de Buffon sur la dégénérescence du continent américain.

Raynal ne peut passer pour un précurseur ni des Tocqueville ni des Michel Chevalier, qui ont eu l'intuition de la puissance américaine. Comme nombre de ses contemporains, il demeure un rhéteur qui mérite le jugement de Sainte-Beuve, il "a été moins grand que célèbre".

---

15. Raynal, *Histoire philosophique...*, livre 18, ch. 34.
16. Raynal, *Révolution de l'Amérique*, 190.

L'Amérique: arrêt sur image. Brissot et le *Journal encyclopédique* devant les événements américains entre 1773 et 1793

Jacques Wagner

> On m'a dit la vie au Far-West et les Prairies,
> Et mon sang a gémi: "Que voilà ma patrie!...
> Déclassé du vieux monde, être sans foi ni loi,
> Desperado! Là-bas, là-bas, je serai roi,
> Oh là-bas, m'y scalper de mon cerveau d'Europe!"
> Jules Laforgue[1]

Depuis les recherches de Robert Darnton,[2] la réputation de Brissot a perdu de son éclat. De son temps, il bénéficia pourtant d'un jugement suffisamment favorable pour attirer l'attention fidèle d'une importante revue littéraire du XVIIIe siècle, le *Journal encyclopédique* (*JE*), et en devenir un collaborateur régulier à partir de 1782 mais surtout vers 1786, au moment où les événements américains produisaient en France des effets sensibles sur les intellectuels et les responsables politiques jusqu'à générer un rêve compensatoire: "Bénissons l'Amérique, écrit Madame Roland et pleurons sur les rives du fleuve de Babylone" (lettre de juin 1788).[3] Le rêve de cette "terre promise" (lettre de 1790)[4] hanta longuement et profondément Brissot qui fit des Treize provinces indépendantes une Amérique à la mesure de son "âme de feu", selon une expression de son *Discours sur la traite et l'esclavage des Nègres*, du 29 février 1788. Il joua, pour le *JE*, un rôle d'informateur très actif et, surtout après la mort de P. Rousseau, fondateur de la revue et principal

1. Jules Laforgue, "Albums", *Revue indépendante*, avril 1888.
2. Robert C. Darnton, "The Grub Street Style of Revolution: J.P. Brissot, Police Spy," *Journal of Modern History* 40: 3 (Sept. 1968): 301-27.
3. *Lettres de Madame Roland*, éd. Claude Perroud, 2 vols. (Paris: Imp. Nationale, 1900-02), 2: 17.
4. *Lettres de Madame Roland*, 2: 80.

rédacteur à l'esprit très classique, l'utilisa comme l'organe d'une agitation politique et philosophique, inspirée par le parti orléanais et les "insurgents" américains, et comme un prolongement de la Société gallo-américaine qu'il instituta le 2 janvier 1787. Dès le 27 février, il est en relation épistolaire directe avec le successeur de P. Rousseau, Ch. Weissenbruck, qui promet d'accepter "tous les articles que la Société lui enverra en faveur de l'Amérique libre".[5] Le 27 mars 1787, il pense au *JE* pour insérer la lettre de J. Adams à Mably.[6] Le 29 septembre 1787, il adresse à Weissenbruck une lettre de remerciements pour la "complaisance" du journaliste "à insérer les articles (sur les E.U.A.) qu'il lui envoyait".[7] Brissot avait de bonnes raisons pour exprimer à Weissenbruck sa "vraie reconnaissance". S'il est vrai que le *JE* se montra très vite réceptif aux événements américains (en avril 1777, il examina un *Exposé des droits des colonies britanniques pour justifier le projet de leur indépendance*; en avril 1779, il proposa un *Abrégé de la Révolution de l'Amérique anglaise*), s'il est vrai qu'entre 1780 et 1784, il recensa 20 titres relatifs aux événements américains et 16 entre 1789 et 1793, c'est surtout à partir de 1785 que l'Amérique voit sa présence s'accroître dans le journal: six titres en 1785, six titres plus quatre lettres en 1786, dix titres plus deux lettres en 1787, sept titres et deux lettres en 1788, soit 37 titres en quatre ans avec une pointe en 1787 et un bon niveau en 1788 qui révèlent sans aucun doute l'efficace intervention de Brissot auprès du *JE*. En 1789, l'attention se relâche en raison de la Convocation des Etats généraux à Versailles. Brissot lui-même quitta le plus vite possible les Etats-Unis dès qu'il apprit la nouvelle. En 1791 et 1792, le journal ne présenta plus rien d'intéressant sur l'Amérique, en dehors des *Nouveaux Voyages de Brissot dans les Etats-Unis*, édition revue de l'ouvrage rédigé en 1788 en complément de celui de 1787. En 1793, on a la surprise de trouver onze titres; mais on s'aperçoit que huit titres relèvent du genre traditionnel du voyage ethnologique, géographique ou naturaliste et trois titres seulement, présentant l'édition définitive des Constitutions américaines, renvoient à l'aspect politique.

Dans le *JE*, la période essentielle quantitativement et sémantiquement correspond donc bien à la période d'activités orléanistes et américaines chez Brissot. Il y a conjonction d'intérêt chez l'un et chez l'autre pour l'Amérique. Y a-t-il pour autant identité de vues, d'esprit et de sensibilité entre Brissot et le *JE*?

---

5. Jacques-Pierre Brissot de Warville, *Correspondance et papiers*, éd. Claude Perroud (Paris: Picard, 1912; 1921), 127.

6. *Correspondance*, 133.

7. *Correspondance*, 161.

La première rencontre en 1780: accord et réticence

Brissot entre anonymement dans le *JE* en octobre 1780 (87-97). Ce dernier a repéré, comme l'a fait au même moment *L'Année Littéraire* (*AL*),[8] l'ouvrage provocateur du jeune homme sur l'Angleterre: *Le Testament politique de l'Angleterre*. Sous ce titre, Brissot examinait, avec un esprit et une gaîté reconnus par les deux journaux,[9] la situation politique de l'Europe et surtout présentait, à la lumière de la guerre d'indépendance américaine, les faiblesses du colonialisme ou plutôt l'illégitimité de tout despotisme.

La perception de son ouvrage varie d'une revue à l'autre. L'*AL* n'exprime aucune réticence à la lecture de "cette pièce vraiment originale". Elle y voit un excellent pamphlet écrit par un politique et un penseur dont les vues sont lumineuses, par un ami de la vérité, traçant sans aménagement, sans exagérations, les malheurs et les fautes de ce pays. Le *JE* est plus circonspect: la plaisanterie lui semble inconvenante pour un sujet aussi grave (10/1780: 87), le sarcasme trop amer (97) et surtout il décèle les illusions de l'esprit de parti dans les réflexions de Brissot: "Nous n'avons pas besoin d'annoncer que c'est un Français qui fait parler l'Angleterre"; le *JE* est trop réaliste pour croire à l'affaiblissement, espéré par toute la France, de la puissance anglaise. Il réplique à Brissot qu'elle possède encore "les trois choses qui seules sont nécessaires pendant la guerre: 1) de l'argent, 2) de l'argent, 3) de l'argent" (97). L'*AL*, au contraire, bénit Brissot d'avoir fait parler une "puissance terrassée" (171).

Avec des teintes différentes mais avec la même joie, les deux revues peignent le dysfonctionnement de la vie politique anglaise, et en particulier insistent sur le thème, familier au *JE*, du despotisme ministériel. L'*AL* plaint le parlement autrefois si respectable d'être "maintenant prostitué" à un ministère qui décide que les colons américains doivent être esclaves ou périr (156). Le *JE*, de même, souligne la fatale inconséquence des ministres d'un peuple libre qui se sont imaginé pouvoir imposer à "leur gré des fers aux alliés de ce peuple" (91). Les deux revues retiennent l'image de la "maison de campagne", moquerie par laquelle Brissot désigne les colonies anglaises en Amérique du Nord.

Mais l'*AL* enlève deux dimensions essentielles au travail de Brissot que le *JE* met bien en évidence parce qu'ils correspondent à sa propre orientation: la perception philosophique de l'histoire humaine et la conception libérale de la vie politique.

En effet, Brissot détecte dans le passé anglais des phases de "singulière frénésie religieuse" (89): les Croisades du XIe siècle, et le *JE* s'émeut de "ce

8. L'*Année Littéraire* (1780) 8, 8: 145.
9. *AL* (1780) 8, 8: 171; *JE* (10/1780): 87 et 97.

portrait hideux des guerres civiles, des disputes et des persécutions que suscita le fanatisme sous le masque de la religion." (90)

D'autre part, Brissot inclut le problème américain dans la question générale des colonies européennes. Avec le Hollandais anonyme, le *JE* avait, dès 1777, évoqué la séparation de l'Espagne et des Provinces-Unies; Brissot étend la remarque à toutes les possessions coloniales de l'Angleterre, de la France et surtout de l'Espagne: le thème philosophique des horreurs perpétrées par l'Espagne en Amérique du Sud transforme l'affaire américaine et lui donne une nouvelle dimension: il ne s'agit plus d'un événement politique anglais mais d'un de ces signes que le temps fournit à la raison humaine pour qu'elle ne désespère pas de voir arriver l'époque de la liberté!

L'indépendance américaine entrait de la sorte dans le discours philosophique que les Lumières tenaient sur l'histoire, tel que le *JE* l'avait extrait de l'abbé Raynal: "Enfin, le temps amène des circonstances, et celle-ci des révolutions heureuses qu'il semblait qu'on ne dût jamais espérer" (*JE*, 1/5/1777: 380); et tel qu'il l'avait découvert chez Chastellux, l'auteur alors célèbre de la *Félicité publique* et dont P. Rousseau entreprit la réédition sur les presses de sa Société typographique à Bouillon: ce discours ouvrait à l'homme le droit au bonheur social; le *JE* remerciait Chastellux de "s'être empressé d'apprendre à la génération actuelle qu'elle avait un espoir légitime à la félicité." (5/1777: 381)

Fort de "cette douce espérance" (381), le *JE* détaille les méfaits de l'empire colonial et y dénonce la source des dépenses et des violences militaires: Brissot fait converger le pacifisme et l'antimilitarisme des Lumières avec l'indépendance américaine.

Plus encore, Brissot noue ce discours rationaliste au discours libéral: la renonciation au système colonial permet "d'introduire dans le commerce une liberté général, d'ouvrir tous les ports à toutes les nations." (92)

Enfin, Brissot amorce le futur développement d'un discours radical fondé sur l'égalité: il introduit le thème de l'esclavage des Noirs, propose d'établir une "parfaite égalité" entre les Anglais, les Irlandais et les Ecossais (91). Le *JE*, contrairement à l'*AL*, fut tout à fait réceptif à l'ensemble de la thématique brissotine; n'y est-il pas préparé depuis 1777 par la lecture de la *Législation* de l'abbé Mably? Il retrouvait aussi chez Brissot l'idée "spartiate" de Mably sur la richesse corruptrice et le commerce destructeur, complétée par la même référence à la Suisse: "Sparte fut libre et puissante tant qu'elle fut pauvre", alors que la Hollande pourtant républicaine tend politiquement vers son déclin, déclare Brissot (*JE*, 10/1780: 95-96).

L'*AL* n'a pas su dégager la puissante énergie dont Brissot a échauffé son *Testament*; elle n'a pas voulu signaler son travail de synthèse idéologique par lequel il incluait l'événement américain dans un pan de la culture et voie de transformation: l'utopie semblait enfin autorisée à quitter la prison de la chimère et à rencontrer la réalité. Du moins, ce fut le rêve de Brissot.

Les prudences méthodologiques du *JE*

Le *JE* conserva, selon sa coutume, une attitude plus réservée, plus froide que Brissot. Il était trop opposé aux thèses d'un J.-J. Rousseau pour accepter facilement de voir dans les événements américains la réalisation d'une utopie, l'avènement de la raison parfaite.

C'est pourquoi il ne cessera de prolonger son enquête pour établir des faits certains, une "histoire fidèle" selon ses termes (4/1779: 58). "Etre plus instruit": ce but le pousse à sélectionner un large spectre d'ouvrages: histoire événementielle, réflexions politiques, analyses économiques, discours académiques, examens juridiques, journaux de voyages ou enquêtes ethnographiques. Il ne néglige aucun genre: "Tout ce qui tend à jeter du jour sur la révolution importante qui fixe l'attention de l'ancien et du nouveau monde ne peut manquer d'être accueilli." (4/1781: 211)

L'histoire événementielle apparaît surtout en 1787. En mai, le *JE* lit l'ouvrage de John Andrews, *The History of the War with America*; en juillet, l'*Histoire des troubles de l'Amérique anglaise* de François Soulès; en août, et en septembre la traduction de l'*Histoire de la Révolution de l'Amérique* par David Ramsay. Le *JE* n'y cherche pas tant le récit des guerres que l'esprit des insurgents. Paradoxalement, il lui paraît "inutile de rappeler les détails de cette guerre encore sous les yeux du public" (5/1787: 421); il espère "qu'on n'attende pas de lui qu'il suive les auteurs dans les descriptions de beaucoup d'événements que le temps n'a pas pu encore nous faire oublier" (7/1787: 64); il répétera le même refus au mois d'août, justifié par la même excuse (8/1787: 64). A cette date, les faits les plus importants sont d'ordre politique: il s'interroge non tant sur la réalité matérielle que sur la vérité spirituelle, sur la signification philosophique de l'événement.

Son recours aux ouvrages historiques signifie d'abord sa volonté de ne pas se contenter de récits partisans: il veille donc à choisir des titres d'ouvrages garantis par la qualité des auteurs. Ainsi D. Ramsay lui paraît digne de confiance pour avoir "occupé dans le gouvernement nouveau des postes importants", avoir eu part "dès l'origine des troubles aux résolutions courageuses qui ont été prises dans les assemblées nationales" et pour s'être trouvé "à portée de suivre les opérations militaires en qualité de médecin des hôpitaux." (8/1787: 64) A défaut d'avoir été acteur et témoin, l'auteur doit avoir eu accès à des témoignages d'acteurs directs: Fr. Soulès est fort apprécié car il a utilisé "des mémoires authentiques que des personnes de distinction ont bien voulu lui procurer"; il a rassemblé des "informations en conversant avec des gens sages et éclairés...qui ont eu part à cette guerre." (7/1787: 62) En outre, le *JE* exige que les auteurs travaillent sur l'excellent principe d'une histoire objective: "ni satire ni panégyrique mais tableau impartial des événements passés", à la manière de Ramsay mais aussi de J. Andrews, à qui il "doit la justice d'avouer qu'il a tâché d'écarter de son esprit et de son coeur tous les motifs, tous les intérêts particuliers capables de le détourner du chemin ouvert par l'impartialité historique." (5/1787: 420) En juillet, le journaliste revient sur cette exigence, à propos de Fr. Soulès qui a su mener son enquête en interrogeant des personnes "de tous les partis, de toutes les nations." (7/1787: 62)

Cette insistance du journal sur la méthode tient à la nature même du sujet traité qui concerne la question classique du meilleur régime, le monarchique ou le républicain.[10] L'*AL* exprime alors franchement la difficulté à aborder ce sujet; son rédacteur se sent mal à l'aise: d'un côté, il doit défendre la monarchie, et de l'autre, soutenir les insurgents américains, pour ne pas se heurter à la diplomatie de Vergennes; il en arrive, contrairement à toute attente, à prôner la tolérance politique. A chacun son genre de gouvernement, lance-t-il, pour tenter d'évacuer toute contradiction: "Nous sommes si libres sous des monarques chéris que dans le temps même où nous félicitons nos amis de jouir d'une liberté qui est plus de leur goût, nous sommes très éloignés de leur porter la moindre envie." (1783, 7, 1: 108) La révolution américaine est, en effet, séduisante, même pour les monarchistes orthodoxes de l'*AL*. Certes, ils refusent la critique américaine de cette "chose absurde et contre nature" qui serait la noblesse héréditaire selon leurs constitutions; certes, ils refusent la critique américaine de la religion dominante, mais ils acceptent de considérer "tout ce que nous pouvons approuver sans risque et que peut-être nous imiterons un jour." (121)

L'Amérique est donc un sujet à risque dans la mesure où sa révolution semblait lancer un défi aux intellectuels français. Le *JE* le sait qui, dès avril 1777, avait averti qu'il constituerait un dossier sur la question sans tenir de discours partisan pour éviter tout dérapage subjectif: "L'impartialité dont nous nous sommes fait une loi dès le commencement de cette grande affaire en rapportant tout ce qui s'écrira pour et contre, nous réduit au seul rôle de relateurs." (4/1777: 280)

Toutefois, le *JE* n'obéit pas uniquement aux contraintes d'une circonstance particulière. Il fait preuve aussi d'un comportement d'historien classique, soucieux de se "tenir toujours soi-même en garde contre les suggestions de l'amour-propre, contre cette prédilection que la patrie sollicite et dont elle fait presque un devoir." (5/1787: 420)

> Une histoire véritablement impartiale de la révolution de l'Amérique, précise-t-il en juillet 1787, devrait être le résultat de toutes celles qu'auraient écrites des auteurs des nations diverses qui ont eu quelque part à la même révolution. Les Anglais certainement n'épargneront pas

---

10. Cf. Voltaire, *Dictionnaire Philosophique*, éd. Julien Benda et Raymond Naves (Paris: Garnier, 1967), 335-37; article "Patrie", écho du débat lancé par Bodin en 1576.

les Français; et ceux-ci ne craindront point de révéler les fautes des Anglais. L'historien le plus digne de foi serait celui qui jouissant de toute sa liberté au milieu des peuples qui n'ont pris aucun intérêt à ces grands différends, écouterait également les deux partis, et nous donnerait ensuite le résultat impartial de leurs diverses narrations. (7/1787: 63)

Bref, devant ce "phénonène politique unique dans l'histoire qui ne peut être qu'un objet de surprise et d'admiration pour les administrateurs des empires et pour la postérité" (1/10/1783: 4), il reste à la fois prudent politiquement et intellectuellement "de sang-froid" (5/1787: 420).

Sa prudence, méthodologique plus que conjoncturelle, le pousse à donner la parole à toutes les parties en présence. Par exemple, de 1781 à 1782, il rassemble successivement les *Pensées sur la Révolution d'Amérique* de Th. Pownall, lieutenant-gouverneur de New Jersey puis de la baie de Massachusetts et membre de la chambre des communes à Londres, partisan de l'indépendance (15/4/1781: 211); en septembre 1781, il présente les *Réflexions impartiales sur l'Amérique*, d'un partisan décidé de l'empire colonial (421-43). Il veille aussi à établir, pour contrebalancer les effets pervers des patriotismes, une alternance entre auteurs français et auteurs anglais; ainsi le livre de Th. Pownall (4/1781) est suivi de celui de Raynal, *Révolution de l'Amérique* (11/1781: 404); en 1782, les *Impartial Reflections on the Conduct of the Late Administration and Opposition of the American Congress* (249-55) sont immédiatement doublées par les *Essais historiques et politiques sur la Révolution de l'Amérique Septentrionale* du célèbre spécialiste de l'administration coloniale à Saint-Domingue, le publiciste Hilliard d'Auberteuil.

Le journal ne se contente pas d'une confrontation virtuelle in absentia. Il repère les ouvrages anglais qui relancent les débats: il note en 1781 que les *Réflexions impartiales sur l'Amérique* sont dirigées contre le doyen de Gloucester, c'est-à-dire l'économiste anglais Josiah Tucker dont il avait lu en janvier 1775 les *Sermons on Political and Commercial Subjects* et dont il avait apprécié les vues indépendantistes (217); de même en octobre 1782, il oppose les *Considérations sur les intérêts de la Grande-Bretagne avec ses colonies d'Amérique* (32) de Jacques Anderson, suggérant que l'Angleterre mette fin à sa souveraineté sur les colonies, aux *Impartial Reflections* d'un anonyme, chaleureux propagandiste du gouvernement londonien (249).

Le journal croise même les deux séries en profitant du débat que provoqua la brochure du philosophe français Raynal sur la *Révolution de l'Amérique* (1/11/1781: 424); en avril 1783, il examine "avec empressement" la *Lettre adressée à l'abbé Raynal sur les affaires de l'Amérique septentrionale* par l'Américain Th. Paine, auteur réputé du *Sens commun* (15/4/1783: 198).

Il donne, à cette occasion, une sévère leçon à Raynal et aux autres auteurs qui se hâtent de "présenter comme prouvé ce qui est précisément en question" (10/1782: 255). L'abbé Raynal

> s'y est pris sans doute trop tôt pour tracer l'histoire d'une des plus grandes et des plus importantes révolutions arrivées dans le monde. Nous ne sommes pas encore à la distance nécessaire pour saisir sans crainte de se tromper les caractères des personnes qui ont agi et les circonstances dans lesquelles ils se sont trouvés... Les relations mêmes des faits sont ordinairement partout moins leur histoire véridique qu'un tableau chargé de couleurs qui les défigurent, qui les présentent tels qu'on a intérêt de les envisager ou tels qu'on veut qu'ils soient offerts au public... C'est au temps seul à dissiper les ténèbres, à écarter les voiles qui masquent la vérité; en se pressant trop, on va au hasard et on s'expose, comme le fait l'abbé Raynal, à exalter fréquemment sans raison et à blâmer sans cause, à célébrer des choses qui ne devaient pas l'être et à se taire sur celles qui méritaient de justes éloges, à changer souvent de dispositions sur les faits et sur les personnes et à n'en peindre presque aucuns de traits fixes et marqués. (4/1783: 199-200)

En 1785, un autre abbé français, l'abbé Mably, se voit réprimandé à son tour par un anonyme Hollandais; le premier numéro de l'année commençait par un compte rendu des *Observations sur le gouvernement et les lois des Etats-Unis d'Amérique* (1/1/1785: 3), prolongé par un second le 15 janvier (202-11); le second semestre reprend en écho, le 15 juillet, cet ouvrage, mais publié à Dublin "avec des remarques d'un républicain" (191). Cet exemple est caractéristique du soin que met le journal à maintenir l'exigence du débat contradictoire. En effet, il utilise cet ouvrage hollandais pourtant fortement marqué au coin du préjugé patriotique. Le journal si constamment attentif à ce piège de l'amour-propre, savait que l'abbé Mably avait indirectement critiqué la constitution hollandaise en félicitant les Américains de "n'avoir point mendié un nouveau maître et de n'avoir pensé qu'à élever un trône à la liberté" (1/1785: 3); le Hollandais répétait dans ses remarques que les Américains devraient choisir un gouvernement monarchique (7/1785: 203), sans que le journal exprime la moindre réserve sur ces points essentiels. Malgré les positions pessimistes du Hollandais sur la nature inadaptée et sur l'avenir fragile de la constitution américaine, le journal accepte son compte rendu parce qu'il y retrouve les critiques de certains aspects trop "populaires", trop démocratiques qu'avait déjà avancés l'abbé Mably, mais surtout une critique de son angélisme moral: celui-ci souhaitait qu'"à mesure que les dignités (des magistrats) sont plus importantes, on leur attribuât des revenus moins considérables". Paroles très philosophiques admet le journaliste (15/1/1785: 203), sous-entendant qu'elles sont peu réalistes; le Hollandais lui permet de préciser sa propre réaction devant les déclamations vertueuses de l'abbé: "Si le raisonnement de Mably avait quelque force, un excellent magistrat serait un prodige." (7/1785: 199)

Ce dernier qualificatif sonne en harmonie avec une hantise des journalistes: la confusion trop courante, trop séduisante aussi, que de nombreux auteurs entretiennent entre chimère et projet politique. Ils craignent que l'Amérique ne relance chez les auteurs français déçus par la réalité française, par l'actualité française, dans ses aspects sociaux, juridiques, économiques et culturels, deux défauts: soit celui d'un Mably, celui d'un "homme de cabinet plus attaché à développer son *Ancien Système* qu'à en concevoir un nouveau d'après les circonstances", pour reprendre les mots du critique hollandais (15/7/1785: 191), soit celui d'un Raynal, dont les "vaines déclamations annoncent plutôt le *Rhéteur enthousiaste* que le sage observateur et l'historien impartial." (1/11/1781: 405)

Le *JE*, à son habitude,–ainsi que je l'ai montré dans ma thèse sur les modes de lecture dans le *JE*, en 1987[11]–cherche à se placer loin des "systèmes américains" mais aussi à résister aux enthousiasmes de l'innovation magique.

Or Brissot de Warville entre dans le *JE* en combattant les systèmes anciens sans résister aux illusions de l'enthousiasme. Dès 1780, sans le connaître, le *JE*, on l'a vu, avait repéré dans le *Testament de l'Angleterre* la propension de Brissot à prendre ses rêves pour la réalité.

L'accord politique du *JE* et de Brissot sur la primauté du droit naturel

Ce que le *JE* admire chez Brissot, c'est sa capacité courageuse à entrer dans le vaste mouvement de réforme des lois françaises que de nombreux avocats ou juristes soutenaient en France depuis quelques années. On sait que dès 1764, Linguet avait lancé l'idée qu'une réforme était "nécessaire". Brissot de Warville, qui fut longtemps un de ses amis, en reprit l'idée et se précipita dans cette voie que d'autres avaient empruntée. Le *JE*, de son côté, suivait avec beaucoup d'attention et de sympathie le travail de ces intellectuels du barreau ou des parlements. Par exemple, en 1781, il présente un *Essai sur les réformes à faire dans notre législation criminelle* de François-Michel Vermeil, avocat au Parlement de Paris, en insistant sur deux aspects novateurs du projet: la perspective libérale qui engage à "respecter les droits de l'homme et à assurer le repos de la société...à venger l'ordre social sans porter atteinte aux droits de l'individu" (15/5/1781: 3); d'autre part, la perspective égalitaire: la loi pénale doit frapper indistinctement tous les états et toutes les conditions (6).

---

11. Jacques Wagner, *Lecture et Société dans le Journal Encyclopédique de P. Rousseau (1756-1785)*, thèse de doctorat d'état, Rennes: Université de Haute Bretagne, 1987.

Le journal déclare ces projets de réformes non seulement utiles mais "nécessaires", reprenant donc à son compte l'ancienne expression de Linguet et s'accorde de la sorte dans ce domaine à l'esprit de Brissot dont il n'ignore pratiquement aucun ouvrage "juridique": en 1782, *Le Sang de l'innocent vengé* qui pose fermement l'idée de la priorité de l'individuel sur le collectif; à la suite de F.M. Vermeil, Brissot courbe le bâton ancien de la loi dans le sens de l'individu envers lequel la société est déclarée avoir désormais des devoirs, sinon la justice ressemblerait à une tyrannie. De ces débats juridiques, se dégageaient deux propositions vigoureusement politiques, remettant en cause l'ancien régime de la société monarchiste: l'égalité doit être la base du droit civil et particulièrement du droit criminel; d'autre part, si la "propriété" devient une dimension qui définit l'individu, la société, outre la légitime exigence qu'elle impose aux individus d'exécuter leurs devoirs, est dans l'obligation absolue de respecter la propriété: celle-ci devient un droit naturel dont la violation détruirait la raison sociale même (*JE*, 15/4/1782: 231-37).

En mai 1782, le *JE* retrouve les idées et les raisonnements de Brissot qui les approfondit dans sa *Théorie des Lois criminelles*. Il leur appose alors, sous l'expression de "philosophie douce" (1/5/1782: 372) le sceau du nouvel esprit qui secoue les conceptions traditionnelles des rapports individus/société. Par exemple, lorsque Brissot examine la question du vol, le *JE* retient le vol de ciboire dans un lieu de culte parce que Brissot refuse d'y voir un sacrilège: ce vol, comme tout autre, s'explique par le besoin (387). Sous ce raisonnement moderne, transparaît le cadre conceptuel autant que sentimental qui fit des Etats-Unis d'Amérique le lieu où s'incarnerait cette "douce philosophie": l'individu n'y était plus soumis à la "fatale loi de la nécessité" (383) qui pousse les pauvres, les victimes de la société, "l'humanité souffrante". En écartant les "préjugés civils ou religieux", en "n'écoutant que la voix de la nature, que le langage de la raison", en abjurant "tout esprit de parti, tout intérêt de secte", Brissot flattait l'esprit cosmopolite du journal qui cite avec plaisir la fière maxime du jeune homme: "Le philosophe se déshonore quand il n'a qu'une raison locale." (381)

Mais dans l'affirmation de sa fierté philosophique, Brissot allait au-delà de la revendication classique d'impartialité. Le *JE* ne détecte pas encore que Brissot, en réalité, emprunte la voie rousseauiste d'un rêve politique qui refuse de confondre utopie et chimère: l'Amérique sera l'incarnation de ce rêve. Alors que, dans la tradition rationaliste d'un Voltaire,[12] toute volonté de réforme se heurtait au scepticisme ("les hommes sont très rarement dignes de se gouverner eux-mêmes")[13] et au réalisme ("L'égalité est donc à la fois la chose la plus naturelle et en même temps la plus chimérique"),[14] Brissot dresse

---

12. Voltaire, *Lettres Philosophiques* et *Dictionnaire Philosophique*, article "Méchant", 301-04.
13. *Dict. Phil.*, art. "Patrie", 336.
14. *Dict. Phil.*, art. "Egalité", 177.

le droit naturel contre le droit positif; sa préférence n'est pas appréciée par tous (*JE*, 11/1782: 119). Ainsi Bernardi, avocat au Parlement d'Aix, abordant le projet d'adoucir la rigueur des lois criminelles, reprend l'attitude classique qui cherche à protéger d'abord "l'administration" de la justice et l'ensemble social en maintenant la peine de mort (15/10/1782: 229); ainsi un anonyme, favorable au dédommagement de l'innocent condamné, reproche à Brissot de mettre en péril l'institution judiciaire par ses arguments. En effet, Brissot ne restreint pas le dédommagement à un calcul réaliste, "indemniser du fruit que l'innocent aurait retiré de ses travaux pour qu'il supporte plus aisément le souvenir de ses peines" (10/1782: 131); il récuse la position réformiste qui vise à conserver la philosophie sociale classique, selon laquelle, résume l'anonyme, "le pacte tacite que les hommes ont fait en formant une société de supporter les maux qui y seraient attachés pour profiter des biens qui en résulteraient, pourrait bien faire douter si le dédommagement...est dû de droit naturel", selon laquelle encore, "un citoyen faussement accusé par l'organe du ministère public est la victime d'un malheur attaché à la condition humaine et que la conservation des individus a rendu nécessaire" (126-27). Brissot souhaiterait que le dédommagement ait un sens moral, qu'il soit un "signe légal de son innocence". Or l'anonyme prétend que "ce n'est pas la justification personnelle qu'il faut avoir en vue" (128).

Brissot renverse la perspective: la société peut être déclarée coupable et l'institution judiciaire doit protéger le citoyen contre les erreurs de la justice.

Le *JE* suit avec sympathie les efforts de Brissot pour desserrer l'étau social qui étouffe l'individu, car ils correspondent aux thèses les plus avancées, les plus ouvertes des Lumières: l'esclavage des peuples est dû à leur ignorance. Les journalistes, en même temps que les écrivains philosophes diffusant le savoir, aident à lutter contre "l'état barbare" de la jurisprudence française. Le *JE* acceptera de nombreux comptes rendus sur ce sujet, composés par Brissot: des *Observations sur Prost de Royer*, récemment décédé (12/1784: 506); un examen du discours de Lacretelle contre le préjugé des peines infamantes (11/1785: 436-61); une réponse à Dom Pedro, moine de Séville, partisan de la torture (9/1787: 128-31); une lettre pour défendre contre le compte rendu du *Mercure de France*, son ouvrage *De la France et des Etats-Unis* (10/1787: 107). La jonction entre Brissot jurisconsulte et Brissot américain devient effective dans le *JE* à ce moment-là.

En effet, en défendant son ouvrage, d'une part Brissot accuse tous les journaux, sauf le *JE*, d'avoir fait silence sur son travail et de l'autre, comme pour éclairer le sens que prend pour lui la Révolution américaine, il évoque l'affaire Hastings: soutenir le mouvement d'indépendance des Américains équivaut dans le principe à attaquer Hastings. Hastings a violé le droit des gens; or il faut punir les maîtres s'ils sont coupables, autant que tout autre citoyen, sous peine de ne plus être en mesure d'empêcher "les gens en place d'être des tyrans et la nation la plus libre de tomber dans la servitude"

(10/1787: 123). L'égalité juridique devant la loi prend une signification politique, grâce à la Révolution américaine; de plus, le dire publiquement, le démontrer dans ses ouvrages, c'est faire preuve de ce courage "américain" qui ne se laisse pas intimider par les préjugés de l'ignorance entretenue par la tyrannie; enfin, c'est contrebalancer, par l'humanité philosophique, l'habitude sociale qui "montre plus de commisération pour les oppresseurs que pour les opprimés" (112). La Révolution américaine étendait aux dimensions d'un continent et d'une histoire ce qu'un Brissot entrevit d'abord dans le cadre de l'institution judiciaire et le généralisait en leçons politiques: le pouvoir, ou les groupes dominants, ou la société en général, ne sont plus à l'abri de la justice (128).

Dès 1785, Brissot avait énoncé les raisons de sa fascination pour l'Amérique:

> Là, l'homme est le fils de ses oeuvres; là, il ne peut y avoir d'injustice autorisée par les lois, d'injustice qui frappe une moitié de la société lorsque l'autre moitié a le secret et le privilège de s'y soustraire; là, il n'y a point de distinction de supplices, pas plus que de rangs; là, point de corps intéressé à soutenir le préjugé; là, il n'est aucun rang où la vérité ne pénètre, aucun esprit que la raison ne dirige; là, l'homme est homme enfin, c'est-à-dire qu'il ne se laisse point mutiler, enchaîner, dégrader, suivant les fantaisies ou les préjugés d'un autre homme. (11/1785: 455)

Cette tirade apparaît inopinément dans un compte rendu que Brissot consacre au *Discours* de Lacretelle *sur le préjugé des peines infâmantes*. L'Amérique s'est transformée en mot-phare, en mot-guide, et surtout en modèle: en Amérique, l'histoire humaine, c'est-à-dire les préjugés qui confisquent le pouvoir au profit des riches et des puissants, n'existe plus; elle a laissé place au "règne universel de la raison" (455).

L'Amérique représente un espace parfait, dont la perfection serait due à l'absence de passé: pays sans trace où s'exerce une raison sans reste, totalement contemporain à lui-même sans réserve d'aucune sorte (ce qui explique l'absence des Indiens dans toute cette fantasmagorie brissotine), vierge: "Dans les anciens gouvernements", ajoute Brissot en pensant à la lourdeur de la présence historique, à la pesanteur du passé, au poids de ce qu'il appelle les préjugés, "dans les états européens et surtout dans la nation française, il subsiste et subsistera toujours malgré les lumières qui les éclairent, une foule d'erreurs, de préjugés et d'injustices qui ne peuvent se dissiper que par une révolution complète." La Révolution américaine démontre que la raison ne peut apparaître que par un effort de volonté radicale car le préjugé dure autant que la société où il naît: "En attendre la destruction de l'effet insensible du temps ou bien des efforts des hommes en place, c'est se bercer de vaines espérances." (455)

Adossé à une perception aussi exaltée de l'Amérique, Brissot s'érige dès 1786 en maître-philosophe post-voltairien sous les applaudissements du *JE*: il convient de détruire les préjugés qui obscurcissent l'esprit humain, à la manière d'un Voltaire mais en outre, il faut détruire "les préjugés politiques" car ce sont "les liens les plus forts de la servitude" (8/1786: 411). Brissot serait de la sorte l'un des rares écrivains à proposer une "histoire populaire", écrite en faveur du peuple (432). Le journal ne cesse de découvrir, dans la plupart des écrits consacrés à l'indépendance américaine qu'il examine chaque année, des idées propres à Brissot, comme si ce dernier était le rédacteur des comptes rendus. Chez J. Andrews, il souligne la force de l'esprit républicain capable de préférer ses convictions personnelles aux dogmes dominants (5/1787: 423); chez Soulès, il remarque le courage à n'être intimidé ni par le riche ni par le noble (7/1787: 62); chez Mazzei, citoyen de Virginie, il retrouve sous une présentation parfaite d'une égalité pure, indépendante de la richesse, du sexe, du privilège, l'écho brissotin d'une société purifée par la raison, constituée d'un peuple libre car "un peuple qui raisonne ne peut être comparé à une multitude ensevelie dans les ténèbres les plus épaisses de l'ignorance et de la superstition" (4/1788: 224); avec Ramsay, avec Chastellux aussi, il insiste sur la richesse économique énorme des Etats-Unis d'Amérique, sur leur immense capacité de commerce que Brissot avait particulièrement illustrée avec l'aide de Clavières dans son ouvrage de 1787.

Avec Brissot, tous les thèmes épars des Lumières (raison, loi, liberté) convergeaient dans un discours cohérent et homogène: la raison signifiait loi universelle pour tous ou égalité et s'opposait aux privilèges; elle signifiait liberté de penser ou liberté de la presse, et s'opposait aux préjugés; elle signifiait liberté de commerce et s'opposait aux conservateurs de la physiocratie; plus encore, elle signifiait liberté à l'égard des circonstances qui déterminent si différemment le destin des hommes. L'Amérique permettait à Brissot d'envisager la possibilité d'une *égalité des chances* parfaitement distribuées à chaque homme: il dénommait cette chance "nature" et la défendit avec véhémence contre Chastellux au cours de son *Examen des Voyages du marquis dans l'Amérique Septentrionale*; il lui interdit de "calomnier la nature"; n'accorder aux Nègres que de la pitié, comme Chastellux, "n'est-ce pas prêter à la nature le projet d'accorder des faveurs à certains hommes, en lui imputant un système d'inégalité entre ses enfants; il n'est qu'un monde pour tous les hommes; les variations qui déparent les individus sont des jeux de hasard, des résultats de circonstances qui varient." La défense des Nègres est aussi métaphorique de son désir propre de n'être plus soumis aux pesanteurs sociales, aux lourdeurs de l'histoire; il ne supporte pas d'entendre le marquis "mettre sur le compte de la nature, cette bonne mère qui nous veut tous égaux, tous libres, tous heureux, un crime qui n'est que le crime d'une barbarie sociale" (11/1786: 430). Sous la pitié de Chastellux, Brissot détectait subtilement un préjugé social exprimant un privilège aristocratique. Chastellux, en effet, pense la société en termes de hiérarchie si bien que la dignité de l'homme devient une "chose comparative": elle serait "d'autant plus grande qu'un homme considère des classes au-dessous de lui; le plébéien fait celle du noble, l'esclave celle de l'homme libre, le Noir celle du Blanc". Brissot proteste vigoureusement au nom des valeurs de la constitution américaine: l'égalité naturelle signifie d'abord la possibilité pour chacun de n'être pas victime des circonstances. Le journaliste est sensible à cet aspect républicain de la pensée de Brissot: "elle est la défense des imprescriptibles droits de l'humanité...elle ne peut que l'honorer aux yeux du sage qui pense que la nature du gouvernement modifie l'homme aux trois quarts et qui sent intimement que l'esclave ignorant et barbare né sur les bords du Bosphore serait un républicain éclairé, s'il était né à Philadelphie." (11/1786: 435-36)

La défense des Noirs dont Brissot, suivi par Condorcet, s'est déclaré le champion dès février 1788, trouve des échos réguliers dans le *JE*: en mars 1788 (*Lettre sur une société pour l'abolition de la traite des Nègres*, 484); en juillet 1788 (*Discours sur la nécessité d'établir à Paris une société pour concourir avec celle de Londres à l'abolition de la traite et de l'esclavage des Nègres*, 53); en janvier 1789 (*Réflexions sur l'esclavage des Nègres*, par Condorcet, 51) Brissot et le *JE* retrouvaient, dans cette question, la cohérence théorique et la générosité humanitaire, propres aux Lumières. Mais il fallait à Brissot plus encore: l'Amérique aurait perdu, à ses yeux, sa séduction de terre vierge si, une fois de plus, des Américains n'avaient sur ce point incarné la raison naturelle. Leur nom: les Quakers.

Les réticences philosophiques du *JE* à l'égard de Brissot

En effet, Brissot se distingue par son amour immodéré pour les Quakers: il transmet au jounal une lettre de Philadelphie qui dénonce la traite des Nègres, pour montrer les effets positifs de la liberté sur l'esprit des hommes: la "générosité exemplaire" des Quakers serait due "à la révolution qui s'est faite dans les idées depuis la séparation d'avec la métropole" (5/1788: 114-16). Avec les Quakers, il estime atteindre la synthèse de tous ses voeux: ces hommes ne dépendraient que de leur volonté; ils ne seraient plus soumis aux circonstances de l'histoire après leur séparation d'avec la métropole; en excluant l'ordre hiérarchique d'une monarchie ou d'une société fondée sur l'argent, ils ajouteraient à la volonté libre qui structure l'être humain la vertu qui protège des effets nocifs du temps.

Tout en suivant Brissot loin dans ses réflexions, le *JE* conserve son sang-froid. Il n'écarte pas les discours qui insistent sur les avantages économiques, comme celui de Chastellux en août 1787 (455); celui de Mallet en août 1788, celui de Marco Lasti sur Americ Vespuce en octobre (265); il apprécie la démarche plus froide mais tout aussi républicaine de Condorcet dans ses *Réflexions sur l'esclavage des Nègres* (1/1789).

De plus, il reproche régulièrement à Brissot son enthousiasme excessif. Brissot est fasciné par l'héroïsme intellectuel: "La dignité de l'homme", écrivait-il dans son *Examen des voyages de Chastellux*, "consiste dans les efforts qu'il fait pour découvrir la vérité, pour la faire régner, dans de grandes idées, dans une volonté forte et constante" et il concluait: "Vouloir avec énergie tout ce qui est bon, tout ce qui est sublime, voilà la dignité de l'homme." (11/1786: 435) Il se détourne de l'esprit brillant des salons et des académies où l'on ne cherche que "le bien-dit" (8/1786: 418) le "clinquant" (11/1785: 444); il vise ainsi Voltaire et Chastellux (8/1786: 411) qui n'auraient manifesté ni grandeur, ni courage, ni chaleur, et seraient restés prisonniers de cette sagesse académique qu'un Lacretelle conseillait à Brissot d'adopter: "J'en suis fâché", lui répond-il. "Certes je m'en défendrai toute ma vie. Sage veut dire modéré dans sa chaleur, couvrant son énergie d'un style entortillé, complaisant dans ses hommages pour les vieux préjugés, pour les oracles à la mode...Pour nous, Européens blasés, il faut de la chaleur pour nous tirer de notre bourbier." (11/1785: 458)

L'héroïsme est un ton mais aussi un courage; l'écrivain doit affronter avec "hardiesse" le pouvoir peu enclin à entendre la vérité (7/1784: 231). Brissot avait été averti par son ami Villar qu'il n'était pas toujours nécessaire, en dépit de l'obligation morale de rester impartial, de "dire tout ce qu'on pense" (lettre du 24/9/1783: 74). Marat lui avait conseillé de respecter "quelque ménagement surtout quand on n'est pas les plus forts" (lettre de 1783). Brissot ne sait pas ou ne veut pas se contrôler. Il aurait trop peur de céder à la "pusillanimité du vulgaire qui, accoutumé à mesurer son respect sur celui des siècles passés, craint de toucher l'idole que des siècles ont honoré de leur vénération." (12/1784: 506)

Avec Th. More, dont il admira l'héroïsme et le projet utopique (11/1784: 481), il estime que le vrai philosophe doit préférer la vertu à la faveur du souverain ou de l'opinion et donc se comporter d'une manière "bilieuse et irascible" selon des termes qui scandalisent le journaliste (5/1783: 15). Celui-ci redoute l'enthousiasme: "avec beaucoup de talent trop d'ardeur nuit souvent", lui rappelle-t-il (21-22). Si politiquement il accepte presque toutes les propositions de l'écrivain, philosophiquement il récuse sa critique de la religion et son goût pour le matérialisme.

C'est pourquoi le *JE* refuse une liberté de la presse qui, trop grande, dégénérerait en licence contraire au bien public. Pour Brissot la mesure de la liberté reste dans tous les cas la recherche du vrai: dans le *JE*, le bien public est avancé comme une limite car il craint que les écrivains, "lorsqu'ils ont à traiter d'un sujet sur lequel leurs lumières et leurs discussions peuvent être utiles au public, ne s'interdisent pas des questions étrangères à cet objet notamment dans des matières où une seule erreur peut exciter contre eux des réclamations de la part de ceux-mêmes qui, dans tout le reste, auraient volontiers applaudi à leurs productions." (7/1787: 208) Le journal déconseillait ainsi à Brissot de mêler religion et politique, politique et philosophie. Brissot pense l'activité humaine en dehors du regard divin et du contrôle religieux. Eclairé par les constitutions américaines, il déclara une fois dans *De la France et des Etats-Unis* que "l'expérience a prouvé que la probité était presque toujours indépendante de la religion." Le *JE* rétorque qu'il aurait pu se dispenser d'une telle provocation qui blesse "ceux que nous appelons nos dévôts" (208-09).

Le journal comprend mal la logique profonde de Brissot qui ressent toute institution comme un obstacle à la liberté et à l'expression de l'individu. Il s'offusquera tout autant des critiques que Brissot lança contre les académies, en pastichant la diatribe de J.-J. Rousseau contre la propriété:

> Le premier qui pour perfectionner les sciences imagina de rassembler ceux qui les cultivaient connaissait peu la nature humaine et l'esprit scientifique. S'il avait jeté un coup d'oeil sur cette foule de corps que chaque état renferme en son sein, il les aurait tous vu agités par le même esprit d'intrigue, de bassesse, de cabale; il aurait vu partout l'homme utile, l'homme supérieur écrasé par la foule des êtres inutiles et médiocres; il en aurait conclu que réunir les savants entre eux, c'était nuire à la science. (5/1783: 13)

Le journal n'apprécie pas cette critique du despotisme des sciences et oppose à Brissot "les avantages que l'on ne peut nier avoir résulté de l'établissement des académies." Il donne alors une leçon d'analyse politique totalement inacceptable pour Brissot: "Quelques inconvénients, vrais ou exagérés, doivent-ils nous empêcher de reconnaître que l'existence de ces corps entretient le goût de l'étude et des sciences? Pour quelques découvertes auxquelles ils ont d'abord résisté combien ne leur en devons-nous pas à eux-mêmes?" (14) Brissot songeait aux résistances des académies à l'égard des théories physiques de Marat. Il exprimait ainsi l'amertume de ces jeunes gens dont les travaux et les opinions rencontraient alors si "peu de confiance" auprès des académiciens, maîtres de l'opinion. Il déchiffrait, dans chaque difficulté personnelle éprouvée à s'insérer dans le réseau intellectuel en France, le signe d'un dysfonctionnement social qu'il souhaite effacer en supprimant tout relief social et en particulier la prééminence du tout sur la partie. Ainsi, il critiquera le code de Catherine II tant admiré par le journaliste, parce que ce code préserve certaines prérogatives du pouvoir et n'établit pas une égalité universelle des peines: le journal veut adapter les peines à la qualité socio-culturelle du coupable car "telle peine agira très puissamment sur une classe de citoyens qui ne ferait sur l'autre qu'une très légère impression." (6/1783: 385) Le *JE* raisonne sur la base d'une société diversifiée et hiérarchisée, Brissot raisonne dans la hantise des "circonstances" qui produisant des différences favoriseraient l'inégalité.

C'est pourquoi il est attiré par le matérialisme pour son aspect moniste. Même s'il récuse certains aspects cyniques d'Helvétius, Brissot adapte à ses besoins la thèse du déterminisme social et éducatif. Son sens de l'égalité naturelle le pousse à voir dans l'histoire des individus un conflit entre leur "génie" naturel et les circonstances: ces dernières répartissent les individus sur l'échiquier social au gré des hasards de la naissance et de l'éducation. Dans le No. 4 de son *Journal du Lycée*, il évoqua la vie de Lord Clive en ces termes: "Né sans fortune, jeté par le hasard dans le commerce des Indes...les circonstances le forcèrent à préférer les armes au commerce. Il se fit grand capitaine, habile négociateur, car le génie est à peu près ce qu'il veut être; les circonstances seules déterminent le point de son vol." (12/1784: 236) Le journaliste se moque d'une pareille naïveté; en supposant un échange absolu des circonstances entre La Fontaine et Condé, il est facile de supposer que La Fontaine grand fabuliste n'aurait pas été un grand capitaine et inversement. Un matérialisme de ce genre rendait Brissot impatient devant les inerties de la société française: la pensée juste n'est pas suffisante pour établir la justice dans la société car celle-ci est constituée de forces capables d'empêcher des réformes qui ne conviennent pas à leurs intérêts. C'est ce qu'il répliqua à Lacretelle (11/1785: 451), c'est ce qu'il dénonça chez Chastellux (11/1786) si véhémentement que le *JE* fut contraint de s'en excuser un mois après (12/1786: 324). L'homme historique est fabriqué par l'environnement: "Qui vous a fait ce que vous êtes? L'éducation, les circonstances" répondit-il (11/1786: 432). De la sorte, l'aristocrate perd toute légitimité mystique: il n'est qu'un produit des circonstances.

Brissot raisonne de la même façon devant le phénomème religieux. Il n'y voit qu'un accident historique n'impliquant aucun sacré tabou, ne justifiant aucune prééminence. A l'école des Américains (10/1783: 6), il a appris "la plus grande tolérance pour les opinions religieuses" (7/1787: 210) qu'il conseille au nom d'une "philosophie du commerce" mais aussi au nom d'une philosophie de l'"humanité" (5/1787: 37): intérêt puissant quelquefois plus fort que l'intérêt personnel ou national. La religion est pour lui synonyme de fanatisme "frénétique": il pense aux Croisades (10/1780: 89), à l'histoire anglaise avant Elisabeth (90) et surtout à l'affaire Calas et La Barre dont "l'affreux supplice où le fantasme entraîna un jeune étourdi pour quelques plaisanteries irréligieuses" révolta tous les philosophes (5/1787: 37). Il cherche par ces rappels voltairiens, non à dénoncer des abus mais à dévaloriser entièrement la religion, à la manière de ce membre de la Société londonnienne contre l'esclavage, M. Clarkson, qui s'exclame au nom des Noirs: "Combien ne doivent-ils pas détester le nom de Chrétien lorsqu'ils voient ceux qui s'en glorifient souillés de crimes abominables? Combien ne doivent-ils pas avoir en horreur une religion qui semble combattre et proscrire les droits les plus naturels de l'espèce humaine et prêcher la férocité, le meurtre?"[15] (*JE*, 11/1786: 85)

Contre ces attaques, le *JE* ne cesse (et ne cessera jusqu'en 1793) de prêcher la réconciliation de la philosophie et de la religion. Il avait fermement souligné son accord à la critique que Mably adressait indirectement aux Américains dès 1777 dans son ouvrage *De la Législation* et qu'il avait repris en 1786 dans ses *Observations sur le gouvernement et les lois des Etats-Unis d'Amérique*. Aucune société ne peut s'établir sur une liberté religieuse totale: seule une religion dominante permet de "former de bons citoyens et de les réunir par la même manière de penser." (1/1785: 205) Le journaliste approuve sans réserve une telle analyse car, contrairement à Brissot, il croit au concours pacifique de la religion et de la politique plutôt qu'à une concurrence meurtrière: la nécessité d'un culte public n'exclut pas de proposer "l'union entre la religion et la philosophie." (5/1777: 385) Le journal s'appuiera, en outre, sur les remarques du républicain hollandais critiquant Mably, pour insister sur la nécessité d'une religion dominante, seule manière de préserver l'Etat "du désordre et de la confusion." (7/1785: 203) Sur la question religieuse, il préfère la position d'Hilliard d'Auberteuil (*Essais historiques et politiques sur la Révolution d'Amérique*): mieux vaut une religion et des parjures impies que pas de religion et des athées honnêtes (10/1782: 265). Le *JE* ne supporterait pas que, sous le label américain, fût réintroduite en France, l'idée baylienne d'une société vertueuse sans l'apport de la religion.

Brissot et le rêve américain

Le *JE* surveille donc avec une attention scrupuleuse les énoncés que, par le biais américain, Brissot cherche à diffuser en France contre la monarchie catholique. Politiquement accordés dans un engagement "populaire" inspiré du libéralisme juridique, économique et politique des Américains, ils diffèrent philosophiquement et psychologiquement.

Dans le *JE*, l'Amérique confirme la volonté de réformes qui anime les intellectuels français; pour Brissot, elle suscite un espoir de changement complet de sa propre condition d'humilié; en 1780, dans son discours couronné par l'Académie de Châlons, il affirmait: "Ce que la justice humaine ne peut encore réparer, c'est l'effet de l'humiliation qui a suivi l'accusé dans tous les degrés de l'instruction." Lui, victime de l'injustice sociale, se sent le frère de ce coupable innocent: "Humiliation! mot inconnu dans ce siècle dégradé, dans ce siècle où l'ignominie perd sa tache quand elle ouvre une

15. Thomas Clarkson, *An essay on the slavery and commerce of the human species* (Londres: Cadell, 1785).

voie à la fortune, où les âmes n'ont plus de nerfs, où l'homme est l'esclave de son supérieur." (5/1787: 34)

L'Amérique le fait rêver au-delà des limites des possibilités nationales, au-delà, ajouterait le *JE*, des besoins français. C'est pourquoi l'attitude du journaliste est complexe. Il souhaite accompagner et soutenir le mouvement de réformes dans la mesure où il lui paraît conforme à l'esprit philosophique: les événements américains lui semblent utilisables moins comme une source d'inspiration que comme une preuve du caractère réaliste de l'esprit de réformes. La raison lui conseille de garder son sang-froid devant des événements qui échauffent trop facilement l'imagination. La nécessité de la réforme ne doit surtout pas se transformer en échappée vers l'impossible chimère: il approuva Mably de ne "s'être point obstiné comme certains philosophes à demander l'impossible, en montrant aux hommes les avantages qu'ils ont perdus sans retour mais de consoler l'humanité en s'occupant de la rendre heureuse même dans la déplorable situation où elle se trouve." (5/1777: 383) Alors que Brissot fait l'éloge de l'*Utopie* de Th. More (11/1784: 484), le *JE* avait naguère refusé d'accorder à l'ouvrage nouvellement traduit par Thomas Rousseau une "réputation qu'il ne peut plus avoir aujourd'hui" et récusé "tous les romans politiques, ces beaux plans de gouvernements que leurs auteurs croient les meilleurs possibles et qui sont impossibles dans la réalité." (11/1780: 162)

Avant 1789, le *JE* s'acharne à contrecarrer la tentative de Brissot de redorer le blason douteux d'un utopisme toujours à craindre du fait de son inspiration rousseauiste ou d'un révolutionnairisme d'inspiration raynalienne. La philosophie rationaliste du *JE* conçoit la réforme comme un mouvement d'adaptation des lois à l'évolution sociale, mouvement appartenant en propre, d'une manière interne, à toute société rationnelle: "Tout ne peut pas être corrompu dans les gouvernements tempérés dont nous parlons. Au sein des abus qui les affligent, on peut remarquer une direction vers le bien qui leur a été imprimée dans le cours des siècles, par leur nature même; direction dont les effets peuvent être suspendus mais difficilement anéantis." (5/1787: 380) Pour le *JE*, l'Amérique ne doit, à aucun prix, sous peine d'un écroulement catastrophique de tout l'édifice du rationalisme classique des Lumières, permettre ni faciliter la séparation de la nature (raison) et de la société.

Au contraire, Brissot, qui récuse ce schéma rationaliste classique, voit dans l'Amérique la possibilité d'un *retour* à l'innocence première, à la vertu originelle qui finira par se confondre avec la figure mythique du Quaker.

Mais cette opposition disparaîtra vers la fin de l'année 1792 devant la menace jacobine. Brissot alors, ne sera plus le jeune homme exalté, chimérique, enthousiaste mais l'homme des "bonnes moeurs", de la paix, de la tolérance, de la sincérité, l'homme de la "vertu", oubliée ou négligée par les Montagnards qu'il traite de "bas intrigants et vils calomniateurs" (1/1793:

53). Au moment où Brissot va mourir, la tête tranchée, au moment où le *JE* va disparaître, dépassé par la dégénérescence qui lui paraît désorganiser les plus belles institutions de la Révolution (33), l'écrivain et le journaliste jettent un dernier regard sur ce qui n'est plus qu'un rêve impossible et dépassé, sur ces Quakers dont l'esprit de la liberté ressemble à la baguette magique d'une fée:

> Elle peut tout, elle fait tout ce qu'elle veut. Elle ordonne et les forêts s'abattent, les montagnes s'abaissent et de riches fermes s'élèvent et préparent l'asile de nombreuses générations tandis que la superbe ville de Palmyre périt et tombe en ruines avec la femme orgueilleuse qui la fonda. (11/1792: 317)

En novembre 1793, par l'intermédiaire de la traduction des *Lettres Philosophiques sur l'histoire de l'Angleterre* (O. Goldsmith), ils chantent une dernière fois les louanges de ces Quakers dont la constitution parfaite offre l'image d'un vrai peuple et non d'une "populace ignorante, imbécile, séditieuse" comme le supposait Mably (11/1793: 512).

Le désenchantement ultime devant une histoire qui "n'est autre chose que celle des malheurs" (11/1793: 356) a poussé le rationaliste prudent qu'était le journaliste encyclopédique à rejoindre l'utopiste rousseauiste que fut Brissot, autour d'un même songe.

L'Amérique est rêvée comme un lieu providentiel où le vouloir, le savoir et le pouvoir seraient enfin réconciliés, où l'individu divisé sous la monarchie serait enfin rendu à lui-même, à la nature. Séparée de la métropole anglaise, l'Amérique fournissait, de manière fantasmatique, un support à l'image d'une vie unifiée, soulagée des inerties sociales et des violences historiques qui l'amenaient inexorablement loin de la nature. Par le biais des Quakers qui finirent par symboliser à eux seuls ce Nouveau Monde tant espéré, Brissot opéra un *arrêt sur image*, comme il souhaita arrêter le mouvement révolutionnaire.

The American War of Independence as Seen by the *Journal encyclopédique*

Joan Lenardon

Is there a point to be made by the simultaneousness of the bicentennial celebrations of the French Revolution with those of the founding of Georgetown University by the Jesuit Bishop, John Carroll in his new United States of America?

And is there a point to be made about the Jesuits' establishing themselves in the first nation in history to begin its existence with the implicit rejection of an established church, a nation whose very Constitution would soon quite explicitly declare such a rejection by the First Amendment? One wonders if the Jesuits had a premonition of the agony that France, the country which had brought about their suppression, was to experience as it wended its way through the desacralization of its political structures.

Although these questions did not become the subject of my presentation, they did influence the form that it finally assumed. In my researching of the years 1789-1793 in the *Journal encyclopédique* (hereafter referred to as the *JE*) about the French Revolution, I had not been overwhelmed by a flood of articles referring to the American War of Independence. Why would this so-called philosophe journal[1] not have given much more space between 1789 and

1. The *Journal encyclopédique* was published uninterruptedly bi-monthly from January 1, 1756 to December 30, 1793, first in Liège, then Brussels, and finally till its fusion with the publication, *l'Esprit des Journaux*, in the unincorporated Duchy of Bouillon. Its founder, Pierre Rousseau was taken with the idea of publishing a journal that would popularize the contents as well as the concepts of the *Encyclopédie*. He succeeded in giving his readers "who were concerned with the progress of letters, religion, and politics during the Enlightenment," a periodical "as significant in representing the liberal point of view as the *Année littéraire* was in representing the traditionalist." See: Raymond Birn, *Pierre Rousseau and the Philosophes of Bouillon*, *SVEC* 29 (Geneva, 1964), 151.

The *JE*'s format consists of: a large section devoted to expository articles and reviews of books covering the panorama of political, religious, social, economic, and cultural facets of life; a section called the *Nouvelles littéraires* (herafter *NL*) that summarized the contents of

1793 to covering a war which seemed to fulfill the noblest expectations of the Enlightenment?

I thus decided to do two things: broaden my sights and note anything which even smacked of those warring and independent Americans; and extend the period of investigation to the decade between 1783 and 1793, that is to say, between the year when the Treaty of Paris formally ended hostilities between Great Britain and her former colonies in North America, and 1793, the last month of which saw the final edition of the *JE*. Within that ten-year period there appeared approximately 161 references to the American War of Independence.

As well, I had set forth certain questions which I felt begged to be addressed. In retrospect I see that at least two of these did function as accurate compasses pointing me in the right direction through the *JE*'s relatively unexplored territory.[2] The first, whether the Americans' break with Monarchy, albeit British, was too radical a move for the *JE* to congratulate; and the second, whether the statutory separation of church and state posed too much of a threat to the basically statist mentality of the *JE*'s editors and the overwhelming majority of the authors to whom it gave space in its pages?[3]

Such insubstantial speculation might never have become embodied in a serious enquiry, had my curiosity about why the Jesuits founded Georgetown in this peculiar American context not persisted: it did somehow alert me to notice the two aspects of the *JE*'s coverage of the emergence of the United States of America which ultimately shaped and informed this presentation.

The *Journal*'s Reporting of the American War

The first was that the "war" in my topic, the American War of Independence, held far less importance for the *JE* than its frequent citations ostensibly indicated. This became apparent as I began to experience how the

---

recently received books and announced the prospectus of forthcoming works; and finally a section called *Principaux événements politiques et autres* (till August 1, 1790, when its name was changed to *Nouvelles politiques*), that concisely rendered the significant political news received from the capitals of Europe, the Middle East, Great Britain, and her American colonies.

2. To be sure, the most functional compass is Dante Lenardon's *Index du Journal encyclopédique* (Geneva: Slatkine, 1976). The *Index* consists of two parts: an enumerated listing of articles in chronological order with their identifiable authors; and an alphabetical arrangement of subjects and authors. (Citations in this paper will be referred to by their number in the chronological part of the *Index*. Subsequent references to the same index item are identified only by page number.) He has also produced the compasses, so to speak, to two other lodes of information about the eighteenth century: *Index de l'Année littéraire* (Geneva: Slatkine, 1979) and *Index du Journal de Trévoux* (Geneva: Slatkine, 1986).

3. See Joan Lenardon, "The Paradox of Revolution within an Etatist Mentality," paper given at the *Colloque: Presse d'élite, presse populaire et propagande pendant la Révolution Française* (University of Haifa, May 16-18, 1988). In press for *SVEC*.

JE itself was perceiving the first dawning of a society, one which, though recognizable in its English provenance, was quite stunningly new to it.

And the second feature of the *JE*'s perception which impressed me was its attitude of surprise and seriousness towards the way in which these thirteen Independent-States (*treize Etats-Indépendants*) adapted to their religious diversity in the New Dispensation as Thirteen United-States (*Treize Etats-Unis*).[4]

My topic had been much too narrow: what the *JE* and perhaps those Jesuits saw was less a war than a revolution.

However, only three times in all of its coverage of what we call the American Revolution, does the *JE* print the specific term, *la révolution américaine*.[5] To give just a few examples, one hears of: "les troubles de l'Amérique Anglaise" (11658), "la rébellion des colonies anglaises en Amérique" (10623), or "cette entreprise la plus extraordinaire dans l'histoire" (13389). In several instances, the editors of the *JE* and their authors, name the event: "l'insurrection américaine" (13091). Elsewhere, they refer to the event as "une guerre" and even as "la guerre de l'indépendance américaine" (12043). It is true that one does hear the simple term, "la révolution" (9764), as well as its various renditions into, for example: "la révolution qui a enlevé l'Amérique à l'Angleterre" (11575), or even as "Quelle révolution inattendue!" (13351)

Only John Adams joins the term, *guerre* with that of *révolution*, to create a cumbersome, though authentic expression of what he perceived and, I suggest, the *JE* perceived, namely, "la guerre et révolution américaine" (11606). How then does one go about releasing from these multitudinous appellations the meaning of that event, which we have come to call, somewhat laconically by comparison, the American Revolution?

The simplest way begins with the realization that very few of these terms denote only the military hostilities which broke out at Lexington on April 19, 1775 and ceased at Yorktown on October 19, 1781. Almost always the *JE* or its authors make these terms connote a much larger phenomenon in the history of humanity, one whose essence seems to have been captured best by John Adams' commodious expression, "la guerre et révolution américaine."

That distinction being made, one might indicate that the reader can still find an extensive though biased reportage of those military hostilities, and of the parts played by their leading military and diplomatic protagonists.[6]

---

4. For the purpose of conveying the *JE*'s emphasis on the unitedness of the Independent-States or Republics, as they are frequently referred to before the adoption of the federative union, the *Journal*'s use of the hyphen is retained.

5. 11606; 13352; *NL* 4/15/85.

6. See 9841 for the *JE*'s résumé of the war. The *JE*'s accuracy measures up well in comparison with "War of the American Revolution, 1775-1783," in *Encyclopedia of Military*

Thus, one could follow the several and apparently not altogether coordinated strategies of the British, after their initial rout at Lexington, Concord and Boston; through their predatory southern campaign to detach Virginia and seal off the rest of the southern colonies from the contamination of the rebellious New Englanders; to their campaign in the northern colonies to entrap the Continental army on the "isle d'Yorck." Why these initial victories of the British failed to culminate quickly in the total suppression of the colonial insurgency receives a military explanation in the *JE*'s exposition of the Americans' innovative tactic of the skirmish within their overall strategy of evading large, frontal battles.

All the main American military engagements are recounted: from the retaking of Boston, through the seizure of Fort Ticonderoga; the victory at Saratoga; the setbacks in White Plains, Long Island, Princeton, and Monmouth; Washington's audacious crossing of the Delaware river to surprise the German mercenaries at Trenton; the reconquest of Virginia and the Carolinas; to the final hemming in of the British at "Yorck-town," and subsequent peace negotiations.

Notwithstanding the *JE*'s undisguised favoritism for the Americans in its reportage of the war, its overall vision does transcend mere anti-British polemic. Indeed through its exploration of causes, the *JE* displays an objectivity, a magnanimity even, towards Great Britain, *agent provocateur*, undoubtedly, of "la guerre américaine," but also the generative matrix of "la révolution américaine."

It is to the exploration of causality that I should like to turn by introducing two authors who, I suggest, sum up most succintly what today we would call the proximate causes for the confrontation between the Bostonians and the forces of General Gage on April 19, 1775.

Raynal and Paine

The first is the abbé Raynal[7] whose opinion is sharply controverted by Thomas Paine.[8] The focus of Paine's letter will be to prove that the French

---

History, ed. R.E. Dupuy (New York: Harper and Row, 1986), 708-25.

7. The abbé Thomas-Guillaume-François Raynal (1711-1796) is identified as "historien, et l'un des philosophes du dix-huitième siècle dont la réputation a jeté le plus d'éclat". He is reputed to have authored the work, *Tableau et Révolutions des colonies anglaises de l'Amérique septentrionale (1781)*. An edition of this work appeared under the title: *Révolutions de l'Amérique* (1781). It was this edition that Paine responded to in his *Lettre* cited below. See: Joseph-Marie Quérard, *La France Littéraire ou Dictionnaire Bibliographique* (Paris: Maisonneuve & Larose, 1964), 7: 472-75.

8. "Lettre addressée à l'abbé Raynal sur les affaires de l'Amérique septentrionale, où l'on relève les erreurs dans lesquelles cet auteur est tombé en rendant compte de la révolution de l'Amérique." (9764) Translated from the English, London, 1783. See also: *NL* 4/15/85 for

historian misunderstood the causes of the break between England and the colonies. (200) According to Paine, the abbé has maintained that:

> De toutes les causes énergiques qui produisirent tant de révolutions sur le globe, aucune n'existait dans le nord de l'Amérique...Tout se réduisait à savoir si la métropole avait ou n'avait pas le droit de mettre directement ou indirectement un léger impôt sur les colonies. (201)

Paine challenges the abbé's "oratorical harangue" on chronological grounds, and pushes the causal date back at least a decade to that of the Stamp Act, which constituted "une usurpation des droits les plus sacrés et les plus précieux des Américains." (201) And although it was revoked the following year, yet another followed, the Declaratory Act which

> attribuait au parlement d'Angleterre le droit de lier l'Amérique dans tous les cas quelconques... Il contenait les semences toutes développées du gouvernement le plus despotique qui fût jamais exercé dans le monde... Les loix demandent obéissance; celle-ci demandait servitude. (202-03)

Paine argues that in failing to see that palpable causes for the rupture existed well before the Tea Act of 1773, Raynal mistakenly reduced all the causes of the war to his "light" tax on tea, and thereby confused: "la cause de la guerre avec la première occasion des hostilités." (203)

Apparent in this particular exchange is, on the one hand, Paine's connecting rights to people, and on the other, Raynal's connecting them to the state. That Paine should castigate the English Parliament for not living up to its historical function is comprehensible in one who has been a beneficiary of that heritage; that Raynal should have missed the point is indicative of a profoundly different mind-set.

Other Proponents of Proximate Causality

The second author who emphasizes proximate causality is François Soulès.[9] He specifies Lord Bute[10] as the cause of "les troubles de l'Amérique

---

a continuation of Paine's rejection of Raynal's authoritativeness on this subject.

9. Identified as one "qui s'est fait en littérature une réputation, principalement comme fidèle et élégant traducteur", in Quérard, *La France Littéraire...*, 9: 224-25. The author of *Histoire des troubles de l'Amérique anglaise* (Paris: Buisson, 1787), he translated many English texts, including Thomas Paine's retort to Edmund Burke.

10. The *JE* and Soulès identify John Stuart, third earl of Bute (1713-1792), as "the tutor of the grandson of George II, the future George III" and as a "zealous Tory who wielded absolute power over his student and George's mother." Although lord Bute resigned as Prime Minister in 1763, he is reputed to have "maintained his influence with George III until the new

Anglaise." (11658) He argues that the Prime Minister was driven by his own political ambition to strengthen the Crown and weaken the Whigs. (67)

Perceiving the New Englanders especially as ideologically related to the Whigs, Bute could not countenance any thought of allowing their representation in Parliament where he feared they would become "partisans-zélés des Whigs, dont ils disent tirer leur origine." (67) He decided therefore to reduce the colonies to utter dependence upon Great Britain through his imposition of the Stamp Act. Even though pockets of American resistance frightened him into revoking it: "Mylord Bute fortifie son parti; un nouvel impôt sur le verre, le papier, le thé, va bientôt apprendre aux Américains qu'on ne leur pardonne point cette révocation forcée." (68-69)

It was this action, Soulès maintains, which provoked the massive resistance from all of the colonies who, following the example of Boston and Massachusetts-Bay, convened their assemblies to demand the reestablishment of their rights.

Although the *JE* devotes another ten pages to Soulès' investigation of causality, it does reject as too narrow the author's primary attribution of the troubles of English America to the personal miscalculation of the Prime Minister. In its view, one which it holds consistently, "il est probable au moins que Mylord Bute n'a fait que hâter une révolution que la puissance des colonies aurait tôt ou tard amenée." (69-70)

There are several authors who, though they too unequivocally acknowledge the provocative character of the Stamp Act, the Tea Act, and the Declaratory Act, argue that the Americans broke with the mother-country only with great reluctance.[11]

Finally, there are two authors who situate the causes of the American Revolution on bases even more narrow than those of a "light tax on tea" or the arrogance of one inept British Minister.

The first heaps most of the blame for disrupting what he construes to have been an idyllic relationship between the brothers American and British, upon Benjamin Franklin: "un politico-philosophe, qu'on vit dans sa jeunesse, apprenti imprimeur rouler dans les rues de Philadelphie une brouette, chargée de papiers imprimés qu'il tâchait de vendre." (13351)

The *JE* peremptorily dismisses this author for allowing the spirit of partiality for his homeland to push him into penning against one of their heroes "une satyre violente contre le politique et le négociateur." (13352)

The other author locates the cause of the Americans' "insurrection" in a childish tantrum which has temporarily beclouded their vision. (14840; 14863)

---

prime minister, George Grenville, made the king promise in May, 1765, that he would neither employ Bute in office nor seek his counsel." (*New Encyclopedia Britannica*, 2: 681)

11. See 11066; 11116; 11575; 11715; 11737; 13091; 14166.

Once that cloud is dissipated, he predicts that they will soon see the light (158-159).

The *JE* quite emphatically rejects both this author's cause and effect in its retort that:

> s'il est un peuple heureux sur la terre, c'est les Américains libres, enveloppés de ce nuage, qui, au lieu d'obscurcir les objets à leurs yeux, leur a fait voir que tous ces beaux privilèges qu'on vante tant ici n'étaient avantageux que pour la mère-patrie. (159)

One can see that the *JE* has allowed the case for proximate causality to be argued, but has not endorsed such a view. From a fuller investigation of its coverage, I suggest that the *JE* regarded the military hostilities between April 1775 and October 1781 as constituting but one climactic point, albeit a most dramatic one, in the development of a people whose history was rooted deeply within their English heritage.

John Adams

No author published by the *JE* more stunningly summarizes what we would today call the remote causes of "la guerre et révolution américaine" than the coiner of this term himself in "Fragment d'un nouvel ouvrage de M. Adams, intitulé: *Défense des Constitutions Américaines*." (11606) This "Fragment" consists of John Adams' piquant explanation of why he is publicizing the extensive letter he wrote to M. l'abbé de Mably.[12]

Adams first tells how he met the abbé at a dinner party in Paris in October of 1782. There, de Mably informed Adams of his intention to write a "history of la révolution d'Amérique" and requested the use of his memoirs. Adams continues:

> Je demandai quelle partie de cette révolution il se proposait d'écrire.–Toute entière, me répondit-on.–Où comptait-il puiser ses matériaux? Ce fut ma seconde question. L'on présumait qu'il les prendrait dans les papiers publics, et qu'il y joindrait les instructions qu'il tirait des particuliers. Je fis quelques objections à ce projet. (134)

Adams indicates that what follows is a translation of their conversation which formed the letter he subsequently sent to the abbé. Adams concludes these preliminary remarks saying that he only encouraged Mably out of politeness,

12. L'abbé Gabriel Bonnot de Mably is identified as "philosophe, politique et historien" in *La France Littéraire*, 5: 404-06. The abbé's *De la Manière d'écrire l'Histoire* appeared in 1783 and his *Observations sur le gouvernement et les loix des Etats-Unis d'Amérique* in 1784.

since he felt he was in no way prepared for this undertaking. Indeed, no one in Europe or in America is capable of writing such a history now.[13]

What is of immediate interest is first of all, the fourfold periodisation of "la révolution américaine" that Adams lays before de Mably with the caution to his self-proclaimed mentor that:

> Sans une connaissance distincte de l'histoire des colonies dans la première période, un écrivain se trouvera toujours embarrassé depuis le commencement de son ouvrage jusqu'à la fin, pour rendre compte des événements et des caractères qui se présenteront à décrire à chaque pas, à mesure qu'il avancera vers la seconde, la troisième et la quatrième périodes. (136)

John Adams dates the first period of the history of "ce grand evénement" from the first founding of the colonies in 1600 to 1761; the second, from 1761 to August 19, 1775; the third, from the battle of Lexington to the signing of the Treaty with France on February 6, 1778; and the fourth, from February 1778 to the culmination of the peace negotiations in the Treaty of Paris in 1783. (135-36)

In the second part of his letter, Adams gathers an exhaustive, one might even say, withering assemblage of basic required readings for the "acquisition of sufficient knowledge" about each of the four periods.[14] Significantly, he ascribes great weight to: "toutes les chartes accordées aux colonies, et les commissions et instructions données aux gouverneurs, tous les codes de loi des différentes colonies, tous les registres de la législature des différentes colonies." (136)

Underscoring repeatedly the necessity to comprehend the constitutive components of the Americans' political life, Adams offers the abbé:

> une clef pour toute cette histoire. Il y a une analogie générale dans les gouvernements et les caractères de tous les Treize-Etats; mais ce ne fut que lorsque les débats et la guerre commencèrent en Massachusetts-Bay, la principale province de la Nouvelle-Angleterre, que les institutions primitives firent leur premier effet. (140)[15]

---

13. However, he does give his compatriots the edge in this matter: "There exists on the new continent a great number of individuals who understand every point relating to a free constitution, infinitely better than the abbé de Mably, and M. de Turgot, however amiable, intelligent and witty they may be."

14. John Adams offers a prodigious amount of documentation on this point, which the *JE* reprints extensively.

15. Once again the *JE* prints Adams' extensive elaboration upon the role of the: local political structures; schools; churches; and militia.

His pedagogical and bibliographical *tour de force* accomplished, Adams closes on a note of genteel self-deprecation: "Voilà, Monsieur, une petite esquisse des quatre sources principales de cette sagesse dans les conseils, de cette habileté, de cette bravoure militaire, qui ont produit la révolution américaine." (140)

The *JE* gives space to many other authors who say as pointedly, though less exhaustively, what John Adams does, namely, that anyone who wants to make sense out of the events taking place in English America since 1775 must go back in history to at least 1600, and then look at this history not merely as a spontaneous American combustion, but rather as a natural development within an Anglo-American culture.[16]

However I am not satisfied that by staying just with these authors, I could do justice to the breadth and depth of the *JE*'s appreciation of this larger phenomenon, *la révolution américaine*. It is, I suggest, through an exploration of what the *JE* fastens upon repeatedly, as fascinating about the Americans' way of life, that one could more reliably demonstrate its basic accord with the long and organic view so elegantly unfolded by John Adams.

If there is one characteristic of the Americans which symbolizes the attractiveness of their revolution for the *JE*, it is the Americans' *esprit républicain*. Granted that in the eighteenth century, the term, *republic*, meant primarily a society in which the monarch's power was limited by that of the people;[17] granted as well that the *JE* and most of its authors subscribe to this meaning. Nonetheless, with regard to its perception of the Americans' *esprit républicain*, the *JE* steps out of that well-defined meaning of renovation into that undefined territory of innovation. One can see this movement towards the more modern understanding of revolution itself in the *JE*'s captivation with: the Americans' keen consciousness of their right to run their own societies; their proven competence to run them well; and their stunning genius to have created not just another bit of exotica, but something truly new in the history of humanity.[18]

---

16. 9764; 9958; 10711; 11066; 11116; 11161; 11302; 11575; 11658; 11715; 13091; 14481; 14840; 14863; *NL* 4/15/85.

17. See Beatrice Fry Hyslop, "The American Press and the French Revolution of 1789" in *Proceedings of the American Philosophical Society*, 104, 1 (February, 1960): 54-85.

18. See: 9764; 10461; 10517; 10711; 11066; 11096; 11242; 11575; 11674; 11737; 12043; 12091; 12616; 13160; 13987; 14166; 14199; 14221; 14378; *NL* 4/15/85; *NP* 7/1/85; *NL* 11/1/85; *NP* 3/15/88; *NP* 2/10/91.

Religious Toleration: an Embodiment of the Americans' *esprit républicain*

The *JE*'s overwhelmingly benevolent and often poignant envy of the Americans' republican spirit will suffuse its extensive examination of their political, religious, social, and economic structures.[19]

One feature which epitomizes this spirit for the *Journal encyclopédique* is the capacity of Americans from so many religious backgrounds to live together in civil accord.[20]

What one author[21] finds so interesting about the lay-out of the city of Philadelphia is that:

> La multiplicité des temples que la tolérance a érigés à la divinité, forme aussi un spectacle intéressant dans cette ville. Chaque secte a le sien; et ce qu'il y a de plus étonnant, les quakers, les anabaptistes, les anglicans, les presbytériens, les méthodistes, les moraves, les luthériens et les catholiques prient leur dieu les uns à côté des autres, chacun à sa manière, sans troubler la concorde qui doit régner entre des concitoyens. (9709)

How the Americans accomplished such an admirable feat is the subject of one of the *JE*'s extensive excerpts from John Andrews' *History of the War with America, France, Spain and Holland; commencing in 1775 and ending in 1783*. (11575)[22]

Andrews seeks to identify the remote cause which impelled the English emigrants to America in the seventeenth century and which still galvanized their resistance to the mother-country in the eighteenth. According to him:

> Persécutés chez eux pour des opinions religieuses peu conformes aux dogmes dominans, leur attachement à ces opinions était si invincible, que, plutôt que d'y renoncer, ils aimèrent mieux abandonner leur patrie, fuir au bout du monde dans les régions les moins habitables, pour y jouir de l'exercice libre et public de leurs sentiments particuliers. (423)

---

19. This paper addresses only a fraction of the material available. Several fruitful lines of research could be carried out if one were to study the manifestations of the Americans' *esprit républicain* under the following headings: political structures; *moeurs*; expectation of the abolition of the slave trade and slavery; economic achievements and prospects.

20. 9709; 9764; 9958; 10532; 10711; 10743; 11575; 11606; 11841; 13091; 13400; 14199; 14221; 14840; 14863; *NP* 5/1/83; *NP* 6/1/86; *NL* 11/15/87; *NL* 5/10/91.

21. "Notices sur diverses contrées de l'Amérique." (9709-2/15/83) Anonymous. The article more generally deals with the physical features of the State of Pennsylvania.

22. London, 1785, 1786.

The hardships which they overcame in their new home prove that they were more than mere enthusiasts for their own opinions. Nevertheless, the force of these opinions perdured so that:

> Le souvenir des causes de l'émigration de leurs ancêtres est encore dans toute sa force chez les habitants de la Nouvelle-Angleterre... Ce que leur enthousiasme tenait de la religion est un peu calmé; mais ce qu'il empruntait de la politique subsiste dans toute son énérgie et sans altération. Il n'y a point de peuple qui soit plus fortement attaché à ses droits et à sa liberté. (424)[23]

Andrews adds that the New Englanders can never forget the harsh treatment they received from the Anglican Church as well as from the Crown, so that:

> Si ce peuple était l'ennemi de la monarchie, il avait encore plus d'aversion pour l'église anglicane. Le traitement rigoureux que les ancêtres éprouvèrent de la part de l'archevêque Laud est ineffaçablement gravé dans sa mémoire, et la douceur du gouvernement ecclésiastique actuel en Angleterre n'a pu encore bannir de son esprit les erreurs et les violences de quelques-uns de ses anciens chefs. Il semble qu'il regarde la hiérarchie comme un corps dévoué au soutien du pouvoir arbitraire, et cite souvent le servile attachement de divers prélats anglais aux maximes absurdes d'une obéissance passive à la volonté du souverain. (426)

Consequently, they incarnated their aspirations to religious and political equality in the very structures of their church order and rejected "tous les rangs et degrés qui accordent un pouvoir spirituel au clergé." (427)[24]

The abbé de Mably also ascribes Americans' unusual treatment of religion to an identifiable historical cause, for as he opines:

> Vos pères ont jeté les premiers fondements de vos colonies dans le temps que l'Angleterre, occupée, ainsi que le reste de l'Europe, des controverses

---

23. The author deplores however, the extravagant attachment of those who "were so determined to protect themselves from any contradiction that they persecuted those who disagreed with them." See also: "Lettres d'un cultivateur Américain"(11841), for Hector St. John de Crèvecoeur's candid acknowledgement that institutionalized religious toleration had a history of its own among the various colonies.

24. The *JE* in one of its rare extensive comments, editorializes that: "Il est évident que, pénétrés de la grandeur et de l'étendue, de l'importance et de la sainteté des fonctions des ministres de la religion, ils ont cru qu'il fallait qu'ils s'y livrassent tout entiers, que les emplois civils ne pouvaient leur causer que des distractions nuisibles, et n'étaient pas compatibles avec l'exercice de piété et de charité, avec le zèle toujours actif du ministère."

théologiques, était déchirée par des guerres de religion. Ils fuirent d'une patrie où régnait le fanatisme; et pleins d'une juste horreur contre l'absurde tyrannie qu'on exerçait sur les consciences. (10352)

Given the basic reason for their emigration, these first Americans understandably: "regardaient comme le comble du bonheur la liberté de servir et d'honorer Dieu de la manière que chacun croirait raisonnable." Far from abating with time, "cette liberté indéfinie de conscience forme encore l'opinion publique et générale de la république." (204)

By contrast, Thomas Paine's explanation for the original emigration to America appears to rely on quasi-theological reasons.

In the second extract of his "Response to *Reflections on the French Revolution*," Paine rejects what he considers to be Edmund Burke's position on the relationship between the church and the state. (13400)

According to Paine: "Toutes les religions sont ou doivent être, par leur nature, douces, tendres, bénignes." How then, he wonders do they become "moroses, intolérantes?" That situation, he claims, "vient de l'union que M. Burke recommande. En joignant l'Eglise à l'Etat, on produit une espèce de mulet capable de détruire et incapable d'engendrer, appellé l'Eglise établie par la loi." (558)

That union provoked so much rancor and irreligion among the English, that they chased the Quakers and other non-conformists to America. Far from insinuating that religion *per se* perturbs the peace of the Body Politic, Paine insists that it is its establishment within that body which causes civil discord.

The *JE*'s editors seem quite comfortable with Andrews and de Mably, both of whom had located the cause of the Americans' penchant for religious toleration in the abusive action of an already existing institutionalized union of church and state; they cannot disguise their uneasiness with Thomas Paine when he finds the mere notion of such an institution absolutely repugnant.

One might be tempted to make too much of the *JE*'s reserve in this area, especially after reading those additional authors who predict moral deterioration and political disintegration to a society which lacks the kind of religio-political cohesiveness provided by an established church. On balance however, I suggest that one would be hard put not to see this journal's utter captivation with the confidence of this multi-religious confederation, that in eschewing the establishment of one church over another, they undoubtedly will form a more perfect union.

In conclusion, I have suggested that the Americans' ability to sustain domestic tranquillity in the midst of religious diversity symbolized for the *JE* their pristine *esprit républicain*. Again and again, the *JE* tells the story of these undaunted people who were born in dissent, made unwelcome within the sacred precincts of the parental home, and then allowed inexplicably to settle on the periphery of, but still within, the British ambit.

There, legitimated, ironically, through the written charters granted them by the same mother-country which had expelled them, these Americans proceeded to enshrine their formerly disruptive dissidences into a string of distinctive societies whose political and religious structures bore unmistakable signs of their English provenance.

Though ill at ease with the absence of an established church among the Americans, the *JE* cannot contain its spontaneous admiration for the Americans' unprecedented achievement in combining religious diversity with political unity.

The *JE*'s overall determination of what caused *la guerre américaine* was best captured by John Andrews who judged that:

> Cet esprit de résistance dont la Grande-Bretagne se plaignait alors amèrement, était donc la pente naturelle et nécessaire de ces colonies qu'elle avait fondées, nourries, et élevées avec tant de soin jusqu'à leur parfaite maturité. (11575)

And lastly, I suggest that it is the *JE*'s unabashed delight with the safe delivery of a robust new society out of the old that best conveys what the *JE* meant by what we have come to call, *la révolution américaine*.

Gallican Liberties and American Freedom

Jacques M. Grès-Gayer

Gallican and American Liberties

> Les Américains semblaient ne faire qu'exécuter ce que nos écrivains avaient conçu: ils donnaient la substance de la réalité à ce que nous étions en train de rêver.[1]

This of course is a judgement by Tocqueville. It cleverly associates the fascination exerted upon some Europeans by the new continent and the utopian character of their approach. They read in the new Republic the realization of the European dream. Though this attitude has been analyzed and discussed at length on the political or ideological levels, one wonders how relevant it is to the religious domain. Or perhaps, to put the question more into focus: what was the French perception, if any, of religion in the new Republic? If indeed America was an utopian way of dealing with their own situation, how did the members of the Gallican Church assess the place of their little sister in the United States?

But what Gallican Church? By 1790 the national Church was severely divided by the reorganization sponsored by the Civil Constitution of the French clergy. Paradoxically the two groups who either accepted it or rejected it claimed to be faithful to the same ideal of Gallican Liberties, those general principles that defined the identity of the French church. Through a constant reference to Early Christianity they developed a moderate ecclesiology that separated the secular and religious spheres, though clearly associating them in the person of the King, and balanced the authority of the Papacy with that

1. Alexis de Tocqueville, *L'Ancien Régime et la Révolution* (Paris: Gallimard, 1952), 199. See also Georges Gusdorf, *Les révolutions de France et d'Amérique. La violence et la sagesse* (Paris: Perrin, 1988), 38.

of the Bishops. The term *Liberties* referred to unalienable rights going back to the constitution of original christendom.[2]

The French Revolution had soon shown the fragility of this conception, since both the non-juror and the constitutional clergy appealed to the same referent. Who were the real defenders of Gallican Liberties? The issue remains complicated and full of contradictions. We shall consider it here from a very limited angle through a confrontation of the Gallican dreams with the reality of American life: how members of the two groups happened to consider the religious situation beyond the ocean, or more precisely, how they interpreted the American model of Catholicism.

The Gallican Church in the New Republic

The comparison will be uneven and piecemeal since in those days Gallicans of all persuasions had more urgent issues to address. Nevertheless, between the pragmatic experience of the French clergy serving in the United States and the more theoretical apprehensions of their colleagues who remained in Europe, a number of general features emerge, which are worthy of attention.

1. French Clergy in America

The first group needs little introduction. It is represented by the limited number of French clergymen who came to participate in the expansion of the new church. Placing themselves under the authority of the first Catholic bishop John Carroll, they served either as teachers with the Sulpicians who founded the Baltimore seminary, or pastors, like Fathers Matignon and Cheverus in Boston. In that sense, they belong much more to the history of the church in America, but since the "Gallican influence" they had developed is taken for granted, it might be of interest to consider them from this different perspective; more precisely, to evaluate their theoretical adherence to the Gallican Liberties given their pragmatic experience in the expansion of the nascent church. In this respect, four themes appear worthy of consideration: church polity, pastoral action, ecumenism, church and state.

2. Gallican Attitudes and American Issues

The first theme deals with ecclesiastical polity. In other words, it tries to discover the underlying ecclesiology of the Gallican missionaries in their new

---

2. To summarize a more complicated issue, see Joseph Lecler, "Qu'est-ce que les Libertés de l'Eglise gallicane", *Recherches de Science religieuse* 23 (1933): 379-410, 542-658; 24 (1934): 47-85.

environment. What strikes the observer is both their faithfulness to an ecclesiology that might be deemed "moderate or classical Gallicanism," and its expression according to the context in which they had to express it. Consider for example their presentation of the role of the papacy: they associated a very clear defense of its importance with a rejection of any exaggeration. Thus in May of 1800, Father–soon to become Bishop–Cheverus of Boston did not hesitate to write: "To believe the Pope infallible is no part of our creed, and no Roman Catholic ever pretended that he is impeccable."[3] Cheverus's defense of episcopacy was not simply typical of an Ancien Régime Gallican, it emphasized the special relationship of the pastor with his flock. Cheverus's biographers have all noted his hesitation in accepting another episcopal appointment either in the United States or in his own country and the reason he gave was that the special bond established between the bishop and his church could not be dissolved.[4]

After Carroll's election, the choice of bishops by their own clergy was not continued, but nothing in the attitude of the Franco-American priests suggests that they were opposed to it. In that instance, of course, this return to the practice of antiquity had been endorsed by the Papacy.

Similarly, if the participation of the laity in the administration of local parishes went further than what might have existed in France, the Gallican clergymen behaved according to local rules and shared with their American confreres a desire to follow these rules with moderation.

A self-evident "Gallicanism," therefore, classical and even subdued. Not only devoid of the aggressiveness of the European model against the alternative ultramontanism, but singularly lacking in any sign of expansionism. The priority here went to missionary work, demanding necessarily some adaptation to the social and political context of the country. How did the French respond to this situation?

The answer in this instance also is that nothing distinguished them from their American colleagues. The communities they constituted worshipped using hymnals and prayer-books, specifically prepared for them,[5] that went much further in their stress on the people's participation than what was then practiced in France.

The Franco-American priests were also most zealous in their relationships with non-Catholic Christians. They were following the example of John Carroll, but did not manifest any difficulty in showing respect and courtesy to

3. Robert H. Lord, John E. Sexton and Edward J. Haddington, *History of the Archdiocese of Boston in the Various Stages of Its Development, 1604-1943*, 3 vols. (New York: Sheed and Ward, 1944), 1: 571.

4. *History of the Archdiocese of Boston*, 1: 691-694.

5. *History of the Archdiocese of Boston*, 1: 593, 694; *Roman Catholic Manual or Collection of Prayers, etc.* (Boston: Manning and Loring, 1803).

ministers of the other Christian communities as well as to the members of their flock.[6] Not only did they take advantage of religious toleration, they also seemingly accepted its values.

Finally, they made a serious effort to accept the separation of church and state as it existed in the country where they exercised their ministry. They had no difficulty in preaching the "entirely spiritual authority of the papacy,"[7] but willingly agreed to participate in the civil activities sponsored by the elected officials of the Republic.

For an American historian, these characteristics are not surprising. They represent the riches and dynamism of genuine American Catholicism, exemplified in the ideas of John Carroll. From an European perspective, this is not so evident since they bore a striking resemblance to the changes imposed upon the French Church by the Revolution. The Gallican clergymen, despite what was imposed in their own country, did not appear to have any difficulty with these four features essential to the proclamation of the Gospel in the new Republic, even if they bore a striking resemblance to the very elements they condemned in the Constitutional Church.

The Gallican Church in the French Revolution

Recent historiography, particularly the works of Bernard Plongeron, has convincingly placed the members of the Gallican Church who accepted the Civil Constitution in a new perspective that reveals many strengths. Not only did they welcome political democracy, but their interpretation of the Gallican Liberties brought them to positions very similar to those American Catholicism came to defend.

1. On the matter of ecclesiastical polity, it is well known that the Constitutional Church advocated a form of democracy in the Church that favored elections of the clergy. This, they contended, was more faithful to genuine Christian tradition, and far from weakening the authority of the pastors, strengthened it. Their defense of episcopacy was at least as strong as the one we might observe in America, and we can find an exposition of the particular relationship of the local bishop to his Church which corresponds precisely to Bishop Cheverus's "marriage" to the Boston church.[8]

2. Their concern for pastoral action encouraged them to develop an authentic liturgical and spiritual life based on lay participation and activity at the local level.

---

6. Annabelle Melville, *Jean Lefebvre de Cheverus, 1768-1886* (Milwaukee: Bruce, 1958): 132-40.

7. *History of the Archdiocese of Boston*, 1: 571. (Cheverus).

8. *History of the Archdiocese of Boston*, 1: 691, 693-94.

3. They also welcomed a form of religious toleration based on the right of conscience and saw it as the best way to foster a reunion of Christendom on the basis of their Gallican interpretation of the Catholic tradition.

4. Their relationship with the state was however more complex. If, in the words of the Metropolitan of Rennes, Le Coz, they saw total "accord between the Catholic Religion and Republican Government,"[9] and valiantly survived the separation of church and state associated with de-Christianization, they remained faithful to an ideal of "Christian Civilization" that necessitated cooperation between the secular and religious powers at the national level.[10]

One could assume, therefore, that for members of the Constitutional Church the nascent Church in America was closest to their ideal, and that despite its numerical weakness, it was extolled as representing the future of a renewed Catholicism. Yet this was hardly the case.

The Constitutional Church and the New Republic

1. Contacts

There was certainly some real interest within the Revolutionary Church for the Catholicism of the new Republic, a concern that is difficult to define since no study has yet been devoted to the topic. A number of passing references suggest that despite their own problems and the difficulties of communication, leading figures of the Constitutional Church followed with attention the development of the Catholic faith in America. The correspondence between Bishop Grégoire of Blois–the greatest among the Fathers of the schismatic Church–and John Carroll reveals Grégoire as anxious to present and defend his own cause as well as to become acquainted with the situation of the American church. This may explain the American Archbishop's rather cool replies.[11]

The same Grégoire perhaps gives us the clue to the Constitutional perception of the American Catholic community. In the second edition of his *Essai historique sur les libertés de l'Eglise gallicane et des autres Eglises de la catholicité*, he surveys the different national churches of the Catholic communion and evaluates them according to how closely they came to

---

9. Claude Le Coz, *Accord de la religion catholique avec le gouvernement républicain* (Rennes, [n.p.n.d.]).

10. Bernard Plongeron, "Permanence d'une idéologie de "civilisation chrétienne" dans le clergé constitutionnel," *Studies in Eighteenth-Century Culture*, vol. 7, ed. Roseann Runte (Madison: University of Wisconsin Press, 1978): 274.

11. *Archives of the Baltimore Archdiocese*, Grégoire Letters (April 10, 1809, September 10, 1810, September 4, 1813, February 5, 1814): 484, 486, 487.

John Carroll's letters to Grégoire printed in the *John Carroll's Papers* have to be interpreted in the context of what Grégoire had written to him.

correspond to the French ideals. Surprisingly, despite his claim to be exhaustive, the French bishop does not seem to consider the North American situation better than that of Catholicism in England. After simply mentioning the institution of the American hierarchy, he gives a few trifling details and concludes:

> On dira peut-être, que les libertés des Eglises étant l'objet de cet ouvrage, les détails qu'on vient de lire n'offrent rien d'important à cet égard. Je suis complètement de cet avis; mais des personnes au désir desquelles il m'est agréable de déférer ayant témoigné leur surprise de ne rien trouver dans la première édition sur les églises catholiques qui sont hors d'Europe, il fallait justifier cette lacune par la disette des faits qui ne sont pas arrivés à ma connaissance, ou plutôt qui manquent en réalité [...] beaucoup de *chrétientés* y sont inorganisées, ou n'ont qu'une forme peu régulière et une existence précaire.[12]

This is a puzzling judgment, one which might certainly be adequate to Africa or Asia, but why America, where the ecclesiastical structures were already present?

A brief return to the four issues considered above might be useful.

2. Issues

1. From the perspective of the Constitutional Church, the origins of the American Church clearly manifested a return to the structure and policy of the early Church. The election of the first bishop of Baltimore by his clergy, his "synodical" action with the members of his presbyterium, the very simplicity of a missionary situation could be viewed as a model of reform and renewal.

2. Similarly, the movement to foster lay participation in worship and the life of the Church at large was seen as a return to genuine Catholic tradition.

3. The Americans' acceptance of religious toleration and their positive use of it could not but be approved by the French Catholics who did the same.

4. For Grégoire, however, these attributes could not constitute an ideal Church since they lacked an essential foundation: without State cooperation, they had developed in the context of "unorganized Christendom." To put it more bluntly, the constructive elements of Gallican liberties present in the American Church were irremediably weakened by the characteristics of American freedom: religious liberty and the separation of Church and State.

---

12. Henri Grégoire, *Essai historique sur les libertés de l'Eglise gallicane et des autres Eglises de la catholicité* (Paris, 1820), 462-63.

Gallican Liberties and American Freedom

When in order to escape persecution the first Sulpicians left France for the New World, their Superior General, M. Emery, detailed in a striking address what they were to expect in their new ministry. They were to be missionaries and serve differently three groups of people: heathen Indians, heretic Protestants and the Catholic minority.[13] This discourse stressed the imperfect aspect of the American religious experience. It reveals a conservative apprehension of the religious situation in the United States, that might as well have been expressed by members of the French Revolutionary Church. They saw themselves as missionaries sent to give, not to receive; to teach, not to learn; and to share their dream, not really expecting its fulfillment.

Their discontent with the situation of the Church in America shows that despite major differences in the interpretation of the Gallican ideal in the national context, members of the French clergy on either side of the Atlantic shared the same utopian vision.

Both saw in the Gallican Liberties an ideal model of the Church which reconstructed the situation of the early centuries. They diverged on practical issues, such as the sharing of ecclesiastical authority, attitudes to religious toleration, or more seriously, the question of a political regime. But they still functioned within the same framework of "Christian civilization," or to be more precise, "Catholic civilization."

American freedom, as they rightly perceived, destroyed the most important of their Gallican principles: the unity of the national Church and its concrete association with the political power.

The more conservative perceived this alliance in terms of *Throne and Altar*,[14] while their adversaries preferred to see it as a cooperation between Church and State. They all rejected a "freedom" that deprived the American Church of its influence upon society. Toleration in that context, far from preparing religious unity, made it totally unreachable:[15] "On sait combien il nous en a coûté pour avoir voulu faire l'expérience de la Constitution civile des Américains," wrote M. Tabaraud in 1803, in his *De la nécessité d'une*

---

13. "Il s'agira dans ce séminaire de former tous les ouvriers apostoliques que la Providence destine à affermir les catholiques dans la foi, à ramener les hérétiques dans le sein de l'Eglise, à porter la lumière de l'Evangile aux sauvages: en un mot à faire régner Jésus-Christ," Jean Leflon, *Monsieur Emery* (Paris, 1944) 1: 163.

14. Dale Van Kley, "Church, State and the Ideological Origins of the French Revolution: The Debate over the General Assembly of the Gallican Clergy in 1756," *Journal of Modern History* 51 (1979): 652-62.

15. Bernard Plongeron, "Les langages théologiques de la tolérance," *Bulletin de la Société de l'Histoire du Protestantisme français*, 134 (1988): 228-29.

religion de l'Etat. "Dieu veuille que nous n'ayons pas à nous repentir de ce système de tolérance religieuse."[16]

Again the non-juror Oratorian expressed a pessimism shared by all Gallicans.

Conclusion

For the Gallicans favorable or opposed to the Republican system, in Europe or across the ocean, the American Bill of Rights was anything but an ideal to be imitated or a dream to be realized. Their own utopian dream was oriented toward the past, all they could think of doing was to offer it to their American brothers. They do not seem to have considered of any value for the future the experience of Catholicism in the new Republic. Or rather, at least one of them did: how else can we explain the moderate if not reluctant endorsement by Cheverus, then Cardinal-Archbishop of Bordeaux, of the Roman condemnation of Lamennais?[17]

Indeed it was left to Lamennais and his disciples to discover the values of American liberties and oppose them to "Gallican Servitudes."[18] It is no coincidence that Henri Lacordaire took the opportunity of writing Tocqueville's eulogy to extol the Christian aspect of American democracy. For this opponent of Gallican servitude, the "American democracy has founded a great people, religious, powerful, respected, free at last."[19]

---

16. Mathurin Tabaraud, *De la nécessité d'une religion de l'Etat* (Paris, 1803): 61.

17. Melville, *Cheverus*, 403.

18. See the "prospectus de lancement de l'*Avenir*" written by Abbé Gerbet in August 1830, in *Articles de l'Avenir* (Louvain, 1830), ii. Marcel Prelot and Françoise Gallouédec-Genuys, *Le Libéralisme catholique* (Paris, 1969): 81.

19. "La démocratie américaine a fondé un grand peuple, religieux, puissant, respecté, libre enfin," Henri Lacordaire, "Discours de réception à l'Académie française," *Oeuvres* (Paris, 1920), 8: 341. On the later influences of this "American mirage" see Claude Fohlen, "Catholicisme américain et catholicisme européen: la convergence de l'américanisme", *Revue d'histoire moderne et contemporaine* 34 (1987): 215-30.

Lafitau, Démeunier and the Rejection of the American Model at the French National Assembly, 1789-1791

Edna Hindie Lemay

If 1492 marks the discovery of America, it was only three centuries later that the New World began to figure in books of history and geography. In fact, La Popelinière introduced the travels of Christopher Columbus and others into his *Three Worlds* (1582), and then wrote briefly of Topinambas, Brazilians and Mexicans in his *History of Histories* (1599). Slowly, the European vision of the outer world extends to include America which appears in a few general works on religion, history and geography in the seventeenth century.[1] At the beginning of the eighteenth century, Lenglet-Dufresnoy devoted almost half his third volume to the American continent, admitting that he knew little of the southern hemisphere.[2] Only with Maclot's geography in 1765[3] did America gain some importance and an extra chapter on the French and English settlements. Three years later, Cornelius de Pauw[4] wrote that no event proved more noteworthy than the discovery of America, though he considered native Americans to be rather degenerate. Writing in Berlin, he might have wanted to keep in line with Frederick the Great's policy of dissuading candidates for emigration. In the eighteenth century, any form of depopulation was considered an impoverishment of the country.

The reason for this long delayed interest in America was that the Orient continued to be the main attraction in literature concerning the non-European world.[5] This is true until the mid-eighteenth century when seven volumes of

---

1. Urbain Chevreau, *L'Histoire du monde* (Paris, 1681); Jean-Baptiste Audiffret, *Géographie ancienne, moderne et historique*, 3 vols. (Paris, 1689).

2. Nicolas Lenglet-Dufresnoy, *Méthode pour étudier la géographie*, 4 vols. (Paris, 1716).

3. Jean-Charles Maclot, *Précis sur le globe terrestre* (Paris, 1765).

4. Cornelius de Pauw, *Recherches philosophiques sur les Américains*, 3 vols. (Berlin, 1768-1769).

5. Geoffroy Atkinson, *Les nouveaux horizons de la Renaissance française* (Paris: Droz, 1935), 10-11; Michel Mollat, éd., *Aspects internationaux de la découverte océanique au XVe et XVIe siècles*, 5e Colloque internat. d'histoire maritime, Lisbonne, 1960 (Paris: SEVPEN, 1966), 34;

Abbé Prévost's *General History of Travel* concern Asia, four volumes Africa and then only four volumes America (1746-1760). Even in Démeunier's book (see below), the references to America are much less frequent than those made to Asia and Africa.

Lafitau, the American "Savages" and the Young Colonies

Nonetheless, America would gradually assume importance in the anthropological vision of the world, "savages" coming to represent the origins of humanity, man in his early steps. Convinced that all men belong to the same human family, during the five years (1712-1717) Lafitau spent with the Indians of North America, he constantly saw in their habits and customs similarities with those of ancient Europeans. Thus he included them in his Europe-centered historical vision of humanity. Moreover, living and working closely with them, Lafitau came to respect them for their qualities, as he explained in dedicating the book to the Duke of Orléans. "Under rough and uncultured appearances, these people reveal a love for their country engraved in their hearts, a natural passion for glory, an immense courage not only in face of peril, but in all circumstances, fearless of death which their education has trained them to accept." As an attentive observer, Lafitau had noted that in spite of an apparent lack of laws, religion and the prime necessities of life, primitive Americans had qualities such as intelligence, imagination, memory and a kind heart. This vision of the American savage, acquired thanks to the "science of habits and customs", would, he hoped, lead to progress in the general knowledge of mankind.[6]

In the course of the eighteenth century, there are relatively few references to Lafitau, but many more to the other Jesuit traveller, Charlevoix, who published a *History and General Description of New France* in 1744. Charlevoix contrasted American "savages" to barbarians, while Lafitau had treated them as the native people of America, different from Europeans. Prévost used both Charlevoix and Lafitau in volume 15 of his *General History of Travel* (1759) on the character, habits and customs of North American Indians. His description of their government gives a glowing picture of their leaders, brave and disinterested, who propose solutions to their people rather than give orders. Crimes being rarely committed, there is no need for criminal justice. Children are never punished because Indians are convinced that man is born free and that no one has the right to restrain his liberty . Over the years, the travel literature tended to reinforce the myth of the "noble savage." In 1758, when

---

Henri-Jean Martin et Lucien Febvre, éds., *L'Apparition du livre* (Paris: A. Michel, 1958), 420-23.

6. Joseph-François Lafitau, *Customs of the American Indians Compared with the Customs of Primitive Times*, ed. and transl. by William N. Fenton and Elizabeth Moore, 2 vols. (Toronto: The Champlain Society, 1974), 1: 2-3.

the Seven Years' war was raging, Goguet referred to Lafitau's title (without mentioning the author) in his book on the *Origin of Laws, Arts and Sciences*.[7] Contrary to Lafitau, Goguet used the ethnographic materials of travellers to America to fill in the gaps of ancient history.[8]

Until then, it could be said that Frenchmen were interested in America mainly for its primitive people. The "noble savage" vision of America obscured that of European pioneers trying to eke out an existence in the face of many physical dangers. However, as the French lost the war against England, home interest in the American colonies grew, far-sighted ministers expecting them one day to be free of the mother country. Americans would come to Europe to rouse interest in their cause and to seek French aid against the common enemy. Franklin came to Paris in 1767 and again in 1769 to attract public opinion in favor of his fellowmen struggling with the English over taxation. On his third trip in 1776, he contacted Vergennes, minister of foreign affairs, since his collaborators (Silas Deane and Richard Henry) had already been in contact with Beaumarchais, supplying arms and munitions to the rebels. In January 1778, Louis XVI agreed to help the Americans and the alliance treaty was signed the following month. Probably at no time in the history of Franco-American relations had there been so much enthusiasm for the younger country. Franklin proved to be an excellent ambassador, won the heart of many leading personalities and entrance into all the leading *salons*. He met Voltaire and the two old men became the idols of Parisian society, both entering into the Lodge of the Nine-Sisters in 1778. Throughout the Constituent Assembly he would always be referred to with much respect.

Now, literature dealt more and more with the young English colonies rather than with American Indians. In 1778, two books appeared on the market, both translated from English. William Robertson's *History of America* dealt with the Indians; Regnier dedicated to Franklin a compendium of the constituent laws of the English colonies.[9] These laws, according to Regnier, provided the framework for the best democracy that ever existed; Franklin was addressed as the chief member of that society of heroes. In 1787, David Ramsay's *History of the Revolution in America* (also translated and published in French) adopted the point of view that the English Americans were treading in the footsteps of their ancestors who led one tyrant to the scaffold and chased the other one from the kingdom.

---

7. Antoine-Yves Goguet, *De l'origine des loix, des arts et des sciences*, 3 vols. (Paris: Desaint et Saillant et La Haye, 1758), 151-55.

8. Edna H. Lemay, "Histoire de l'antiquité et découverte du nouveau monde chez deux auteurs du XVIIIe siècle", *SVEC* 153 (Oxford: The Voltaire Foundation, 1976), 1313-28.

9. Claude-Ambroise Regnier, *Recueil des loix constitutives des Colonies anglaises, confédérées sous la dénomination d'Etats-Unis de l'Amérique-Septentrionale*, traduit de l'anglais (Philadelphie et se vend à Paris, 1778).

Démeunier and America

Thus from a twofold point of view, America entered the scene of travel literature, offering an anthropological vision of early mankind and a revolutionary vision of a free people. Thanks to Lafitau on one hand and to the American Revolution on the other, both these aspects were treated by a young French author arriving in Paris in 1771. To make a living he translated English travel accounts and, five years later, published *Esprit des usages et des coutumes des différents peuples*.[10] Did he conceive the book thanks to a solid acquaintance with travel literature, or did Panckoucke suggest it since, when it appeared, he sent it to Voltaire? Whatever the answer, Démeunier made an original contribution to the study of man. Whereas Prévost had dealt with the world geographically, he took the same material but rearranged it in a thematic ethnographic approach, within which he divided humanity chronologically: savages, barbarians and civilized men, a classification that would continue to be used throughout the nineteenth century.

In his introduction, Démeunier recognized Montesquieu as his guide in the field of comparative studies, but failed to pay tribute to Lafitau to whom he is indebted for the "savage" stage of mankind, making at least 26 references, explicit or not, to his work. For Démeunier, American Indians are living representatives of mankind in its early stages. His "savage" is a proud and independent being, living close to the animal stage, eating scantily and often in hiding, drinking strong beverages and revealing coarse, brutal and instinctive manners: in short, man living in a state of nature. Nevertheless, in his social anthropological study of man, nowhere does he hint that the "savage" stage is the ideal one. As man progresses in time and in space, it is evident that the main objective of all human history is to reach the civilized stage as witnessed in Europe and especially in Enlightenment France.

Ten years later, American Indians were relegated to a few lines when Démeunier undertook the study of contemporary America in his tour of the world written at the request of Panckoucke: the two volumes on "Political Economy" in the *Encyclopédie méthodique*. The section on America was published separately in 1786 and again in 1790, so as to advertise the constitutions of the thirteen American states.[11] The principles on which the young nation was founded derived from the English charters: no taxation without representation; religious toleration; free press, etc. Because Americans grew up with these principles, they believed in human dignity and so were

---

10. Jean-Nicolas Démeunier, *Esprit des usages et des coutumes des différents peuples*, 3 vols. (Paris: Pissot, 1776).

11. Démeunier, "Economie politique et diplomatique", *Encyclopédie méthodique*, 2 vols. (Paris: Panckoucke, 1784 et 1786) and the separate editions, *Essai sur les Etats-Unis* (Paris, 1786); *L'Amérique indépendante*, 3 vols. (Gand, 1790).

unlike other people: thus their revolt against the mother country. Briefly, Démeunier gave the story of the American War of Independence[12] as fought mainly on the sole grievance of taxation. At no time in history, ancient or modern, had a revolution been as important or as rapid as in America. Evidently, Démeunier grasped not only the difference between the American and French Revolutions but believed that the American constitutions, written at the end of the eighteenth century, had benefitted from the enlightened philosophy of the period and from English laws. He also put the accent on "destiny" which had placed the United States in the Northern hemisphere, the temperate zone, attracting "active and free peoples," as opposed to the Southern hemisphere which, with its more fertile and richer soil, under a hotter sun, made men more apt for slavery. In like manner, the United States and England, countries of the North, are contrasted with Spain ruined by the wealth of the mines and subject to absolute government. In his remarks on the American constitutions, Démeunier derided "men of letters" who criticized the defects without remarking on how well they suited the country, making feasible some form of political life.

Therefore, as an anthropologist Démeunier saw the importance of the American "savage" in an historical vision of mankind. Now, for the elected deputy of the Third Estate, the American political establishment became the offspring of the best England had to offer, the American Revolution being the fulfillment of English revolutionary aims a century earlier. The myth of the "noble savage" slowly became the myth of the "noble white American" revolting against the wrongs of his own people. The United States being governed by the civil laws of England, their constitutions were applicable nowhere outside of America. Europe might well admire them but not imitate them, though at times American laws might be useful to Europe still suffering from many unjust regulations, the remains of feudal times. Démeunier referred to Mably, Richard Price and Turgot, criticizing what each had to say concerning the American constitutions. He noted, in his publication of 1790, that in view of the American character and spirit, molded by the English constitution, no other type of democracy would have suited the former colonies. However, in spite of the recent, unrealistic propaganda in favor of "absolute liberty," Démeunier believed that few people were ready for it.

Examining the American act of confederacy, Démeunier found it superior not only to any constitution of ancient history, but to the Dutch and Swiss constitutions as well. Congress was admirable for the way it conducted the war, prepared the peace treaty and maintained its authority over the inhabitants, concerned only with their independence. Now, at the time when each state needed only to tend to its own affairs, it was important that the

---

12. Démeunier, *L'Amérique indépendante*, 1: 21-31.

executive be strengthened, a measure which Washington himself was in favor of, and concerning which Démeunier proposed solutions. No doubt that under the circumstances, he was echoing the opinion of Thomas Jefferson whom he had consulted for his study, and, as a member of the Constitution Committee at the National Assembly, he was alluding to the French political situation.

However, if a country of thirteen states loosely tied together needed a stronger confederacy, absolute governments would use armed soldiers to enforce their rule: a situation far from ideal. If the misdeeds of American citizens, who were not punished, were compared to those of chiefs of state elsewhere, certainly the latter, more numerous, would prove much more destructive of human dignity. Démeunier's last remarks concern several topics of direct interest to the French National Assembly, such as the electoral system, government finances, commerce, organization of the navy, etc.

In the few lines devoted to the American "savages," Démeunier launched a cry of alarm in their favor. Pushed off their territories by the European drive westward, they were the victims of civilized men who had themselves suffered from arbitrary taxes raised by the mother country. As a future revolutionary, Démeunier claimed for these unfortunate people, deprived of their lands, the justice due to all men. As Robespierre who later would claim political rights for all free men, colored or not, so as not to tarnish the principles of the French Revolution, so Démeunier invited Americans to consecrate their revolution by granting liberty and independence to the "peaceful men living in the forests of America".[13]

Démeunier was undoubtedly the only deputy at the French National Assembly to have acquired such a well-documented vision of both types of Americans, primitive and civilized, thanks to the literary sources available. His colleague, four years younger than he and a lawyer in Toulouse, Barère de Vieuzac, was also a literary man who wrote various eulogies for the *Académie des Jeux Floraux*, including one on Rousseau in 1787-1788 for which he won a prize. In his introduction to the newspaper, *Le Point du Jour*, started during the summer of 1789, among the references to Greece and Rome, Sweden and Switzerland, Barère emphasized the English model as being very useful for Europeans though far from perfect.[14]

When he turned to the American continent, Barère found many more chances for reform and regeneration because here was a new and empty land where the "holy voice" of nature could be heard. There, men could receive a good education without learning bad habits. English fanatics had been converted into "gentle, philosophical Christians." Commerce flourished in spite of English prohibitory laws. Last but not least of all the factors favoring

13. Démeunier, *Essai sur les Etats-Unis*, 86.

14. Bertrand Barère was founder and editor of *Le Point du Jour*, published in Paris from 1789 to 1791. See *Discours préliminaire*, iii-xvii.

American freedom was the presence of Benjamin Franklin. Comparable to a biblical figure, founder of the human race, Franklin was the Socrates of modern times to whom America owed so much. However, the unknowing initiator of the French Revolution was Vergennes, wanting to inflict a defeat upon England. The noble generals and common soldiers he sent to America would come back to France imbued with the American way of life and so unconsciously promote revolution in France.[15]

If not a great orator at the Constituent Assembly, Démeunier was very important as a member of the Constitution Committee, intervening frequently in the discussions as moderator, anxious to conciliate various points of view. Of humble origins, educated for the church which he left to pursue a literary career in Paris, he had fared quite well under the *Ancien Régime*, acquiring various posts and pensions. Undoubtedly pushed into politics by the important people he was acquainted with thanks to the Lodge of Nine-Sisters and other social circles, he was a practical man typical of the great majority of Constituent deputies. He never referred to America in his speeches.

The National Assembly and America

1. Political Issues

In fact, it was Mirabeau who made the first reference to the New World when, on July 23, 1789, in a debate on the establishment of a bourgeois militia, he described the Americans as having divided their uninhabited lands into so many states. People were free to choose their own form of government provided they remained republican and within the confederacy. The image was vastly simplified but very appropriate for the kind of rhetorical effect in which Mirabeau excelled. He seems to have forgotten the original inhabitants to see only numerous European settlers, each with his plot of land to cultivate on his own, in short, the dream of many Frenchmen. However, this optimistic vision worked both for and against the American model according to the character of each orator.

The summer of 1789 was the best time for bringing in the American myth, when the first and most important conquests of the Revolution were achieved. Thanks to La Fayette and his American contacts, Champion de Cicé, the archbishop of Bordeaux, reported on the works of the Constitution Committee by referring to the Declaration of Human Rights (July 27, 1789). "This noble idea", he said, "conceived in another hemisphere" where France had helped the Americans to gain freedom and which now shows France "on which principles

15. *Le Point du Jour*, April 27 to June 17, 1789.

we should depend for the conservation of our liberty."[16] As the committee program was drafted, the United States showed how useful a bicameral legislature could be, an argument used at length by Lally-Tollendal on August 31, 1789, when he added that it would be absurd for France not to follow suit. However, other deputies, such as Lanjuinais and Sallé de Choux, argued to the contrary: France could adopt a unicameral legislature because the royal veto, serving as a counter-power, replaced the American senate. In the wake of Champion de Cicé, other young liberal nobles claimed that since the United States served as an example in the New World, France should be an example to the universe.

On the night of August 4, Leguen de Kerangal proposed to follow the example of English America: a country of land-owners oblivious of the feudal system. If the vision was overly optimistic, it was in tune with the revolutionary enthusiasm of that evening. Leguen was realistic enough to speak of "English America," thus acknowledging the American debt to England in New World manifestations of liberty. Rabaut de Saint-Etienne, a Protestant pastor from Nîmes who, with his father, had spent years trying to smooth out differences between the two religious communities in the south, had come to Paris to negotiate Protestant civil rights in 1786. Now, he claimed that if the French, as the Americans, intended to regenerate themselves, then a declaration of human rights was absolutely necessary, thought he did suggest more than a servile imitation (August 18). Not everyone, however, favored a declaration in August 1789. Some deputies thought it dangerous.

A faithful servant of the royal government over the past 30 years, Malouet, had last served in the capacity of navy intendant at Toulon. Little inclined to what he called "metaphysical presentations," Malouet thought them dangerous because, above all, people needed a good efficient government catering to their everyday needs. The situation in the United States was quite different. Americans had taken man in the heart of nature and presented him to the universe in his original state. This had been possible because recently founded American society was composed of property owners already accustomed to equality. Knowing neither luxury nor poverty, hardly aware of the burden of taxation and social prejudices which ruled French life, never having experienced any form of feudalism on the land they worked, "such men were undoubtedly prepared to receive total liberty: their tastes, their customs, their situation called for democracy." And then like many a colonial administrator ever since, Malouet reminded his audience that France was composed of a "multitude of propertyless men who eke out an existence by hard work." It was too early for Frenchmen to be granted the freedom Americans rightly enjoy

16. This and all subsequent quotes and references to the speeches at the National Assembly, as indicated by the date, are in the *Archives parlementaires*, 1e série, 1789-1799 (Paris, 1881).

thanks to various local and historical reasons (August 1, 1789). This does not mean, added Malouet, that such Frenchmen have not an equal right to liberty. However, he believed that in a great empire where men lived at different social levels, justified boundaries to natural liberty were as important as granting more liberty. He thought it essential at first to tend to such difficult tasks as improving the conditions of the poor and giving more chances to everyone by reform measures. In other words, Malouet never understood that men live not only by bread, but by ideas too. Liberty stirred masses in the hope of a better future, while fulfilling their material needs was a never-ending proposition. A lesser-known deputy, Crenière, an iron merchant from Vendôme, thought a declaration of human rights would be absurd for France. His fairly long speech is full of ideas taken from Rousseau concerning the difference between the constitution of a nation and its institutions.

Barnave used the same argument as Malouet two years later when, after the flight to Varennes, he sought to defend the monarchy in a long and important speech which was much applauded. He criticized those who advocated a republican form of government in imitation of the United States where the circumstances were so different. He presented his vision of the inhabitants, spread thinly over the land whose boundaries were the forests, having all the customs, simplicity and sentiments of "an almost new" people, "almost" solely occupied by agriculture and other simple tasks which make men pure and natural, removing them from artificial passions which cause revolutions in government. This idealized picture of America was undoubtedly drawn to convince his audience that the model could be of no use to Frenchmen.

2. Economic Issues

In 1790, references to America concerned practical aspects of the business world rather than revolutionary ideals and principles. As a matter of fact, one-third of the total references to America at the National Assembly concerned economic relations. Many deputies (Delattre d'Abbeville, Dupont de Nemours, Lechapelier, Malouet, Mirabeau and Pétion) stressed the importance of encouraging commerce with the United States on the grounds that good business makes good friends. On September 3, 1790, Condorcet lectured on the evils of an excessive emission of paper money which Americans had been forced to use when fighting for their liberty, their lives and their property. Such was not the case in France where men were crowded together into close quarters and divided into two classes of which one sought revenge for years of oppression suffered from the other. In other words, the effects on the French economy would be far worse than had been the case in America.

The commercial topic involving a great deal of discussion concerned American tobacco, the purchase of which should not hinder the French from adopting a system of complete liberty in the growth of their own. Free commerce could only benefit all parties. In this connection, it may be recalled that Jefferson, when he arrived in Paris in 1784, had hoped to liquidate the American debt to France by improving the commercial treaty between the two countries. Tobacco growing interested some members of the clergy. On April 6, 1790, Abbé Coulmiers, an active "progressive" member of the National Assembly, boasted of the superior quality of American tobacco which France bought to mix with her own. This commerce afforded a profit of 24 million pounds to the states of Maryland and Virginia and almost 4 million to France. It was the only commercial tie with the United States, the power in the New World whom France had aided in the rebellion against England, a friend to be kept through good business. Should France stop buying American tobacco, the risk would be great of losing the benefits of past efforts and expenses: America would soon forget French interests and, being of the same blood, language and religion, go back to the mother country. On November 13, 1790, Abbé Coulmiers requested an indefinite postponement of the matter after quoting Jefferson, who had written that "tobacco growth was always ruinous for a country, draining lands and ruining agriculture."

In mid-November 1790, Abbé Maury spoke at length against free growth of tobacco, defending the purchase of the American produce which France paid for with various types of merchandise such as spirits, wine, oil, soap, etc. In a professional manner he explained how the free growth of French tobacco would profit the working man less than wheat grown on a national basis. Though the United States and in particular Virginia grew the best tobacco in the world, Abbé Maury referred to Franklin and the states of Virginia, Carolina and Maryland to prove how harmful tobacco growing was to the soil and how the United States were gradually giving preference to wheat fields. The same argument was used by the marquis d'Estourmel in favor of maintaining the tax on American tobacco in order to discourage French farmers from cultivating this harmful product (November 30, 1790). However, other nobles (Briois de Beaumetz, d'André) wishing to encourage Franco-American commerce sought to reduce import taxes. Finally, a conciliatory measure was adopted slightly reducing the rates (February 13, 1791).

3. Human Rights Issues

In 1791, during the heated discussions concerning the French colonies in America, Lanjuinais made a rather interesting reference to North America, where the only distinction between citizens was that of free men and indentured servants. The latter, Lanjuinais rather ironically compared to slaves, a term which hypocritical American ideology would not use. However, in the United States all freemen, regardless of the color of their skin, had equal civil rights; such was the case when slaves or indentured servants had acquired their freedom. In the Spanish colonies, not only did colored people have access to all political rights, but free Negroes might hold political office. Then in a few lines, Lanjuinais advocated the mixing of races which, by crossing the spiritual intelligence of one with the physical strength of the other, would make for all the good qualities needed of active citizens entitled to full civil rights. This speech was made on the very day (May 12, 1791) when the Assembly voted on the question of the colonies and only a minority followed the arguments of Lanjuinais.

During the same month of May 1791, the debates on the death penalty and the bicameral legislature occasioned several references to America, which had not abolished the first and had maintained the second. On May 30, Prugnon curiously distinguished between American political wisdom, acquired in recent times thanks to the English heritage, and Chinese maturity dating back centuries to the times of primitive men. However, he made no reference to a closer race of primitive men, the American Indians. Against the death penalty and claiming a better criminal justice, Pétion noted the next day that Americans rarely condemned to death and nowhere in the world were crimes less frequent and criminals treated with greater kindness. In America, not only did the wicked repent but virtuous Quakers devoted their lives to consoling and converting men who had the misfortune to be serving prison terms.

America was also admired for its equal inheritance rights (Dupont de Nemours in May 1791) and for its respect of the laws (Barnave in June). When discussing orders of chivalry in July, Anthoine, a member of the Jacobin club, approved of the abolition of the Order of Cincinnatus. If Frenchmen were wise and enlightened, they would immediately abolish all such orders and distinctions among men, acknowledging only personal merit (July 30, 1791). On August 13, Barnave remarked that the American constitution was much shorter and therefore more adaptable to circumstances. In an important speech he said that the French constitution had actually reached two hundred articles because they thought it necessary to go into many more details than the Americans as to the functioning of government. Ten days later Robespierre and Pétion praised America for its freedom of the press. Pétion mentioned the pamphlets, newspapers and other literature read by all men during the debates raging on the new federal system in America. People read, heard and examined this very polemical literature, but no troubles ensued and they remained faithful to the confederacy. Reason, he said, will always rule a free people never to be mistaken for stupid men languishing under despotic rule.

4. Constitutional Issues

As the months passed and revision of the constitution was undertaken, the question of a divided legislative body once again came to the fore. In

September 1789, the vote had been massively in favor of a single-chamber body, but now there seemed to be doubts about the wisdom of such a form of government. On May 10, 1791, rather than refer to Montesquieu and the past in favor of two chambers, Buxot pointed to the United States where the leading legislators had preferred a system of two equal chambers in which the same class of men sit, voted in by the same law. Under the influence of Franklin, Pennsylvania had at first adopted a single chamber legislature, but after the Revolution gave it up for the bicameral system of two equal chambers. Franklin himself later admitted his error and the new Congress, once the constitution was written, adopted the bicameral legislature which Buzot was advocating for France, now that its constitution was ready. During these debates, at one moment Lanjuinais exclaimed, referring to Franklin and his unicameral legislature: "This system is excellent for philosophers, but not for men still subject to their passions; and passions will continue to dominate men for years to come."

The next day (May 21, 1791), Pétion reminded the Assembly that to divide the legislature into two equal sections is not at all the same thing as voting for deputies sitting in two separate chambers as in England where the members of each chamber have different rights, privileged deputies sitting in the first chamber and commoners in the second. The American Congress began its career like the French Assembly since absolute union of all deputies was equally necessary to draw up a constitution. Once that constitution was made, only one of the thirteen states kept a single chamber legislature. Now Congress itself met as a single body, dividing into two sections for discussion and meeting again to conclude. Pétion reminded his audience that he had already advocated this system in the early days of the Assembly, referring to the American constitution. His opinion on the matter had not changed.

Such was not the opinion of Dr. Salle from Nancy, who saw no reason for fearing hasty debates in a single chamber, nor did he fear a majority opinion which some thought should be counterbalanced. The American example was unsuitable for France. How can one possibly undertake to compare a new nation with an old one in need of regeneration? How to compare federated republics spread out over lands whose boundaries are lakes, rivers and deserts, and a vast but tightly knit monarchy where the government necessarily has to be centralized and capable of rapid decisions? Moreover, Dr Salle added, France could be considered to have the equivalent of the American system since its executive power, endowed with a suspensive veto over legislative decrees, acted as the equivalent of the second chamber (May 21, 1791).

The same argument rejecting the American model was used by Lechapelier on August 29. When peaceful Americans, living widely spread out over a vast territory, examine their constitution, it is to prevent rather than encourage revolution. In highly populated France, men live "pressed together" in close quarters; turbulent characters, they avidly seek change and often aim much further than is necessary. Hence, a periodical constituent assembly would always entail a revolution: he proposed June 1, 1800 as a date for the next one. Malouet, already very critical of the 1791 constitution, immediately expressed disagreement as he hoped for an earlier revision. The American constitution was based on habits and customs prior to the Declaration of Independence. The "people" having replaced the "prince," nothing of their past was destroyed and they could build up a better future keeping in mind the interests of all. If such a constitution was liable to periodical examination by national conventions, it was preferable to wait to have enough experience before doing so. In France the situation was quite different. A completely new regime needed the free consent of all men and sufficient experience to justify its success. Both factors were still lacking, according to Malouet, who by now was strongly in opposition.

Pétion proposed to define the term 'convention' as an assembly authorized by the people to make and reform its constitution. Therefore, a national convention was a constituent assembly and not a legislative one: the two must not be confused because their powers were very different. Even in England, where sometimes king and parliament jointly modified the constitution, this did not mean that political liberty was guaranteed. A better example to follow was America, "the freest country in the world, where human rights were best known, best developed because reason and knowledge had suffered the least from superstition and experience had founded the best government" (August 29, 1791).

Like the references to Rousseau, so those to the United States were used by all parties at the Constituent Assembly. If everyone admired the new nation, all knew that it could not be used as a model for revolutionary France whose past was so different. It was not without reason that the best scholar on America, Démeunier, a practical man, not a dreamer, never referred to that land. Those who did refer to America either rejected it completely because it was inappropriate to France, or spoke of it in glowing terms as a democracy which all nations should aim for in a more or less distant future. It was in such terms that a deputy who never spoke at the National Assembly, Lenoir-Laroche, wrote in 1795, in his *Spirit of the Constitution*: "Americans were the first people to seek the foundations of their institutions in the nature of man and who, before asking how to act dealt with what should be done."[17] Then in a long paragraph he gave a very idealistic picture of Americans who, when they land in the new country, seem to lose all their bad habits of the past. Thus it was much easier for them to reach political perfection, which no Frenchman could possibly envisage.

---

17. Jean-Jacques Lenoir-Laroche, *De l'esprit de la Constitution* (Paris, an III, 1795).

It was fourteen years later when an observer of contemporary events would try to assess the American model during the French Revolution. J.B. Suard wrote about Brissot's letter on the constitution and commerce of the United States[18] which at the time had been harmful. There was no reason to criticize American democracy so bitterly today because at the time enthusiastic admirers thought it could be imitated in France. How to reconcile the fact that for some America was a paradise and for others a land of greed and ill faith? How to make Brissot's enthusiastic description of American ways and customs agree with governmental tolerance for the considerable abuses of a great number of businessmen? How can such abuses allow commerce to grow and prosper?

Suard believed the answer lay in the American social order and wealth. Some sort of democracy always existed in America. It was founded by Quakers and Presbyterians who knew neither feudal rights nor royal privileges. Local administration and the participation of property owners in legislative affairs had, over the years, created a public spirit of independence which, together with good moral conduct were encouraged by the rural life Americans led. However, none of this was a guarantee of honest commercial dealings. In America, men were of two types: the first accepted democracy and followed its ways, the others were only interested in becoming rich. The positive aspects of America were acknowledged by Brissot, but the two, good and bad, co-exist "under a government of constant morality where immorality is not rare". It was wrong of Brissot to have sought to undermine French institutions on the basis of the American example. Though his vision of America was not exaggerated, he went astray in wanting to apply it to France. If democracy was successful in America, that did not mean it could function in France.

Suard summed up what most admirers of America felt at the National Assembly. Their image of the new nation whose inhabitants were either "noble savages" or "virtuous farmers" ploughing the soil they owned, could not possibly apply to France, prisoner of her past having to seek regeneration in other ways.

---

18. Jean-Baptiste Suard, *Mélanges de littérature*, 3 vols. 'Lettre sur la Constitution et le commerce des Etats-Unis' de Brissot (Paris: Dentu, an XII, 1803), 3: 160-71.

Des guerres d'Amérique à la Révolution Française: le théâtre de Billardon de Sauvigny

François Moureau

Les divisions chronologiques sont trompeuses: c'est avec les écrivains de l'Ancien Régime que se fit une bonne part de la littérature révolutionnaire, cette "carmagnole des Muses" dont un ouvrage récent a traité en détail.[1] L'auteur dont je voudrais parler dans ces pages est un excellent exemple de transferts idéologiques entre l'univers de la monarchie française et celui de la Révolution. Edme Billardon de Sauvigny a une place modeste dans l'histoire littéraire comme l'un des pères du "style troubadour" avec sa délicieuse *Histoire amoureuse de Pierre le Long* (1765) illustrée par Greuze et ornée par Philidor de romances "médiévales" accompagnées à la harpe.[2] Cet ancien militaire, nommé en 1776 censeur de la Police, perdit ce poste de confiance en 1788 pour avoir assez légèrement autorisé l'*Almanach des honnêtes gens* de Sylvain Maréchal. Pendant la Révolution, il reprit du service à la Garde nationale, où il exerça divers commandements dans la cavalerie. Monarchiste avant 1789, patriote ensuite, il se convertit au bonapartisme en 1797: un itinéraire qui fut loin d'être rare en ces périodes compliquées.[3] Ennemi des philosophes, mais surtout de Voltaire, et "protégé" de Rousseau, il appartient à partir de 1781 à la Loge parisienne des Neuf-Soeurs, rendez-vous de l'élite littéraire du temps.[4] Juste avant la Révolution, on le retrouve dans la mouvance des Orléans et de Mme de Genlis, au milieu du bouillonnement des "feuillistes" qui s'agitent au Palais-Royal en faveur de la branche cadette et des

---

1. *La Carmagnole des Muses*, J.-Cl. Bonnet, éd. (Paris: Armand Colin, 1988).
2. Edme Billardon de Sauvigny, *Histoire amoureuse de Pierre le Long et de sa très honorée dame Blanche Bazu* ("Londres" [Paris], 1765).
3. La notice: "Sauvigny" de Michel Gilot pour le *Dictionnaire des journalistes (1600-1789)*, éd. J. Sgard (Grenoble: PUG, 1976), 339-41, corrige les nombreuses erreurs de biographes anciens. Billardon avait un frère abbé, lui-même écrivain, avec qui on le confond parfois. On lui attribue aussi certaines oeuvres de Chevrier ou d'autres auteurs.
4. Alain Le Bihan, *Francs-maçons parisiens du Grand Orient de France (fin du XVIIIe siècle)* (Paris: B.N., 1966), 75.

idées nouvelles. Rédacteur du *Journal des dames* en 1764,[5] puis en 1786-1789 du *Magasin des Modes nouvelles*, Billardon essaie de sortir ses lectrices de la frivolité; il se vante de les faire penser. Parmi d'autres, il représente assez bien l'écrivain polygraphe de la fin des Lumières, besogneux, ami de la vie simple à la Rousseau et fréquentant les Grands, plein du vocabulaire de la sensibilité nouvelle: bienfaisance, liberté et laudateur de la monarchie bourbonienne. Cet apologiste de la société communautaire rurale de l'Ile d'Ouessant et du village de Hautpont en Auvergne[6] vit à Paris, où il a son "Ermitage" et son Ermenonville à deux pas de la Comédie-Française.[7]

La carrière théâtrale de Sauvigny a cependant une cohérence qui a en grande partie échappé aux rares chercheurs, qui, comme C.D. Brenner[8] ou G. Chinard,[9] se sont occupés de son oeuvre. S'il participe à un courant, bien connu aujourd'hui par les travaux d'Anne Boës,[10] qui renouvelle la tragédie française par le recours à l'histoire nationale, s'il rivalise en ces domaines avec de Belloy et Marie-Joseph Chénier, si, au moment de la Révolution, il participe dans *Du Théâtre sous les rapports de la nouvelle Constitution*[11] à la curée contre une Comédie-Française chargée de tous les maux de l'Ancien Régime,[12] s'il combat d'autres institutions comme l'Académie française, coupable à ses yeux dans une "Courte esquisse d'une longue dénonciation à faire" d'être un repaire aristocrate et d'avoir méprisé le "sublime et cher Rousseau", si, en un mot, Billardon de Sauvigny patauge dans les conventions d'époque, il y a chez lui deux constantes originales: la haine de l'Angleterre et l'amour des peuples de l'Amérique.

Ce vent dominant qui vient de l'Atlantique se combine dans son théâtre à un fort courant né du cyclone rousseauiste: une *Mort de Socrate* de 1763, où il n'est pas malaisé de voir le philosophe genevois crucifié, une *Rose ou la Fête de Salency* de 1771 qui réalise, sur le mode mineur, le projet de réjouissance rustique dont rêvait la *Lettre à d'Alembert*, et, la même année, un *Persifleur* joué à la Comédie-Française: "La morale a maintenant ses

---

5. *Journal des dames*, "Bachaumont", t.2, 25 novembre 1764. Fait ignoré de Nina Rattner Gelbart, *Feminine and Opposition Journalism in Old Regime France: Le Journal des Dames*, (Berkeley: Univ. of California Press, 1987).

6. Gilot, 340.

7. "Quai des Célestins, chez la baronne d'Andelot" en 1776-1777; "rue de Vaugirard, chez la marquise d'Escars" en 1777-1778, etc. (Gilot, 340).

8. Clarence Dietz Brenner, "A neglected Preromantic: Billardon de Sauvigny", *Romanic Review* 39 (1938): 48-58. Pour l'essentiel, étude de l'aspect "troubadour" de son oeuvre.

9. Billardon de Sauvigny, *Vashington ou la Liberté du Nouveau Monde*, éd. Gilbert Chinard (Princeton: Princeton Univ. Press, 1941).

10. *La Lanterne magique de l'histoire: essai sur le théâtre historique en France de 1750 à 1789*, (SVEC 213) (Oxford: The Voltaire Foundation, 1982).

11. Paris: Cussac, 1790.

12. *Moralités historiques et allégoriques en vers sur les événements les plus intéressants pour la Nation française* (Paris: Prault, an VIII), 36-38: ouvrage lu au Portique Républicain.

hypocrites comme en avait autrefois la religion".[13] Mais Billardon n'a pas rencontré l'Amérique par le truchement de Rousseau, sauf peut-être dans son éloge du sauvage américain venu plutôt de Montaigne.[14] Billardon a pu connaître *La Découverte du Nouveau Monde*, livret lyrique que Rousseau composa en 1739 et qui ne fut publié qu'en 1776.[15] En toute hypothèse, la réconciliation finale des Indiens et des conquistadors espagnols relevait de l'unanimisme conclusif du style d'opéra plus que d'une réflexion politique originale. Au XVIIIe siècle, de Rameau à Voltaire (*Alzire*) ou à Piron (*Fernand Cortès*), qu'elles soient orientales ou occidentales, les Indes sont d'abord galantes. Le mythe américain de Billardon a une autre origine.

Il repose sur un patriotisme français que renforcèrent la Guerre de Sept Ans, celle de l'Indépendance américaine et plus tard les Coalitions révolutionnaires: l'Angleterre en était l'adversaire fantasmatique. On comprend mal que *La Prussiade* (1758) de Chevrier ait pu lui être attribuée; en revanche, on imagine bien que ce chevalier des Ordres du Roi, historien zélé des fastes nationaux, "depuis Clovis jusqu'à saint Louis" (1785, 4 vols.), soit l'auteur de *Réflexions en vers sur l'héroïsme* (1756), d'un éloge de la noblesse commerçante et militaire, *L'Une et l'Autre* (1756), complément de l'ouvrage à la mode de l'abbé Coyer, on comprend qu'il ait composé un poème épique comme *La France vengée* (1757). Au théâtre, il donne une *Gabrielle d'Estrée* (1778), créée à Versailles, et surtout un *Agrippa d'Aubigné* (1783),[16] préambule à la réconciliation nationale de l'Edit de Tolérance. En ce siècle anglomane,[17] et sans même remonter à la Guerre de Cent Ans où l'histoire médiévale lui peint pourtant les premières roueries d'Albion, Billardon voit dans l'Angleterre l'instrument privilégié du mal moral, l'île aussi qui a refusé une terre d'exil au Citoyen de Genève.

---

13. Edme-Louis Billardon de Sauvigny, *Le Persifleur* (Paris: Delalain, 1771): Préface.

14. Voir, par exemple le *Discours sur les sciences et les arts* (Jean-Jacques Rousseau, *Oeuvres Complètes* (Paris: Gallimard, 1964), 3: 11: "Je n'ose parler de ces Nations heureuses qui ne connaissent pas même de nom les vices que nous avons tant de peine à réprimer, de ces sauvages de l'Amérique dont Montaigne ne balance point à préférer la simple et naturelle police").

15. Rousseau, *La découverte du Nouveau Monde*, *O.C.*, 2: 811-41. Edition originale: "Londres" (Bruxelles: Boubers, 1776). Voir notre: "Rousseau librettiste de Jean-Jacques", *Les Ecrivains français et l'opéra*, éd. J.-P. Capdevielle et P.-E. Knabe (Cologne: DME, 1986), 87.

16. Billardon de Sauvigny, *Agrippa d'Aubigné*, comédie en un acte et en vers, non représentée sur une scène publique, dans *Les Après-soupés de la société* ("Sybaris" et Paris, S.d. (1782-1783)), t.5, cahier XIX. Arsenal: Rf 82931 (5).

17. Josephine Grieder, *Anglomania in France, 1740-1789. Fact, Fiction and Political Discourse* (Genève: Droz, 1985). Dans *Les Amants français*, Billardon présente un Français ami de l'Amérique et très critique sur "l'anglomanie" ambiante (I,i et xii) (*Les Après-soupés*, t.3).

Hirza* ou *Les Illinois

La geste américaine présente dans le théâtre de Billardon va d'*Hirza ou les Illinois* en 1767 à *Vashington ou la Liberté du Nouveau Monde* en 1791. L'Angleterre y joue son rôle; mais, au-delà, et avant de revenir à nos pièces américaines, on notera que le fait britannique participe à la théâtralisation du politique que Billardon met en scène dans ses divers écrits. Opéra historique, ce *Péronne sauvée* représenté en 1783 à l'Académie royale:[18] le livret traite du siège de la ville en 1536 par les armées de Charles-Quint; Billardon y introduit des Anglais "qui voulaient s'emparer de Péronne par surprise".[19] Héroïsme contre trahison, la dialectique pédagogique est en marche. Sous le Directoire encore, après le 13 vendémiaire an V, Billardon, "chef de bataillon, commandant des compagnies près le Corps législatif", se pose en accusateur de l'Angleterre dans sa *Prestation du serment des vétérans militaires près le Conseil des Anciens*:[20] il y condamne le gouvernement anglais comme "le plus atroce de tous et le plus lâchement artificieux" (1), et l'Anglais, "qui, dès les premiers jours de notre Révolution, a constamment soudoyé nos ennemis intérieurs et extérieurs", "qui calcule froidement combien de milliers d'hommes il va sacrifier encore à ses vues dominatrices et mercantiles." (2)

Tout cela ne met certes pas l'ancien "censeur de la Police" en totale opposition avec les divers pouvoirs qu'il sert. Certains détails le prouvent: la tragédie d'*Hirza ou les Illinois* fut vraisemblablement imprimée et diffusée aux frais du Ministère de la Guerre. Dans tous les exemplaires consultés,[21] la page de titre porte un cachet au chiffre redoublé (LA) qui se rencontre aussi sur l'édition originale du *Siège de Calais* de Buirette de Belloy[22] joué deux ans plus tôt et imprimé sur ordre du gouvernement pour soutenir le patriotisme anti-britannique. De surcroît, les Archives de la Comédie-Française témoignent qu'entre 1767 et 1780 plusieurs centaines de militaires furent envoyés par leurs supérieurs aux représentations d'*Hirza*.[23] A la fin du mois de mai 1789, les Comédiens jouèrent la pièce à la Cour:[24] le vent

18. Créé le 27 mai 1783, musique de Nicolas dit Alexandre Dezède. Il en existe une analyse récente par Michel Noiray, "L'opéra de la Révolution (1790-1794): 'un tapage de chien'?", *La Carmagnole des Muses*, 363.

19. Billardon, *Péronne sauvée*, "Préface", in *Les Après-soupés*, 4: 28.

20. Billardon, *Prestation*... (Paris: Ballen, s.d.), 4 p., in-4° (Arsenal: Rf 13576).

21. Archives de la Comédie-Française: ex. en maroquin rouge, dauphins poussés aux quatre coins, lettre "P" au dos. B.N." Yf 11968. Arsenal: 8° B. 13564; 8° B 13481 (2); Rf 13564; Sorbonne: H.J.r. 33 (2) (in-8°).

22. B.N.: Yf 6705. La Bibliothèque nationale possède dix-sept exemplaires de cette "édition" (dont quelques contrefaçons).

23. Dossier Sauvigny: 375 en 1767, 100 en 1768, 376 en 1770 et 233 en 1780. L'administration militaire payait une livre par place.

24. Archives de Comédie-Française: Dossier Sauvigny. Lettre de Billardon aux Comédiens-Français, 23 mai 1789.

américain souffla un moment sur Versailles, en même temps que celui des Etats généraux.

Si l'utilisation politique de l'oeuvre de Billardon est évidente, s'il fut un agent assez conscient de la propagande française contre l'Angleterre, il n'en est pas moins l'un des exemples les plus originaux de l'influence du rêve américain sur le théâtre français des Lumières. La tâche n'était pas évidente, tant la tradition théâtrale donnait de l'Amérique une image stéréotypée limitée à quelques "airs des sauvages" et autres entrées de ballets. Au contraire, l'oeuvre de Billardon tente, souvent avec maladresse, mais avec une belle constance, de montrer une Amérique contemporaine, réelle et modérément idéalisée, ce qu'il appelle "le plaisir de peindre un pays et des hommes nouveaux".[25] La tragédie révolutionnaire de *Vashington ou la Liberté du Nouveau Monde* sera l'aboutissement, d'ailleurs équivoque, des pièces américaines antérieures. L'Amérique est le "Nouveau Monde", c'est-à-dire l'enfance du monde. Le "protégé" de Jean-Jacques, qui n'a jamais traversé l'Atlantique, y anime des êtres de la nature sous la forme de tribus indiennes dont *Hirza* raconte les contacts avec la "civilisation" européenne.

Il s'agit sans doute de son chef-d'oeuvre, une pièce qui, quoi qu'en ait dit Voltaire, jaloux de ce qu'elle fît ombrage à ses *Scythes* en 1767,[26] est la première "tragédie" sur un sujet américain moderne. On y remarque une attention à la couleur locale, à la vérité historique, qui, à l'époque du drame bourgeois et de la tragédie historique, fait d'*Hirza* le modèle d'un nouveau genre: la tragédie historique à sujet contemporain (*Major e 'proximo' reverentia*). Jouée à la Comédie-Française, dans l'enceinte de la tradition, mais par quelques acteurs d'élite, dont Lekain dans le rôle du chef de guerre Hiaskar, Molé dans celui de Monréal et Mlle Dubois dans le rôle-titre,[27] la pièce utilise le décor grandiose des chutes du Niagara, lieu sacré de la civilisation des "Sauvages", où trente ans plus tard Chateaubriand fit un pèlerinage magnifié par les *Mémoires d'Outre-Tombe*: [28]

> On voit dans l'enfoncement, écrit Billardon, le Saut de Niagara; d'un côté, des rochers, des cabanes et quelques arbres; de l'autre un tombeau élevé

---

25. Billardon, *Hirza*, "Préface", i.

26. Voltaire, *Les Scythes*, *Théâtre*, éd. Moland (Paris: Garnier, 1877) 4: 259-334. Voltaire soupçonne les Comédiens-Français d'avoir mis en scène *Hirza* pour faire tomber sa pièce (Best. D 14179). Chacun des deux auteurs s'accusa du plagiat (voir plus bas la polémique sur le cinquième acte).

27. Liste des acteurs dans l'édition originale (n.p.). La maladie de Mlle Dubois survenue après la première perturba la série de représentations (*Mercure de France*, juillet 1767, 192-93).

28. Chateaubriand, *Oeuvres Complètes*, éd. Maurice Levaillant et Georges Moulinier (Paris: Gallimard, "La Pléiade", 1951), t.1. (Livre VII, ch. 7-9), 241-48.

sur des piliers matachés,[29] et décorés de chevelures en forme de trophée; au pied du tombeau est un autel sur lequel sont les armes du défunt, ses flèches, son casse-tête, son manitou.[30]

Il faudrait rechercher dans les descriptions et les gravures illustrant les ouvrages sur les Indiens de l'Amérique septentrionale, de de Bry à Lafitau ou à Charlevoix,[31] la source d'un tableau aussi précis, qui s'inspire aussi d'une mode du "barbare" et du "primitif" que l'art contemporain–je pense aux peuples asiatiques dessinés, peints et gravés par Jean-Baptiste le Prince[32]–fait peu à peu transiter vers le théâtre, témoin tel costume "brut" de Lekain interprétant le tartare Gengis Kan.[33] Car c'est bien d'une tragédie "primitiviste" qu'il s'agit dans *Hirza*: "Les Sauvages...suivent presque machinalement les impulsions subites du coeur, ces premiers mouvements de la pitié qui nous rendent généreux et bons," et Billardon poursuit après avoir cité Rousseau:[34] "Ces Sauvages, uniquement occupés de la chasse ou de la guerre, ne connaissent à peu près que le physique de l'amour."[35]

Si les Illinois n'ont pas encore découvert le sentiment amoureux, cet art de dissimuler la pulsion sexuelle, ils ont déjà été corrompus: "les Sauvages, accoutumés à vivre avec les Européens et si souvent trompés par eux, sont devenus très méchants", rapporte Billardon informé par "plusieurs officiers du Canada".[36] A l'origine, la pièce s'intitulait *Les Sauvages*; le changement de titre peut s'expliquer par le fait que ces "sauvages" n'en sont plus

---

29. Adjectif absent de Furetière, Richelet, "Trévoux" et Littré; non répertorié dans Huguet, le *Dictionnaire de l'Académie* et le TLF.

30. Billardon, *Hirza* (I,i), éd. de 1767, 3. A comparer au décor "sauvage" des *Scythes* de Voltaire: "Un bocage et un berceau avec un banc de gazon; on voit dans le lointain des campagnes et des cabanes". Dans *Hirza*, I.i, le chef Hiaskar évoque ainsi le fleuve sacré:

Triste Niagara, séjour craint de nos Dieux.
Vous, rochers menaçants, et vous, flots furieux,
Qui des monts inégaux couvrant les vastes cimes
Tombez en mugissant d'abîmes en abîmes,
Vous avez vu briser le calumet de paix.

31. Thédore de Bry, *Histoire de l'Amérique ou Nouveau Monde*, 13 parties (Francfort/Main, 1591-1634); Joseph-François Lafitau, *Moeurs des Sauvages américains comparées aux moeurs des premiers temps*, 2 vols. (Paris, 1723); Pierre-François de Charlevoix, *Histoire et description générale de la Nouvelle France*, 3 vols. (Paris, 1744).

32. On citera ses dessins des populations sibériennes (1761) gravés pour le *Voyage en Sibérie* (1768) de Chappe d'Auteroche. Entre autres, un magnifique "Kamtchadal en costume de cérémonie" (Louvre, Cabinet des Dessins, inv. 34612).

33. Dans *L'Orphelin de la Chine* (1755) de Voltaire. Tableau: *Lekain en Gengis Kan* par Simon-Bernard Lenoir (1774) (Musée de la Comédie-Française).

34. Rousseau, *Discours sur l'origine et les fondements de l'inégalité*, *O.C.*, 3: 155: "...qu'est-ce que la générosité", etc.

35. *Hirza*, "Préface", iii. L'expression de "physique de l'amour" est tirée de Rousseau, *Discours sur (...) l'inégalité*, 157.

36. "Préface", ii.

véritablement et que Hirza l'héroïne s'ouvre à l'amour en même temps qu'aux maléfices de la civilisation.[37] L'intrigue est vue du côté des Indiens: Thamar, père d'Hirza et chef des Illinois, a été lâchement tué par les Français. Sa fille veut le venger en sacrifiant quarante prisonniers français ou son assassin présumé, Monréal. Or elle aime un déserteur français, transformé en coureur de bois, qui pratique à la tête des Illinois une guérilla efficace contre les Anglais et les Iroquois: ce héros canadien qui a appris l'art de la guerre moderne aux Indiens, n'est autre que le fils de Monréal. On s'attendrait à un débat manichéen renouvelé pour partie du *Cid*. De fait, le mal est du côté de la civilisation: les Français de Québec, qui ont rompu la trêve, furent les agresseurs des Illinois. Monréal fils prend le parti des "Sauvages". On révèle que le véritable meurtrier de Thamar était le chef félon, le "tyran de Québec" (I, i), Fontalbar,[38] celui-là même qui avait déterré la hache de guerre.[39] Il y a dans cette intrigue quelque chose du *Cleveland* de l'abbé Prévost publié entre 1731 et 1739 et qui fut l'un des plus grands succès de librairie du siècle.

Billardon a hésité entre deux dénouements: celui de la tragi-comédie classique où les héros positifs sont sauvés–ce fut la version que l'on joua d'abord à la Comédie-Française[40] et qui fut imprimée–, celui qui convenait le mieux à cette pièce désespérée, à cet adieu à la "sauvagerie", le suicide final des héros.[41] Voltaire venait de choisir cette dernière "catastrophe" dans sa tragédie des *Scythes*;[42] Billardon révisa sa pièce dans ce sens, ce qui fournit au seigneur de Ferney l'occasion de crier au plagiat (Best. D 14317). En tout état de cause, cette chute convient mieux au ton général de la pièce, évocation

---

37. "Préface", vi. Le 9 novembre 1765, Marin "approuva" la pièce sous ce titre, ainsi que le remarque Billardon en conclusion de sa "Préface" (vi).

38. Ce nom à consonance espagnole (souvenir des conquistadors) qui s'oppose à celui de Monréal (à connotation française, monarchiste et canadienne) n'est pas choisi au hasard. Il évite de toute manière de trop délicats rapprochements avec les réels vaincus de Québec tombée en 1759 sous Montcalm et avec la chute de Montréal l'année suivante. Le conflit entre les troupes réglées des villes et les coureurs de bois ne dut cependant pas être indifférent à l'ancien militaire qu'était Billardon. Ce thème rejoint d'ailleurs le "rousseauisme" du texte qui met en contradiction la "vertu" des Indiens et de leurs alliés avec la "corruption" des citadins.

39. "La hache des guerriers reposait sous la terre;
Thamar l'a retirée, hélas! pour mon malheur" (I,iii).

40. Les comptes rendus de presse le prouvent: *Année littéraire*, 1767, t.8, Lettre 8, p. 184: "...la pièce finit par une sage leçon de Monréal à son fils".

41. Pendant la maladie de Mlle Dubois, Billardon corrigea le texte pour la reprise. Voir les comptes rendus du *Mercure de France*, août 1767, 197: "catastrophe entièrement différente"; juillet 1767, Vol. 2, 197: Hirza veut tuer Monréal, son fils s'interpose et reçoit le coup de poignard. Hirza se suicide.

42. (V,v): Obéide se frappe et, ensuite, Athamare, son amant, se saisit du même "fer" pour se suicider. Le parallèle avec la "catastrophe" de *Hirza* est évident; c'est pourquoi Billardon prit soin de préciser à la fin de sa "Préface" que sa pièce avait été "approuvée" en novembre 1765, avant la rédaction des *Scythes*. Cela ne l'empêcha pas de modifier son dénouement dans un sens qui n'est pas étranger à la tragédie de Voltaire.

élégiaque de la vie sauvage des peuples de l'Amérique du Nord et renonciation au mythe positif de la colonisation européenne. *L'Année Littéraire* de Fréron y vit avec son habituelle finesse le renversement des valeurs occidentales: ce Monréal qui trahissait sa patrie et sa religion, ce renégat amant d'une sauvageonne, "mélange désagréable de tendresse et de férocité",[43] n'enseignait rien de bon. Le *Journal encyclopédique*, au contraire, retrouva dans cette tragédie sauvage "la nature dans toute son énergie", "un des bons tableaux du coeur humain que la philosophie ait tracés".[44]

La destinée de la pièce n'était pas close; la Guerre d'indépendance américaine lui redonna curieusement une actualité qui faisait des Illinois et des renégats français la métaphore prémonitoire des Insurgents. C'est le sens d'une lettre inédite de Billardon aux Comédiens-Français; il leur écrivait le 12 décembre 1779 à propos de ces oeuvres "dont le but est l'amour de la patrie":

> C'est à ce titre que je demande la représentation des *Illinois*. En ne changeant rien au plan général de cet ouvrage, j'en ai placé l'époque au moment où les Insurgents secourus par les Français ont secoué le joug de l'Angleterre. La renaissance de notre marine, l'enthousiasme de la nation, la sagesse du gouvernement, le succès de M. le comte d'Estaing, tous ces tableaux si dignes d'un coeur patriotique sont couronnés par une action encore présente au coeur des Français, je veux parler du dévouement de l'immortel d'Assas.[45]

Hirza fut en effet reprise en janvier suivant; on l'avait jouée en province et à l'étranger.[46] La nouvelle version de la tragédie parut chez la Veuve Duchesne,[47] puis dans *Les Après-soupés*.[48]

Les Nègres et *Les Amants français*

La fusion du rêve américain et de la geste anti-coloniale et anti-britannique se marque dans d'autres oeuvres contemporaines de Billardon. Elles indiquent une dérive de plus en plus forte vers la nouvelle nation américaine au détriment des populations amérindiennes d'origine, comme si

---

43. *Année Littéraire*, 1767, 8: 184-87.

44. *Journal encyclopédique*, 15 septembre 1767, t.4, 3e Partie, 111.

45. Archives de la Comédie-Française: Dossier Sauvigny. Le chevalier d'Assas mort en 1760 avait été le modèle héroïque de la Guerre de Sept Ans.

46. Edition avignonnaise de Bonnet sous l'adresse parisienne de Ruault en 1776, 39-(1)p. (Archives de la Comédie Française); édition hollandaise en 1780 pour une représentation à La Haye (La Haye: H. Constapel, 1780). (Philadelphie: Rosenbach Foundation).

47. *Hirza* (Paris: Veuve Duchesne, 1780). (Washington: Library of Congress).

48. *Les après-soupés*, 4: 1-84.

la naissance de cette société libérée de la corruption européenne rejetait en dehors de l'histoire la civilisation précolombienne, esquisse maintenant inutile de la jeunesse du monde. Pendant ces années, l'Américain se métamorphose de colon en citoyen. On mesure ce passage dans deux comédies de Billardon, *Les Nègres* et *Les Amants français*, ouvrages destinés à des théâtres privés–au comte d'Artois peut-être–, dont la musique ne fait pas le moindre charme. La comédie en un acte et en vers des *Nègres* sur une musique de Dezède, futur collaborateur de Billardon pour *Péronne sauvée*, fut écrite "à l'occasion de la paix" (Traité de Paris, 1782):[49] la scène est à Saint-Domingue près du Cap entre des planteurs anglais de la Jamaïque et leurs équivalents français. Une jolie gravure de Binet, l'illustrateur de Rétif, représente la scène de nuit (un enlèvement) qui forme le fond de la pièce. Dans cette plantation de cannes à sucre, les esclaves sont un peu plus qu'un décor: ils vivent une espèce de pastorale créole qui n'annonce guère d'élan émancipateur.

> Moi travailler matin et soir,
> Moi battu quand il plaît à Maître,
> Esclave à li pour toujours l'être,
> N'y plus songer quand moi te voir,

chante le nègre à sa négresse (sc.i). De fait, la pièce célèbre la réconciliation franco-britannique grâce au roi–Louis XVI–qui a rendu "la liberté des mers".

> Pour danser, vivent nos amours,
> Les noirs dansent mieux que les blancs,

proclament dans le divertissement final colons et esclaves mêlés. Mais le nègre Azor–homonyme de l'humanoïde de Marmontel et Grétry–[50] fait son rôle de "nègre commandeur" et veille, fouet en main, à ce que l'ordre règne dans ce sabbat bien organisé. Nous retiendrons pour notre propos que la réconciliation se fait entre colons, en dehors des mères patries, et sur le dos des esclaves.

Les Amants français sont de peu antérieurs aux *Nègres*.[51] Billardon écrivit cette comédie en deux actes et en vers "à l'occasion des avantages remportés sur mer et sur terre par les Français et les Etats-Unis de l'Amérique dans la Virginie" (allusion aux victoires de Chesapeake et de Yorktown à l'automne 1781). Le thème américain est sous-jacent; dans le divertissement final un Anglais et une Anglaise jouent le rôle des nègres dans la comédie précédente

49. *Les Après-soupés*, 5: 1-54 et 5 p. de musique, gravure de Binet.
50. André E.M. Grétry et Jean-François Marmontel, *Zémire et Azor*, comédie-ballet créée à la Cour en 1771. Azor y est un être mi-homme mi-bête que l'amour transforme (souvenir de *La Belle et la Bête* de Mme Leprince de Beaumont).
51. *Les Après-soupés*, 3: 1-48 et 2p. de musique signée "Mme L.".

en chantant avec "l'accent du pays". *Les Amants français* célèbrent la geste américaine des soldats de Louis XVI:

> De Grasse et Rochambeau, Saint-Simon, La Fayette,
> Et tant d'autres guerriers dont la gloire est complète" (II,vii).

Le "chevalier français", "proctecteur généreux des prisonniers anglais" (II,vii), va au secours d'un "peuple libre et sage" (II,viii).[52] Le mythe américain se combine à l'exaltation des valeurs nationales françaises, aujourd'hui monarchiques. La voie "révolutionnaire" du *Vashington ou la Liberté du Nouveau Monde* est déjà frayée.

Vashington* ou *La liberté du Nouveau Monde

Abdir, tragédie mystérieuse représentée sans grand succès à la Comédie-Français et peut-être étouffée par le pouvoir politique, n'est qu'une redite de ces sentiments. Elle fut jouée quatre fois du 26 janvier au 12 février 1785 sous le nom d'*Agir*, "drame tragique en quatre actes", réduit à trois dès la seconde représentation.[53] L'impression s'en fit chez la Veuve Duchesne (Brenner 10960), mais aucune des bibliothèques que nous avons consultées, dont les Archives de la Comédie-Française, n'en conserve d'exemplaires.[54] Le tirage fut vraisemblablement confisqué et détruit. Ecrite en pleine réconciliation franco-britannique, cette tragédie "tartare" racontait sous un voile léger l'histoire du capitaine anglais Asgill–"Agir", puis "Abdir"–fait prisonnier à Yorktown, condamné à mort et gracié sur intervention de Vergennes.[55] Les mauvais traitements infligés aux captifs par les troupes britanniques avaient alimenté la propagande française au moment des guerres d'Amérique. On a vu que *Les Amants français* y faisaient allusion, *Vashington* en fera un tableau d'ouverture pompeux avec l'évocation des sévices soufferts par les Américains à la suite de la prise de Charleston (I,i). Le journaliste du *Mercure de France*,

---

52. L'écho des affaires américaines sur une intrigue française se retrouve dans une comédie bordelaise de 1780: *Les Nouvellistes* de Pierre de Montagne dont l'intrigue est fondée elle aussi sur les nouvelles que l'on attend d'Amérique et sur l'enthousiasme qu'elles provoquent: voir notre article, "Journaux et journalistes dans la comédie française des 17e et 18e siècles", *La Diffusion et la lecture des journaux de langue française sous l'Ancien Régime*, éd. Hans Bots (Amsterdam et Maarsen: APA-Holland University Press, 1988), 166.

53. Archives de la Comédie-Française: Dossier Sauvigny. Feuille comptable sous le nom d'*Agir*, titre que l'on rencontre dans la correspondance de Billardon (17 et 19 octobre 1784) (Moureau, "Journaux et journalistes", 166).

54. Catalogues et fichiers dépouillés: Paris, Bibliothèque nationale, Arsenal, Opéra, Institut, Mazarine, Sorbonne, Bibliothèque de la Société des Auteurs et Compositeurs dramatiques; Londres: British Library; Etats-Unis: NUC.

55. Gilbert Chinard fait l'analyse de la pièce dans son édition de *Vashington* (xx-xxii).

qui signalait que le sujet venait de donner lieu à une adaptation romanesque,[56] n'hésitait pas dans cette tragédie "tartare" à désigner Vazir-Kan comme le "chef des Insurgents":[57] un Vazir-Kan sous lequel se déguisait bien peu le personnage de George Washington lui-même!

L'idée d'une pièce sur le héros de l'Indépendance était dans l'air. Billardon ne la réalisa que six ans plus tard, pour son adieu à la scène. Joué sur le Théâtre de la Nation–l'Odéon actuel–où s'étaient regroupés les ex-Comédiens-Français fidèles à une certaine tradition[58] et qu'avaient abandonnés Talma et ses amis, *Vashington*–prononcé à la française, écrit: "Vazington" dans l'imprimé et même orthographié "Wargenston" dans les Archives du Théâtre-Français[59]–fut un assez éclatant désastre. La fragilité de l'idéologie de son auteur, ses contradictions, ses illusions équivoques s'y font clairement jour. Cette tragédie en quatre actes–une coquetterie de Billardon déjà signalée–eut deux uniques représentations les 13 et 14 juillet 1791. Les dates étaient choisies à dessein, on s'en doute, pour célébrer le premier anniversaire de la Fête de la Fédération où La Fayette et la Garde nationale, dont Billardon était un officier supérieur, avaient un moment représenté la nouvelle légitimité "révolutionnaire". L'acte III se passait dans la "salle du Congrès" des Etats-Unis, copie conforme de l'Assemblée nationale française; le dernier acte avait pour décor:

> une grande plaine sur les bords de la Delavarre (*sic*) nommée le champ de la fédération. Tous les préparatifs sont faits sur l'autel de la patrie, on voit en forme de colonne la table d'airain, sur laquelle est le traité d'alliance avec les Français.

Si l'intrigue de la pièce est fondée sur des événements en partie réels, cette Fête de la Fédération américaine est de l'invention de Billardon. Derrière Washington se profile La Fayette, et derrière le héros français de l'Amérique le parti modéré qui voit dans la Fédération le but et le bout de la Révolution. Imprimée chez le libraire parisien Maillard d'Orivelle, à l'enseigne du "Contrat social",[60] cette pièce "révolutionnaire" est de fait un

56. Charles-Joseph de Mayer, *Asgill ou les Désordres des guerres civiles* (Amsterdam et Paris, 1784) in-12, XII-130 p.

57. *Mercure de France* (5 février 1785): 131.

58. Marvin Carlson, *Le Théâtre de la révolution française* (Paris: Gallimard, 1970). Carlson voit dans la représentation de *Vashington* une tentative de ce théâtre pour "réfuter l'accusation de tendances aristocratiques dont il était objet". (117)

59. Dossier Sauvigny. Pièce comptable. Recettes: 2821 et 1312 livres.

60. M. de Sauvigny, *Vashington ou la liberté du Nouveau Monde*, Tragédie en quatre Actes (Paris: Maillard d'Orivelle, 1791).

manifeste en faveur du *statu quo*.[61] En avril, pour mesurer sa popularité, La Fayette avait démissionné du commandement de la Garde nationale, démission reprise dès le lendemain. Le 17 juillet, les pétitionnaires venus déposer sur l'autel de la Patrie au Champ de Mars leur demande de déchéance du roi furent dispersés par la Garde nationale. Entre-temps, Louis XVI avait fui à Varennes et l'Assemblée était agitée de mouvements divers sur l'avenir du monarque-citoyen et du régime que fondait la Constitution de 1791. La Garde nationale et La Fayette étaient les garants de la monarchie "régénérée". Washington se vit enrôler dans le parti.[62] Celui qui fut honoré avec Thomas Paine, plus carrément "révolutionnaire", du titre de citoyen français par décret du 26 août 1792[63] n'en demandait pas tant. Y avait-il chez Billardon l'idée d'une alliance franco-américaine cimentée par la Guerre d'indépendance et le renouveau de la France qui faisait de son monarque, héros américain autant que La Fayette, le père de la Constitution et l'image modernisée du "chevalier français"? *Vashington ou la Liberté du Nouveau Monde* qui critique les "tyrans", l'Angleterre, "vil instrument des rois" (I,i), et fait l'éloge des vertus américaines, hommage aux valeurs antiques et au monde chevaleresque, va certainement dans cette direction. Gilbert Chinard a conduit une analyse minutieuse de cette tragédie, de ses sources historiques américaines, de ce que Billardon y ajouta,[64] je n'y reviendrai pas. Si la pièce, qui fut un échec, ne contribua guère en France à la mythification d'un Washington en fait moins connu que Franklin sur les bords de la Seine,[65] malgré le battage publicitaire fait autour du buste de Houdon en 1785,[66] elle nous importe pour d'autres raisons. Elle témoigne des difficultés qu'eurent les hommes de la Révolution à assimiler leur propre passé intellectuel et moral. En 1790, Billardon attaque la Comédie-Française; l'année suivante, il se range dans le camp des Anciens de la troupe. Plus grave, il superpose et connote, sans le moindre rite de passage, trois images différentes: le "Sauvage" américain, vertueux et fidèle, le colon émancipé, patriote et chevaleresque, le "héros français", matrice commune de ce véritable retour aux sources. Hirza, Monréal fils, "Vashington" et La Fayette sont les répliques d'un même modèle moral. Des deux côtés de l'Atlantique règne un déisme pacificateur;[67]

---

61. Le *Journal de Paris*, N° 194, 13 juillet 1791, note qu'il s'agit d'une "pièce de circonstance" et que "des allusions (sont) faciles à saisir".

62. "Vazington" le déclare: "La force des Etats naît du maintien des lois" (III,vi).

63. Collation originale aux Arch. Nat.: A 117 (Cat. exp. Paris, *Washington*, 1947, n° 13).

64. *Vashington*, xxiv-xli et les notes historiques, 65-69.

65. "Laurens" (Henry Laurens) le fait remarquer à "Vazington":
"Emule du grand homme, immortel comme lui".

66. H.H. Arnason, *Jean-Antoine Houdon* (Paris: Edita-Denoël, 1976), 78-82.

67. "L'Orateur" du Congrès:
"Mon corps est dans les fers; mon âme n'est qu'à moi.
Ou mon hommage est libre, ou la loi n'est qu'un piège

l'ambassadeur de France qui clôt la tragédie avec Vashington apporte sa caution à ce beau rêve. Mais il est le représentant du roi de France, alors que la pièce brocarde les tyrans; en cet été de 1791, l'équilibrisme idéologique vit ses derniers beaux jours.

Billardon n'est pas le génie dramatique méconnu que les historiens de la Révolution cherchent depuis deux siècles. Il semble même que celle-ci ait stérilisé son talent. Les événements allaient plus vite que le théâtre, le spectacle était naturellement dans la rue, et les fantaisies idéologiques devinrent vite justiciables du tribunal révolutionnaire. Billardon eut l'honnêteté et la prudence d'en rester là, dans l'attente du "restaurateur" offert par Brumaire. En loyal disciple de Rousseau, il a cru que la "liberté" viendrait du "Nouveau Monde", de ces terres vierges où la pensée sauvage, l'esprit pionnier et les vertus oubliées en Europe pourraient à leur tour perfectionner la Nature et laver l'Humanité des péchés de l'Ancien Monde. C'était déjà d'un "La Fayette nous voilà!" que rêvait Billardon, d'une France "régénérée" par l'Amérique. Bonaparte qui voulait faire l'Europe à sa manière se chargea de renvoyer dans les oubliettes de l'Histoire ce séduisant trompe-l'oeil de théâtre.

(...)
Les prêtres consacraient ces moyens corrupteurs" (III,ii).

Musique et verbe à l'époque révolutionnaire: autour du culte de Franklin et de La Fayette

Béatrice Didier

"La Révolution et la contre-révolution se sont faites en chantant", écrivait très justement L. Guichard.[1] Les pouvoirs révolutionnaires ont favorisé cette activité musicale et l'ont orientée. La musique vocale a été mise à l'honneur plus encore que la musique instrumentale, parce que le message qu'elle transmet est explicité par le sens des paroles. Le chant permet aussi à tout homme, même non musicien professionnel, de s'exprimer. Il y eut une naissance quasi spontanée de chansons, mais il y eut aussi tout un système de commandes, parfois fort autoritaires, à en croire Grétry.[2] Le Comité de Salut public suscite des créations et opère un choix, décide la mise en musique par le Conservatoire, la publication, la diffusion.

On est parfois méfiant à l'endroit de la musique révolutionnaire, peut-être justement parce qu'il s'agit d'un art au service d'une idéologie. Cette musique est mal connue, malgré les travaux de Constant Pierre, de Julien Tiersot, de Léon Guichard, de Jean Mongrédien, de François Moureau et d'autres chercheurs;[3] il est très difficile–sauf quelques chansons–de pouvoir l'entendre; il existe très peu d'enregistrements. Et pourtant elle mérite notre attention, non seulement dans des perspectives d'histoire des mentalités et d'histoire de la musique, certes; mais aussi parce que quelques-unes de ces oeuvres atteignent une réelle beauté.

---

1. Léon Guichard, *La musique et les lettres au temps du romantisme* (Paris: P.U.F., 1955). Nous tenons à marquer ici notre dette envers ce livre et son auteur, auquel cet article est dédié.

2. André E.-M. Grétry, *Réflexions d'un solitaire* (Bruxelles: Van Oest, 1919).

3. Voir Constant Pierre, *Hymnes et chansons de la Révolution. Aperçu général et catalogue avec notice* (Paris: Imprimerie nationale, 1904); Julien Tiersot, *La chanson populaire et les écrivains romantiques* (Paris: Plon, 1931), *inter alia*; L. Guichard, *La Musique...*; Jean Mongrédien, *La musique en France des Lumières au Romantisme* (Paris: Flammarion, 1986); François Moureau et Elisabeth Wahl, *Chants de la Révolution* (Paris: Hachette, 1989). Voir aussi *Catalogue de l'exposition Benjamin Franklin et la France*, Bibliothèque Nationale.

Les musiciens, dont souvent l'activité avait commencé avant la Révolution et se poursuit après, ne sont pas médiocres. Citons au moins Méhul (1763-1817), auteur du *Chant du départ*, de l'opéra *Stratonice* (1792), Lesueur (1760-1837) qui sera le maître de Berlioz, auteur d'Hymnes et de l'opéra *La Caverne*, très novateur (1797), Gossec (1733-1829), qui écrivit un opéra *La reprise de Toulon* (1796) et de très belles marches funèbres, Catel (1773-1830), Grétry (1741-1813) célèbre par son *Richard coeur de Lion* (1784) utilisé par la propagande royaliste, mais qui composa aussi dans la droite ligne de l'esprit républicain, Cherubini (1760-1842), l'auteur de l'admirable *Médée* (1797), et de chants révolutionnaires, enfin, et sans prétendre épuiser la liste, Devienne qu'on est en train de redécouvrir, l'auteur des *Visitandines* (1793). Si tous ces musiciens "professionnels" ont écrit des hymnes pour les fêtes de la Révolution, il faut aussi souligner que l'oeuvre musicale peut-être la plus connue de cette époque, *la Marseillaise*, pour ses paroles, comme pour sa musique, est l'oeuvre d'un "non-professionnel", Rouget de Lisle. L'exaltation patriotique a suscité la création chez des individus qui n'étaient pas des musiciens de métier, comme elle a suscité l'héroïsme d'armées qui n'étaient pas non plus celles des militaires de carrière.

Les thèmes de la musique révolutionnaire; Franklin, La Fayette

Venons-en aux poètes dont les strophes sont mises en musique par les Méhul, Bossec, etc. Là aussi ils ont souvent produit avant et après la Révolution. Citons Lebrun-Pindare, Ducis, Désorgues, Coupigny, Ginguené, et surtout Marie-Joseph Chénier dont le lyrisme s'accorde si bien avec le style des Hymnes révolutionnaires et qui a beaucoup composé: pour les Fêtes de la Fédération, de l'Etre Suprême, etc. L'écho de la Révolution américaine se serait peut-être davantage fait sentir chez son frère André Chénier, qui quoique favorable aux débuts de la Révolution ne travailla pas à ses fêtes, et que la Terreur guillotina, au moment où elle organisait systématiquement ces grands programmes festifs. Son poème *l'Amérique*, tel que nous pouvons l'imaginer et le reconstituer d'après les fragments qu'il a laissés, ne se contentait pas d'évoquer Christophe Colomb et de lui faire condamner à l'avance l'esclavage. A. Chénier prévoyait aussi de "Parler prophétiquement des treize Etats unis...quelles sont ces treizes femmes...vêtues de telle manière ...avec un tel visage...dansantes et se tenant par la main."[4] Il avait lu avec soin des textes qui étaient de nature à alimenter son imagination: "M. de Chastellux écrit avoir vu chez Mme Brech, la fille de M. Franklin, deux mille deux cents chemises faites par les dames et les demoiselles d'Amérique pour les soldats

4. André Chénier, *Oeuvres poétiques*, éd. Moland (Paris: Garnier, 1884), 2: 138.

américains. Chacune avait son nom... Ce lin qui sera trempé des sueurs qui couleront pour la liberté"[5]

Les thèmes de cette musique révolutionnaire sont beaucoup plus variés qu'on pourrait le croire. D'abord, les divers événements de la Révolution, 14 juillet, 10 août, 21 janvier, 9-10 thermidor, etc. Et comme la Révolution essaie de se créer une mémoire, tout en abolissant celle de l'Ancien Régime, elle scande son temps par des anniversaires de ces événements fondateurs, qui chaque fois donnent lieu à des créations musicales. Les victoires de l'armée sont chantées et d'autant plus que le pays est assiégé de l'extérieur et de l'intérieur: bataille de Fleurus, reprise de Toulon. La Révolution qui supprime les saints a ses héros: Marat, Viala, Le Pelletier, pour lesquels sont composés cantiques et complaintes. Essayons de voir, parmi ces nombreux thèmes, la place des Etats-Unis.

Signataire de la Déclaration d'Indépendance, inspirateur de la Constitution de Pennsylvanie, premier ambassadeur américain à Paris, initiateur de l'amitié franco-américaine, savant, philosophe, éducateur, homme d'Etat, Franklin avait tout pour fasciner le public français, et il est, de beaucoup, la figure américaine qui est le plus à l'honneur dans la musique révolutionnaire.

Il semble d'abord être lié à une des chansons les plus populaires de la Révolution, le fameux *Ça ira*, qui a connu plusieurs versions et dont les premières n'étaient nullement sanguinaires. Le fameux refrain serait emprunté à un tic verbal de Franklin, du moins est-ce ainsi qu'il a été perçu, presque dès son origine. La chanson apparaît en 1790, au moment de la Fête de la Fédération, à partir d'un rythme de danse de Ladré déjà connu sous l'Ancien Régime.[6] Voici ce qu'en dit la *Chronique de Paris*, du 4 mai 1792: "Et Franklin répétait *Ça ira*. Plusieurs de nos révolutionnaires se sont rappelés le tic du législateur de Delaware; et c'est ce qui a donné lieu à notre chant patriotique, à notre *Ranz des vaches*." Sébastien Mercier, en 1797, dans le *Nouveau Paris*, se fait l'écho de la même tradition: "Le mot *Ça ira* était, d'ailleurs respectable par son origine; nous l'avions emprunté au célèbre Franklin; c'était son expression favorite dans le plus fort de la Révolution d'Amérique".

Sa mort est l'occasion d'un *Eloge* prononcé par Condorcet le 13 novembre 1790,[7] et d'une véritable "apothéose", pour reprendre l'expression de G. Chinard.[8] La relation de "l'Eloge civique" qui lui est rendu le 21 juillet 1791 en est la preuve (*Mercure de France*, 8 octobre 1791). Mais le culte de Franklin ne s'arrêtera pas là. Il se poursuit pendant toute la Révolution, l'an II, l'an III. Et il est l'occasion de diverses créations musicales. Des couplets civiques sont

---

5. Chénier, *O.P.*, 2: 159.
6. B.N., Rés. Ye 3155; C. Pierre, 315.
7. The Library of Congress, LE 3026F8C7.
8. *L'Apothéose de Benjamin Franklin*, Gilbert Chinard, éd. (Paris: Librairie orientale et américaine, 1955).

chantés pour l'inauguration des bustes de Franklin, Voltaire, Buffon, Jean-Jacques Rousseau, Marat, Le Pelletier dans la salle de la section populaire et républicaine d'Avre libre. Les paroles en sont du "citoyen Dourneau-Démophile" sur l'air "Je suis Lindor" et paraissent, l'an II.[9] Il a été créé une "section Franklin". Elle plante un "arbre de la Liberté" et chante sur l'air "aux Armes Citoyens", des couplets de Mollin. "Cet arbre qui debout s'avance..."[10]

On trouve la présence de Franklin dans plusieurs hymnes et chansons de la Révolution. Ainsi dans *La lyre républicaine ou recueil des hymnes et chansons patriotiques*.[11] Le *Chansonnier de la Montagne* par différents auteurs[12] contient un "Hymne aux Bienfaiteurs de l'Humanité d'Aristide Valcourt". S'adressant fictivement à Franklin, il s'écrie:

Ton art à la foudre étonnée
Déroba l'électricité
Et de l'Amérique enchaînée
Tu préparas la liberté

Le poète Piis, qui est loin d'être médiocre et dont on connaît par ailleurs l'inspiration de poète alchimiste, y célèbre Franklin comme le patron des imprimeurs.

L'autre figure, liée à l'histoire de la Révolution américaine que l'on voit apparaître souvent dans la musique révolutionnaire, mais peut-être davantage pour son rôle au début de la Révolution française que pour son équipée outre-Atlantique, c'est La Fayette, objet tantôt d'exaltation et de louange, tantôt de sarcasmes et d'ironie, suivant les partis politiques.

Des couplets sont chantés à M. le Marquis de La Fayette présent à la bénédiction des drapeaux du district des Cordeliers, le 13 août 1789: "Prêts à jouir de sa noble conquête..."[13] Dans la version de 1790 du *Ça ira* que nous évoquions ci-dessus à propos de Franklin, La Fayette est présent; les deux héros de l'Indépendance américaine se trouvent ainsi rapprochés:

Par le prudent La Fayette
Tout trouble s'apaisera
(...)
La Fayette dit: Vienne qui voudra!

---

9. B.N. Ye 42225; C. Pierre, 1079.
10. Archives Nationales, D XXXVIII, 5; C. Pierre, 1350.
11. Impr. des Ecoles républicaines, an III, Ye 26958.
12. Favre, an III, in 12, Ye 17630.
13. *Album des muses*, 1790, Ye 11675; C. Pierre, 210.

Le patriotisme leur répondra
Sans craindre ni feu ni flamme.[14]

Une "Ode en marche nationale pour être chantée en choeur et à grand orchestre" par Florida Tomeoni est dédiée à La Fayette.[15]

Constant Pierre signale trois chants à La Fayette sur l'air "Avec les jeux dans le village", d'une part des couplets à M. de La Fayette, commandant général de la Garde nationale parisienne;[16] d'autre part, sur le même air, une "chanson sur le brave La Fayette".[17] Enfin un "Hommage à M. le marquis de La Fayette, maréchal des camps, garde de la troupe nationale parisienne" par M. G. D... et qui débute ainsi: "Trop grand pour employer la brique".[18]

Une "Chanson martiale sur l'heureux retour des patriotes Bordelais", de 1790, écrite sur l'air *Vive le vin, vive l'amour*, "Voulez à nous, chers concitoyens", par Sarade, comporte un refrain à la louange de La Fayette.[19] Il arrive aussi que La Fayette figure dans des oeuvres plus satiriques. Ainsi dans ce "Pot Pourri national ou le Miroir de la Vérité", de 1789: "Ces Vive le Roi m'impatientaient"[20] ou dans le "Dialogue entre Le Roi, La Reine, La Fayette, Bailli, L'Assemblée". Les *Actes des Apôtres*, le journal royaliste qui reproduit beaucoup de chansons, est précieux pour le sujet qui nous occupe. On y trouve un "Honneur à Lafayette", sur l'air de Malborough (1791), dans le 8ème volume.[21] De la même année, 1791, la chanson les trois visions sur l'air: "*L'avez-vous vu mon bien-aimé*: Avez-vous vu le cheval blanc que monte

---

14. Mais dans une version suivante, La Fayette est supprimé, remplacé par "baïonettes" et "Liberté", cf. Moureau et Wahl, *Chants de la Révolution*, 7 et 47.

15. *Chronique de Paris*, 13 juillet 1790, 776; C. Pierre, 4.

16. B.N. Vm7, 1643 à 16434 recueilli dans Vm7, 7092; C. Pierre, 360.

17. Bibl. du Sénat, carton 6, cote 210; C. Pierre, 360*.

18. Vm7, 7094 et 16512, Bibl. Sénat, carton 6, cote 274; C. Pierre, 363.

La Bibliothèque du Congrès (Performing arts, Music) contient un curieux *Recueil de dix-neuf chansons républicaines populaires* de 1791 sur divers sujets, prise de la Bastille, Necker, etc. (M1730.R27 Case) avec une "Chanson sur le Brave La Fayette":

A la prudence de Minerve
Joignant le courage de Mars

et cette conclusion:

Pour servir sagement la France
Louis pouvait-il mieux choisir?

Ce recueil contient aussi un Hommage à M. de La Fayette, par M. D... sur l'air *Avec les jeux dans le Village*. Il s'agit donc des mêmes textes que C. Pierre a trouvés à la Bibliothèque du Sénat, mais il ne signale pas cet exemplaire de la Bibliothèque du Congrès.

19. Archives Nationales, AD VIII, 35, pièce 13; C. Pierre, 399.

20. Ye 30615 et Rés. Ye 3137; C. Pierre, 219.

21. N° 224, p. 12; C. Pierre, 468.

La Fayette?"[22] Et encore, toujours de 1791, "les faits et gestes remarquables de feu M. La Fayette," pot-pourri sur l'air "Mottié, va, t'en Limagne".[23]

En revanche, on constate que des personnages comme Jefferson, Washington, Paine, sont pratiquement absents (sauf découverte toujours possible) de la chanson et de l'hymne révolutionnaire. Peut-être cette absence même ne manque-t-elle pas d'intérêt. La chanson, en particulier, est un reflet assez exact de la mentalité populaire de l'époque: le peuple est vite pris par des problèmes de subsistance, par la guerre avec les pays voisins, les événements quotidiens de la Révolution à Paris, et oublie quelque peu, à mesure que les temps deviennent plus durs, le modèle de la Révolution américaine. Si Franklin semble échapper à cet oubli, cela n'en est que plus remarquable et s'explique, je pense, à la fois par sa mort qui permet l'entrée aux Champs Elysées et l'idéalisation; mais aussi par la diversité de sa personnalité qui répond à des tendances essentielles de l'esprit de la Révolution. Il répond à l'exaltation de l'image du peuple, plus particulièrement de l'artisan: il a été ouvrier typographe. Il a été journaliste, et on sait l'importance que prit ce domaine de l'écriture sous la Révolution; il a été savant, et la Révolution française a exalté le développement des sciences; il a été un éducateur, et la Révolution vient réformer totalement l'enseignement. Il a été législateur, et la Révolution a enfanté plusieurs constitutions.

Les thèmes éternels attirent peut-être davantage les musiciens et les poètes de la Révolution française. Elle célèbre la jeunesse et la vieillesse, les époux, l'agriculture, l'Etre Suprême, et lorsque l'on évoque un événement ou un personnage particulier, c'est presque toujours pour en tirer une leçon plus générale. Cette tendance moralisatrice est en grande partie responsable de notre incompréhension. Nous nous méfions des abstractions et nous concevons la poésie, depuis Rimbaud surtout, comme une illumination individuelle. Mais la conception de la poésie à cette époque est différente. La poésie révolutionnaire a été préparée par toute cette poésie d'idées, cette poésie philosophique qui fleurit pendant le XVIIIe siècle et dont Voltaire n'est certes pas le seul représentant.

Les formes musicales

Pour ce qui est des formes musicales aussi, la Révolution est l'héritière du Siècle des Lumières: elle lui est redevable de ces formes où la fusion de la parole et du verbe est constante: la chanson, l'ode ou la cantate, l'opéra. Aucune époque ne peut créer des formes absolument *ex nihilo*; mais ces formes ont été profondément modifiées par les changements du contexte

22. *Actes des Apôtres*, Vol. 9, n° 247, 15; C. Pierre, 495.
23. Actes des Apôtres, Vol. 10, n° 292, 12; C. Pierre, 565.

politique, de la réception de l'oeuvre, du public. Ainsi, la chanson politique, jusque-là clandestine, éclate maintenant au grand jour, devient un élément actif de la vie publique. Les modes de sa transmission ont changé en même temps que son contenu. Ainsi s'explique ce phénomène du remploi des airs dont nous venons de voir quelques exemples et qui s'est fait systématiquement, aussi bien avec des airs religieux, en particulier les Noëls, parce qu'ils étaient connus de tous.

Si le développement de la chanson est peut-être ce qui est le plus frappant, le lieu où s'exprime le plus une certaine spontanéité populaire, la création des Hymnes n'en demeure pas moins aussi un élément fondamental de ces Fêtes révolutionnaires dont on a, depuis déjà quelques années, souligné l'importance et la nouveauté. Production immense que Constant Pierre a recensée le premier. Mais il y a encore à découvrir à ce sujet, en particulier en province et à l'étranger. La forme strophique y est en général vigoureuse. Le refrain permet une reprise collective du chant, tandis que les strophes, plus difficiles d'exécution, étaient chantées par des musiciens. Le refrain assure la cohésion des participants.

La limite entre la rue et le théâtre n'existe plus. Les chansons sont souvent reprises dans le mélodrame, les hymnes peuvent être représentés sur la scène, après l'avoir été en plein air. Ce qui est le plus neuf, du point de vue forme, ce sont peut-être ces scènes lyriques et patriotiques, un peu comparables au "fait historique" qui d'ailleurs est souvent scandé lui aussi par des chansons. La "scène lyrique et patriotique" est un pot-pourri, composition rapide, qui permet à la fois d'informer et de galvaniser la foule.

Mais à côté de cela, la forme d'opéra traditionnelle continue à être pratiquée et avec une grande effervescence. On reprend des opéras antérieurs, en modifiant les paroles parfois, on écrit de nouveaux opéras sur des thèmes d'actualité ou sur des thèmes antiques. Comme pour le théâtre proprement dit, la multiplication des lieux de spectacle contribue à cette fécondité. *Lodoiska* (1791) de Cherubili, *Stratonice* (1792) de Méhul, *La Caverne* (1793) de Lesueur, et surtout la *Médée* (1797) de Cherubini, ou encore l'*Ariodant* (1798) de Méhul sont des oeuvres marquantes où, comme l'a bien souligné J. Mongrédien, souffle un esprit de liberté qui remet en cause la séparation des genres et prépare l'opéra romantique.

Les rapports chant-parole

Chansons, hymnes, opéras sous toutes ses formes aboutissent à une exaltation de la voix et de cette unité chant-parole. Il serait naïf d'en rendre responsable la seule Révolution; les transformations de l'opéra français au XVIIIe siècle, l'influence de l'opéra italien cher aux Philosophes, la réforme de Gluck avaient préparé cette transformation du rapport chant-parole. Les études très précises de J.L. Lam ont montré à quel point les compositeurs, si bousculés fussent-ils par l'événement, ont systématiquement travaillé à faire coïncider accent musical et accent du mot dans les Hymnes.[24] L'accent organise la mobilisation de la respiration du corps tout entier par le chant. C'est par cette concordance de l'accent que se crée l'unité musicale, idéologique, émotive de tout un groupe.

Pour que cet effet soit possible, il fallait aussi que les paroles fussent audibles, ce qui suppose un effort à tous les niveaux. Les poètes doivent utiliser un langage relativement simple, les musiciens renoncer aux vocalises et à l'ornementation compliquée, les exécutants doivent enfin fournir un effort de respiration et d'articulation. Et d'autant que ces hymnes, ces chansons sont chantés souvent en plein air. Un élément neuf dans la musique révolutionnaire, c'est l'augmentation des masses vocales. Il fallait faire de l'effet, frapper l'audition, avoir un maximum de participation. Que l'on imagine l'étendue du Champs de Mars lors de la Fête de la Fédération, par exemple. Les choeurs de la Révolution ont atteint un nombre jusque-là jamais égalé. Berlioz, Wagner, Mahler s'en souviendront.

Il faut aussi souligner combien ces manifestations musicales ont pour un temps freiné cette coupure que tout le XVIIIe siècle avait préparée, entre professionnels et non-professionnels. Sans pour autant s'imaginer que par la grâce de la Révolution, tous les Français sont soudain devenus musiciens, et tout en se rappelant que les professionnels étaient fortement, et autoritairement, mis à contribution, le développement de la chanson et du chant choral ont permis l'exécution, l'expression musicale à l'homme de la rue. Nous avons évoqué les diverses versions du *Ça ira*; il y eut aussi de multiples versions de *La Marseillaise*. Chacun pouvait composer une Marseillaise avec les paroles qui lui convenaient, entraînées par la puissance rythmique de cet air universellement connu. L'alliance parole-musique aide, suscite l'invention et la fantaisie, l'air étant déjà donné il suffit de changer les paroles; inversement, sur un slogan, sur ces paroles forcément répétitives de la propagande révolutionnaire, on peut, sans connaître la musique, intégrer des airs simples, articulés par le rythme fortement marqué qui caractérise le slogan.

Il faut aussi rattacher à l'ensemble de cette situation, l'essor que prennent sous la Révolution les instruments à vent. Gossec sur ce point est tout à fait novateur dans sa *Marche lugubre*. L'unité chant-parole est soutenue et rythmée de préférence par des instruments à vent et à percussion. Ainsi est remise en cause la hiérarchie qui donnait la première place aux instruments à cordes, ainsi se trouvent réapparaître des instruments populaires–tels le serpent–que les ensembles baroques utilisaient et que le classicisme avaient éliminés. Berlioz là aussi s'en souviendra. On a supposé qu'une influence maçonnique

---

24. J.L. Lam, *Poésie et musique des Fêtes révolutionnaires* (Thèse, Clermont-Ferrand, 1980).

avait pu avoir son rôle dans cette préférence des révolutionnaires pour l'instrument à vent. Beaucoup de professeurs du premier Conservatoire étaient maçons. Mais il y a également des raisons simplement pratiques: robustesse, volume sonore qui sont des qualités fondamentales pour le plein air. Or comme ce sont les mêmes musiciens qui écrivent pour les Fêtes nationales et pour l'opéra, la musique dramatique a profité aussi de cet élargissement de l'orchestration.

Les Fêtes ont eu une influence considerable sur l'évolution de la musique, et en particulier de cette unité parole-musique que nous avons étudiée ici; dans la fête, les strophes sont, selon l'expression de Léon Guichard, "non seulement mises en musique, mais mises en scène." Et cela implique une dramatisation du Verbe dont tout le discours musical, et aussi bien l'Opéra bénéficient. Grâce aux Fêtes, la phrase musicale et verbale étroitement fusionnées, sont entraînées dans une action et dans une organisation dont David fut souvent le génial ordonnateur. Les Fêtes sont rarement statiques: ou bien elles ont un caractère processionnel, ou bien, si elles demeurent à une place définie, des chanteurs, des groupes vont évoluer. D'autre part la fête est essentiellement destinée à être vue autant qu'entendue; son succès dépend directement de l'abondance des spectateurs et de leur participation active. Tous ces facteurs sont évidemment pris en compte par les poètes et par les musiciens.

Pour des raisons idéologiques, la Révolution a donc privilégié l'unité chant-parole, lui a donné une priorité dans les Fêtes et dans les spectacles, dans l'enseignement. Les dirigeants, ce faisant, ne pensaient vraisemblablement qu'aux nécessités de la propagande. Mais tout se tient, les conditions de composition modifient l'organisation même de l'oeuvre. Ils ont permis à la parole et à la musique de connaître une harmonieuse collaboration, d'atteindre à une force, une puissance nouvelles, dans une mise en scène où gestes, costumes, décors n'étaient pas négligés. Ils ont ainsi, avec des succès inégaux je veux bien, contribué à la création d'un art total où tous les sens sont concernés, où la distinction entre exécutants et public s'abolit, où tout devient mise en scène de la voix. Tel modeste couplet à Franklin qui, isolé, pourrait nous paraître une assez pauvre poésie, ne peut se comprendre qu'en se reportant à ce mouvement qui le magnifie et le dépasse, d'apothéose de la voix, organe irremplaçable de la fusion de la parole et du verbe.

Notes on the contributors

Régis Antoine, whose doctoral thesis was on French Writers and the Antilles (1979), taught in Guadeloupe and St. Nazaire, and now teaches French literature and the literature of the French West Indies at the University of Nantes. He has published on the Revolutionary period in the Antilles, on Saint-John Perse, Césaire, and literary dissidents.

Béatrice Didier holds a doctorate in French literature from the University of Paris, and has taught at the University of Paris-VIII since 1969. Her numerous publications have focused on Diderot, Rousseau, Stendhal, George Sand and other writers of the late eighteenth and early nineteenth centuries, on literature and music during the same period, on diaries and autobiography, on feminine writing, and on editing manuscripts. She is the editor-director of *Corps écrit*, of several collections for P.U.F., and her most recent book is *Ecrire la Révolution 1789-1799*.

Jean Ehrard is a well-known Enlightenment specialist, who wrote doctoral dissertations on the idea of nature in eighteenth-century France and on Montesquieu's art criticism (1963 and 1965). He is the author of many books and articles on literary and historical topics, including works on the eighteenth century, on Montesquieu, Diderot, Marmontel, the Encyclopedia, Marivaux, and the French Revolution. He is the secretary of the Société française d'Etude du Dix-Huitième Siècle, and professor emeritus at the University of Clermont-Ferrand, where he is associated with the Centre de Recherches Révolutionnaires et Romantiques.

Jean-Jacques Fiechter is a Swiss historian, who received his doctorate from the University of Lausanne in 1965. He has combined a career in multinational business with academic and literary pursuits. His recent works include books on Gouverneur Morris, on Régula Engel, and on the Duc de Lauzun. He is currently working on Rochambeau's campaign.

Claude Fohlen, a noted French historian, studied at the Universities of Bordeaux, Toulouse and Paris, where he earned his doctorate in 1955. He has been a visiting guest professor at a number of American universities, while holding a chair at the University of Paris-I. His many works include a number of books on economic history, on regional history, as well as eight on the United States, the most recent of which appeared in 1988 (*Les Etats-Unis au XXe siècle*). He is one of the foremost interpreters of America in France.

Jacques Grès-Gayer studied philosophy, theology, history and political science in Rome and Paris. He holds a doctorate in theology from the Institute Catholique and one in history from the University of Paris-Sorbonne (1981). His publications include several articles on theological and historical topics in the seventeenth and eighteenth centuries, and he is working on a book on early ecumenism (Paris and Canterbury). He teaches in the department of Church History at the Catholic University of America.

James Hennessey, S.J. studied at Loyola University, Woodstock College, and the Catholic University of America, where he received his doctorate in history in 1963. He has taught history and church history at various institutions, and has been Professor of the History of Christianity at Boston College since 1977. In addition to numerous articles and contributions to journals and encyclopedias, he has recently published two books on American Catholics.

Edna Hindie Lemay studied in Egypt and in the United States, and holds a doctorate from the University of Paris-Sorbonne (1974). She has been working at the Ecole des Hautes Etudes en Sciences Sociales under François Furet since 1970, where she also teaches. She has contributed many papers and articles on the eighteenth and nineteenth centuries, on ethnology, constitutional history, and sociocultural history. Her book, *La vie quotidienne des députés en 1789*, appeared in 1988.

Joan Lenardon, who holds a Master's in European Studies from Hunter College, has been teaching at the Faculty of Theology of the University of Western Ontario, St. Peter's Seminary, since 1965. Her published papers have centered on church and state issues in France, on the *Journal encyclopédique*, and on the *Année littéraire*.

François Moureau received a doctorate in literature from the University of Paris-Sorbonne in 1977 and teaches at the University of Bourgogne in Dijon. He has specialized in the history of the theater in the seventeenth and eighteenth centuries, and has published works on Dufresny and Watteau, as well as numerous articles on Italian theater in France, and dramatic literature by Diderot and Rousseau, among others. He holds administrative positions with various French societies for the study of the eighteenth century, and is director of a research group on travel literature at the University of Paris-Sorbonne.

Daniel Price studied at Loyola, St. Louis, and Gregorian Universities before receiving his doctorate in history from the University of Chicago in 1981. His dissertation was on Jesuit preaching in Paris in the mid-eighteenth century. He has taught at Xavier University and is now director of Corporate On-Site Programs at the Union Institute in Cincinnati.

Aurelia Roman studied in Bucharest, in France and in the United States, and holds a doctorate in French literature from George Washington University. She has taught in Washington and at Georgetown University's School of Foreign Service for many years. Her research and publications have centered on Ionesco, on French civilization, and on pedagogical issues.

Madeleine Simons received her doctorate in French literature from Johns Hopkins University. Her published works include articles on eighteenth and nineteenth-century authors, on semiotics, and books on Rousseau and Stendhal. She is currently working on medieval iconography. She is now a professor emerita at Georgetown University.

Louis Trenard, a French historian, studied at Lyon, from which university he earned his doctorate in 1955. He has taught at the Universities of Clermont-Ferrand and Lille, where he is now a professor emeritus of modern and regional history. He has held many positions in French historical societies and is director of the *Revue du Nord* as well as editor of *l'Information historique*. His numerous publications have focused on the history of ideas, sociocultural history, and regional history. His most recent work is *Histoire de la Révolution française dans la région lyonnaise*.

Jacques Wagner has studied at the University of Haute-Bretagne (Rennes), where he received his doctorate in 1987 with a thesis on reading and society in the *Journal encyclopédique*, and where he now teaches. He has published on the eighteenth-century writers, on the press, and on America as viewed in the *Journal encyclopédique*.